Reproductive Justice

REPRODUCTIVE JUSTICE: A NEW VISION
FOR THE TWENTY-FIRST CENTURY

*Edited by Rickie Solinger,
Khiara M. Bridges,
Zakiya Luna, and Ruby Tapia*

Reproductive Justice

An Introduction

Loretta J. Ross and Rickie Solinger

UNIVERSITY OF CALIFORNIA PRESS

University of California Press, one of the most distin-
guished university presses in the United States, enriches
lives around the world by advancing scholarship in the
humanities, social sciences, and natural sciences. Its
activities are supported by the UC Press Foundation and
by philanthropic contributions from individuals and
institutions. For more information, visit www.ucpress.edu.

University of California Press
Oakland, California

Library of Congress Cataloging-in-Publication Data

Names: Ross, Loretta, author. | Solinger, Rickie, 1947–
author.
Title: Reproductive justice : an introduction / Loretta J.
Ross and Rickie Solinger
Description: Oakland, California : University of
California Press, [2017] | Series: Reproductive justice :
a new vision for the twenty-first century ; 1 | Includes
bibliographical references and index.
Identifiers: LCCN 2016046912 | ISBN 9780520288188 (cloth :
alk. paper) | ISBN 9780520288201 (pbk. : alk. paper) |
ISBN 9780520963207 (eBook)
Subjects: LCSH: Human reproduction—Law and
legislation—United States. | Reproductive rights—
United States. | Reproductive health—United States.
| African American women—Health and hygiene. |
Women's rights—United States.
Classification: LCC KF3760 .S65 2017 | DDC 342.7308/5—dc23
LC record available at https://lccn.loc.gov/2016046912

Manufactured in the United States of America

25 24 23 22 21 20 19
10 9 8 7 6 5 4 3

For the SisterSong family and my son, Howard Michael Ross, without whom much of my life would not have been possible. May Ruby and Dean live in a world where reproductive justice prevails.

CONTENTS

Introduction

The two of us, Loretta and Rickie, joined forces to write *Reproductive Justice: An Introduction* so that we could introduce the concept of reproductive justice to new audiences. As a scholar (Rickie) and an activist (Loretta), we believe that we have made a book that will contribute to the exciting upsurge of reproductive justice activism and scholarship. We have read each other's articles and books and followed each other's work for years with respect and admiration. Making this book has deepened both our regard for each other and our commitment to the principles of reproductive justice.

We chose to write this book in the form of a primer because it is an explanation of the basic elements of our subject. *Reproductive Justice: An Introduction* offers an expansive explanation of reproductive justice so that readers can learn about this creative vision for achieving human rights protections. The primer will also help readers understand how reproductive justice is significantly different from the pro-choice/antiabortion debates that have dominated the headlines and mainstream political conflict for so long.

LORETTA

For years, as a human rights and reproductive rights activist, I have needed historical and sociological information and analysis to support my work. But I have had a hard time finding studies of reproduction in America that did not marginalize women of color. Most of the work by white writers supplied few, if any, perspectives on women of color, quite often treating them as afterthoughts instead of putting their stories anywhere near the center of the narrative. As a Black feminist, I am committed to focusing on the powerful role of colonialism and white supremacy in determining reproductive destinies. Without these perspectives, a great many historical treatments leave almost everything unexplained. I value Rickie's work because for more than twenty-five years, she has produced deep, analytical writing about the intersection of race, gender, sovereignty, and class. As a world-class historian, she carefully details the experiences of women of color facing political, economic, and cultural forces inimical to the concept of reproductive freedom and autonomy. When Rickie invited me to write this primer with her, I trusted that together we could offer this emerging knowledge about reproductive justice in its most powerful form, with lucidity, authenticity, and an incisive critique of white supremacy and capitalism.

Presenting and preserving our two voices in this project was a challenge and a joy. Because I was present when the reproductive justice framework was created, I offer a first-person voice and more than two decades of experience promoting this new vision for reproductive activism. My years as one of the leaders of SisterSong Women of Color Reproductive Justice Collective gave me the opportunity to witness the excitement of building a new movement centered on the needs of women of color grappling with issues of pregnancy, birth, abortion, and parenting. This radical, fresh vision brought thousands of new voices into the movement. The reproductive justice vision spread out like exploding fireworks to touch off new understandings of the intersections of many issues in the lives of women of color.

Rickie's voice is that of a disciplined and compassionate historian. She bravely reinterprets historical facts, paying attention to voices and perspectives of those most marginalized by privilege and power. Her precise language and attention to detail offer an authoritative example of what history looks like when the lives of marginalized women are centered in the lens.

RICKIE

Writing *Reproductive Justice: An Introduction* with Loretta is the culmination of my work as a historian of reproductive politics in the United States. I have been writing books for decades, preparing myself, without even quite knowing it, for this collaboration. My books have been serial efforts to answer the same group of questions: Who gets to be a "legitimate" mother in the United States? (And who do authorities consider "legitimately" sexual?) Who is denied maternal legitimacy? What do race and class have to do with "legitimate" and "illegitimate" maternity? What do the government, the church, the community, and the family have to do with deciding and *enforcing* answers to these questions? How have answers changed over time? And perhaps most important, how does the maternal "legitimacy" of some persons depend on and guarantee the *illegitimacy* of others?

For example, for decades, TV shows, movies, and other cultural expressions typically portrayed white, middle-class, heterosexual, married women as the mothers we all want to be and to have: "legitimate" mothers. So what are Americans to think about persons who do not have all of these assets and resources to bring to motherhood? Our political culture conditions us to regard these mothers as inappropriate, "illegitimate" mothers in comparison. It underwrites the idea that motherhood is a class privilege, properly reserved only for women with enough money to give their children "all the advantages," a deeply antidemocratic idea. Here we can see how the nobility of white, middle-class maternity depends on the definition of others as unfit, degraded, and illegitimate. In turn, poor mothers have been branded illegitimate because they do not have the resources that middle-class mothers do.

When I became aware of Loretta's work and the intersectional, reproductive justice analysis she was developing along with others, I knew that my work was finally "at home." Listening to Loretta's lectures, reading her work, and paying attention to the arena she was helping to define added up to an intellectual and political home base for me and my work in a way that the disciplines of history and women's studies have not been. An intellectual and political location that draws on human rights, justice, lived experience, uncompromising analysis, and straightforward language feels like the sturdiest, truest place to work.

As a white, Jewish teenager learning about the Holocaust, I began to learn about other brutal histories of dispossession and degradation, cultural destruction, and death. I began to learn at the same time, through the civil rights movement, what fighting for dignity looks like and about the power of voice. Since that time, I have looked at champions of resistance as models. Loretta has been an extremely important teacher and model for me for two decades, articulating a constructive, human-rights-based politics of resistance that envisions the dignity and safety and meaningfulness of each person's life. This opportunity I've had—to be an ally—has been profoundly important, helping me to see the deep connection between developing respect for others and oneself.

· · ·

We begin this book with a history of reproductive politics in the United States because as reproductive justice activists and scholars, we understand that the past explains a great deal about the present and also shapes the future. When politicians, judges, and policy makers make decisions that affect our lives, for example, by enacting or upholding laws that restrict access to various kinds of reproductive health care, they are building on the past. The Hyde Amendment, which prohibits the use of federal funds for abortion, profoundly curtails a poor woman's decision making in ways that are consistent with—and further encode—older laws, policies, and social norms that aimed to deny reproductive dignity to poor women.

Public discussion of reproductive politics today typically excludes references to race, despite the fact that this terrain has always been deeply racialized in the United States. Reproductive justice activists and scholars argue that if we continue to deny the 500-year history of racialized reproductive law and policy— fashioned and deployed to maintain a country dominated by "white people"—then the legacy of racialized reproduction will flourish in the twenty-first century and beyond.

Reproductive justice presents a real and present engagement with the world of reproductive politics that produces new forms of knowledge and different understandings of history. As you will read, reproductive justice is full of free thinking that has inspired many women of color and progressive white allies to imagine a world in which people's human rights are respected and protected when they make decisions about whether to become a parent.

Our mutual journey as friends and collaborators has left neither of us untouched. We have been enriched by this process and are honored to offer our readers this collaborative gift.

A NOTE ABOUT LANGUAGE AND GENDER

This book recognizes the limits of traditional, biologically based binary definitions of gender at the same time as it chronicles and analyzes histories that these definitions have produced. We have mostly used the term "woman" when discussing legislation in the past that used language targeting women and mothers. When we write about the present, we use terms such as "people who can get pregnant and give birth" as well as "woman." Our language reflects a range of gender identities and the diversity of people's lived experiences. Our language choices are based on several principles. First, as reproductive justice authors, we do not want to duplicate the prejudices that make transgender people invisible and vulnerable. Inclusive language reflects a commitment to the idea that not everyone who can get pregnant and have children is a woman (traditionally, a person with female body parts who presents herself as female), and, in addition, that not all women can or do get pregnant and give birth. So "woman" as a general term is both too narrow and too broad.

Second, reproductive oppressions are not about genital anatomy. Reproductive oppressions stem from a determination to exercise power over vulnerable persons and achieve goals that have nothing to do with the well-being or interests of individual reproducers. Third, reproductive decisions (such as whether to have an abortion or to use contraception) and parenthood are not about anatomy or body parts. Reproductive decision making is about the *lived experience* of individuals, including, for many persons, their drive to possess reproductive autonomy as part of their achievement of full personhood.

"Woman," then, (a person who presents herself as female and may have a vagina and ovaries) does not describe the identity of all persons who can or will get pregnant and give birth and mother a child. A transwoman generally cannot get pregnant, and trans men may be able to. Further, "woman" does not describe the identity of all persons who decide whether to have an abortion or use contraception. Physician Cheryl Chastine explains: "We must give primacy to people's understanding of themselves. We can't advocate that each pregnant person be able to effect the best decision for themselves—while simultaneously insisting that people who aren't cisgender [persons who present themselves in ways that are consistent with their official gender-identification at birth] should go along silently with language in which they don't exist."[1]

There is, of course, the danger that excising the term "woman" in order to include transgender persons in our reproductive justice analysis can have the effect of effacing the particular lived experiences of *women,* as societies have traditionally defined and recognized this category of persons. Certainly the experience of being a woman has generally included being targeted for various kinds of sexual and reproductive oppressions and brutalities. "Woman" is also a self-defined category, especially for those denied the recognition of their full humanity, who embrace the term as a particular marker of gender identity.

For some, overeffacement of the term "woman" can constitute a form of erasure that is also incompatible with the principles of reproductive justice. This book's histories of traditionally female-identified persons demonstrate how politicians, lawmakers, policy makers, the judiciary, and ordinary people have used the sexuality and fertility of traditionally defined women to achieve specific demographic, political, and cultural goals—including male supremacy—in ways that have depended on and guaranteed the subordination of these women to traditionally defined men. It may be complicated and tricky to accomplish, but we are committed to writing as inclusively as we can in the present moment of rapidly changing terminology and conventions.

These observations about the politics of gender and language (here and elsewhere) are being freshly developed in the twenty-first century. This book applies the new insights inconsistently, sometimes using "women and girls" and "mothers," sometimes using the term "individuals" and "parents" and other gender-neutral words. Let's say this text is one ragged beginning to the project of defying the gender binary and recognizing the need to develop acute attentiveness to the politics of language in this domain.

ONE

A Reproductive Justice History

Reproductive justice is a contemporary framework for activism and for thinking about the experience of reproduction. It is also a political movement that splices *reproductive rights* with *social justice* to achieve *reproductive justice.* The definition of reproductive justice goes beyond the pro-choice/pro-life debate and has three primary principles: (1) the right *not* to have a child; (2) the right to *have* a child; and (3) the right to *parent* children in safe and healthy environments. In addition, reproductive justice demands sexual autonomy and gender freedom for every human being.

At the heart of reproductive justice is this claim: all fertile persons and persons who reproduce and become parents require a safe and dignified context for these most fundamental human experiences. Achieving this goal depends on access to specific, community-based resources including high-quality health care, housing and education, a living wage, a healthy environment, and a safety net for times when these resources fail. Safe and dignified fertility management, childbirth, and parenting are impossible without these resources.

REPRODUCTIVE JUSTICE AND
HUMAN RIGHTS

The case for reproductive justice makes another basic claim: access to these material resources is justified on the grounds that safe and dignified fertility management, childbirth, and parenting together constitute a fundamental *human right*. Human rights, a global idea, are what governments owe to the people they govern and include both negative rights and positive rights. *Negative rights* are a government's obligation to refrain from unduly interfering with people's mental, physical, and spiritual autonomy. *Positive rights* are a government's obligation to ensure that people can exercise their freedoms and enjoy the benefits of society.

Reproductive justice uses a human rights framework to draw attention to—and resist—laws and public and corporate policies based on racial, gender, and class prejudices. These laws and policies deny people the right to control their bodies, interfere with their reproductive decision making, and, ultimately, prevent many people from being able to live with dignity in safe and healthy communities.

The human rights analysis rests on the claim that interference with the safety and dignity of fertile and reproducing persons is a blow against their humanity—that is, against their rights as human beings. Protecting people against this interference is crucial to ensuring the human rights of all because all of us have the human right to be fertile, the human right to engage in sexual relations, and the human right to reproduce or not, and the human right to be able to care for our children with dignity and safety.

This history of reproduction in the United States pays attention to the ways that women have always been determined to make secret decisions, pursue bold options, share information and resources, depend on the support of sisters, friends, and strangers, and take the risks they needed to take to make the reproductive decisions they could make. Sometimes these efforts were successful, sometimes not. Indeed, the reproductive options that fertile people have are always structured by the resources they have—or do not have.

Understanding the historical, legal, and technological contexts in which women have lived their reproductive lives is key to understanding how women have seized particular spaces for managing their fertility. This means understanding how women have avoided conception and how they have had children and been mothers when they wanted to. This kind of information allows us to understand how women have been responsible mothers when they had children in the midst of the life they had, in the midst of the community they lived in. The crucial point here is that no matter what kinds of regulations the government, the church, the family, or other authorities created, girls and women have always done what they could to shape their own reproductive lives. These assertions have particular meaning for the lived experience of women of color, whose reproductive capacity has constituted both a key engine for white power and wealth historically and a touchstone for those who want to distinguish the "value" of women's reproductive bodies by race. These perspectives make clear that women of color have been targeted in distinctive, brutal ways across U.S. history.

The reproductive justice framework derives its vital depth from drawing attention to the persistence of this history—the ways that the history of white supremacy operating in a capitalist system penetrates and misshapes the present. "The past is never dead," William Faulkner famously said. "It's not even past."[1] In this case, past abuses of women's reproductive bodies live on in contemporary harms and coercions, stimulating reproductive justice activists to define the arena of reproductive dignity and safety in terms of human rights. Keeping in mind the impacts of this history, reproductive justice activists and theorists focus on the lived, embodied reproductive and whole-life experiences within their communities of people who can become pregnant and give birth.

We cannot understand these experiences of fertility and reproduction and maternity separate from our understanding of the community—the social context—in which they occur. When we assess the extent to which a group of fertile and pregnant persons are reproductively healthy and the degree of this group's access to affordable reproductive health services, we can understand the relationship between health, health care, poverty, community empowerment, and the experiences of individuals. We can see the connection between reproductive health and well-being and the right to be a mother or a parent. We can see how the economic and cultural health of the community structures the degree of safety and dignity available to fertile and reproducing persons. These perspectives demonstrate the limits of the marketplace concept of free, unimpeded individual "choice" and turn us toward a human rights analysis.

This first chapter recounts the history of the thirteen original colonies and the United States and the resistance by women of color that gave birth to the reproductive justice framework. This chapter makes the case that knowing this history is crucial for understanding what animates and defines the contours and content of reproductive justice and the activist movement associated with its claims. It is a history that shows how colonizers, enslavers, employers, and the state, among other entities, have *used* reproductive capacity to pursue goals associated with power, wealth, status, and property, creating difficulties and particular degradations for fertile and reproducing persons because of their sex and gender and their capacity to give birth to new life. It highlights the histories of people of color regarding reproduction and parenting because of racial slavery, immigration restrictions, persecution and genocide of Native populations, and other forms of racism in the original thirteen colonies and then the United States. It also highlights the history that women of color have made as they have responded to official policies, cultural assumptions, and casual practices.

This history calls attention over and over to the vulnerabilities of people without institutionalized power. It shows, for example, how some groups have been unable to prevent rape and its consequences; how some were unable to avoid official and unofficial programs of sterilization; how many people were unable to control when they got pregnant or decide whether to stay pregnant and whether or not to be the parents of the children they gave birth to. We see how, as enslaved persons, parents were unable to protect their children from sale or to assert their authority as parents. After white settlers and armies began moving westward across the North American continent, many Native Americans lost their land and also lost their pregnancies and children to genocidal wars and forced marches, and then to the boarding school system that aimed to drain Native culture from the minds of children who were being remade as "Americans." Many people lost their fertility to coercive, race-based sterilization programs. All of these brutalities and indignities and others constitute a catalog of reproductive injustices: they name the reproductive dangers that many persons experienced in the past and that many continue to experience, in updated forms, today. And they define the remedies that mark out the meanings of reproductive justice, in contrast.

By the last third of the twentieth century, a number of factors fueled movement building by feminists of color who focused on matters they would soon associate with reproductive justice. These included the influence of international and U.S. antiracist and feminist-led human rights movements. Movement activists organized against laws and policies that amounted to official reproductive abuse of people of color and their communities. Abuses included coerced sterilization; welfare and fostering policies that punished poor women for "illegitimate" motherhood; and the Hyde Amendment, which denied federal aid to poor women seeking abortions. In other words, reproductive justice was born from the claims of women of color that they had the right to be sexual persons and to be fertile. They claimed the right to decide to become parents and the right to the resources they needed to take care of their children. They also claimed the right to manage their fertility by having access to contraception and abortion services. And they made the case that the reproduction-related abuses of the 1960s and 1970s, the 1980s and 1990s and beyond constituted the direct legacies of a long history of reproductive abuse, reaching back into the slavery regime and earlier. They also drew on their own histories to define the fundamental human rights of all fertile and reproducing persons.

This opening chapter provides a reproductive justice history of reproduction in the United States. It chronicles interactions over time between official efforts to bring reproduction under the control of the state (and other authorities) and the efforts of ordinary people to define, to seek out, to claim, and to hold on to reproductive safety and dignity. These interactions embed some recurrent threads; first, that to achieve its most fundamental goals, *every* government depends on the reproductive capacity of people who can give birth. Government goals might include encouraging reproduction in order to build adequate labor and military forces. From the perspective of European settlers in North America, official laws and policies were crucial to achieving these kinds of aims. The second thread shows that laws and policies were quickly fundamental to racializing the colonies and then the nation, establishing (and fortifying) the primacy of whites. Laws and policies associated with population defined racial groups and boundaries between them, fixing exactly who was enslaved, who was free, and who was native. Over time, every pregnant woman and every baby born was racialized, marked for inclusion or exclusion, as the founding fathers and their heirs defined and protected the national identity of the United States as a "white country." Over time, white settlers and then white citizens used the law to express their sense of the incompatibility of heterogeneity and democracy.

Racializing the nation depended on the development of a culture and a politics—and a body of law—that declared that white babies had a different, dearer, and nonnegotiable value compared to nonwhite babies and that enforced those different values. Culture and laws were meant to identify which female bodies (and their babies) were marked for which kinds of administration and management by the state.[2] In time, these laws constituted a formidable population-control structure and included antimiscegenation laws, immigration laws, and laws criminalizing contraception and abortion. After slavery ended and the babies of African Americans no longer automatically increased the wealth of slave-owning whites, laws encouraged the sterilization of many women, frequently poor women of color. And welfare laws punished the pregnancy and childbearing of the same women. The government has also created a variety of laws over time that have separated children from their mothers. These have given the state both the power to decide what constitutes a good mother and the capacity to act against the motherhood of women defined as falling short of that standard, even when that standard might embed and depend on racial and class biases. Crucially, although officials wrote these laws and others in language that called for policing the sex, reproductive, and maternal experiences of *individuals,* in fact, the laws have had the effect of punishing whole *communities.*

A reproductive justice lens helps us explore this history by revealing the impacts of these kinds of state strategies on the lives of individuals and communities over time. This makes a reproductive justice history distinct from national histories that ignore the short-term or long-term consequences for women and their communities of the slavery regime, the program of Native genocide, anti-Asian immigration restrictions, the Mexican "repatriation," and the colonization of the Americas, the Pacific Islands, and the Caribbean. Many histories have traced the progress of women toward personal reproductive autonomy.

This reproductive justice history does not foreground the concept of individual choice. On the contrary, using the reproductive justice framework, this chapter makes the case that individual choices have only been as capacious and empowering as the resources any woman can turn to in her community. Indeed, this history considers the impacts on women *and* their communities when state policies use women's bodies as "mechanisms of oppression against [their own] communities": for example, when an enslaver used sexual force to impregnate an enslaved woman or when birthing occurs under conditions that are deeply alienated from community traditions or interests.[3]

Historically, the absence of adequate reproductive health services has rigorously structured the lived experiences of generations of women of color and their communities. This history calls attention to the colonizing and modernizing processes that separated women from family and community traditions and resources. For example, when gynecological and obstetric medicine emerged as male-dominated, professionalized specialties, traditional women-centered knowledge and experience could be sidelined and then officially outlawed, and some enslaved women served the new experts as guinea pigs.[4] In the process, midwives were discredited and their age-old traditions degraded or lost. Public policies consigned particular pregnant and parturient women to underfunded public health programs, and standardization of obstetrics required that some women give birth in deteriorated public institutions under dangerous and alienating conditions. Health-related and other impacts rippled across and damaged communities for generations.[5]

Reproductive justice clarifies the need for protection from coerced sex and reproduction and also from coerced suppression or termination of fertility. The reproductive justice/human rights framework makes claims on the incarceration system, the immigration system, and the health care system, for example, to block institutional degradations associated with fertility, reproduction, and maternity or parenthood, and to recognize and protect the reproductive health and parenting rights of persons under their purview. Indeed, the human rights framework embeds a key corollary or foundational principle whose absence has degraded and damaged millions of women across U.S. history: health care, including reproductive health care, is properly a human right, not a commodity for purchase.

COLONIZING NORTH AMERICA AND
RACIALIZING THE NATION

In the colonial period, from the time of the first white European settlements until the ratification of the U.S. Constitution, population growth was crucial to the success of the North American colonial project and to the emergence of the new nation. From the white settlers' point of view, population growth among Europeans was crucial for establishing, developing, enlarging, and defending their land claims, their accumulation of wealth, and their political control of the settled territories. From their point of view as well, removal of the Native population that obstructed European settlement was mandatory, as was rapid population growth among enslaved Africans, who provided the hard labor necessary to realize the full range of Europeans' goals.

European settlers pursued a combination of pronatalist and antinatalist strategies to encourage population growth of African Americans and discourage population growth of Indians. Together, these strategies amounted to *population control,* a crucial aspect of establishing "the legal meanings of racial difference."[6] The first law using reproduction for this purpose was passed in 1662 in the Virginia Colony. It overturned the English common law tradition that defined the status of the child—slave or free— as following the status of the father. Now in Virginia, and soon in other colonies, the new law said that the status of every new baby would follow the status of its mother, not its father.[7] This apparently simple change guaranteed the growth of the unfree population and ensured the longevity of the slavery regime. The law made the fertility of the enslaved woman into the essential, exploitable, colonial resource. Her pregnancies, whether the result of rape or love or something else, engrossed the holdings of her owner. A generation later, in 1692, the Virginia Colony clamped down on the births of racially "mixed" children, outlawing intermarriage, marking all racially indeterminate children as "illegitimate," and forcing them to work for many years as bonded labor. They were forbidden throughout their reproductive years to have children legally or to inherit property.[8]

These laws depended on the complete subordination of enslaved women, including their submission to rape by their masters. Enslaved women did not have any of the sexual, relational, or maternal rights that white females could generally claim, such as the right to choose their sexual partners, the right to enter into a legal marriage, the right to mother and protect their own children, or even the right to *know* their own children.[9] Indeed, research has shown that nearly one out of three children living in the Upper South in 1820 was gone in 1860, sold away to new "owners" in the Lower South and farther west.[10] This is crucial: the catalog of rights enumerated here begins to describe how, at the beginning, the absence of reproductive dignity and safety were key to definitions and mechanisms of degradation, enslavement, and white supremacy.

Enslaved women were often worked viciously hard, far into their pregnancies, despite owners' calculated financial interest in producing the next generation. Many women, near the end of their term and exhausted, lost their pregnancies right in the fields, an event that was all too common since profit-maximizing owners refused to allow enslaved midwives to attend or to call in physicians to supervise, even when such attendance was routine for their own kin.[11]

On Louisiana sugar plantations, pregnant women worked sixty to seventy hours a week "while standing or stooping over cane shoots in ninety-degree temperatures." As a result, they suffered from insufficient blood supply to their placentas, typically suffered from hypertension, had a high percentage of miscarriages and stillbirths, and gave birth to tiny babies. High levels of infant mortality meant that many women were not nursing after completing a pregnancy. As a result, they resumed monthly periods much sooner than they would have if the babies had lived and nursing had continued, suppressing subsequent fertility for the duration. Inadequate diets caused a woman's milk supply to be poor, leading mothers to wean their babies early, another cause of frequent pregnancies at shorter intervals.[12] Women were also forced to do reproductive labor, nursing the babies of other women. All of these practices and others harmed the health and longevity of women and their babies, many of whom were born tiny and vulnerable.[13]

Sometimes mothers who left the fields to nurse their babies were threatened with the whip. One owner is reported to have established a rigid schedule for infant feeding. Apparently the enslaved women on this plantation were able to stand together, however, and force the owner to accept the feeding schedule they had devised.[14]

Indeed, as this case illustrates, even within such a brutal context, enslaved women sometimes found ways to band together in their own interests, including sharing information and materials with each other about how to control fertility.[15] Having many reasons to avoid pregnancy, they taught each other which herbal contraceptives and abortifacients were effective. Midwives among them performed secret abortions. These efforts reflected women's determination to resist: many refused to produce a new slave for the master and refused, as well, to consign a potential child to a life of enslavement. Sometimes a woman might even kill her newborn to save that child from a horrible life enchained to slavery. Each of these acts constituted a woman's claim of full personhood—her linkage of her reproductive life to human freedom.[16]

At the same time that the slavery regime produced laws, policies, and practices that made sure that the African American population would grow, government officials pursued antinatalist programs to reduce Native populations. The key program was, of course, using warfare to kill, to conquer, and to remove populations. But Christian missionaries also had a significant impact on the reproductive lives of Native peoples and communities in the eighteenth and early nineteenth centuries. Determined to "civilize the heathens," missionaries disrespected traditional Indian reproductive practices that had, for centuries, defined and marked birthing rituals and the connections between these rituals and maturity, manhood, womanhood, and other basic elements of culture.

Typically, missionaries focused on ameliorating the deficiencies they saw in Native women, including their lack of knowledge of European birthing and child-rearing practices and their lack of traits associated with European femininity. For example, when the religious proselytizers discovered that some Cherokee women had political and economic authority—traditional powers derived from their capacity to bring forth new life and change the shape of the community—missionaries focused on redirecting all authority away from women and into the hands of men. Equally devastating to the status and power of women within the traditional Indian matrilineal kin network, missionaries inserted themselves into the community as "surrogate parents" with supervisory responsibilities over the "new Christian family."

Throughout much of the nineteenth century, both before and after the Indian Removal Act of 1830 (a federal law permitting the government to use its military to eject Native populations from their traditional lands in the Southeast in order to provide new lands for new cotton plantations to be worked by enslaved labor), federal officials pursued policies of genocide—the ultimate population-control policy. The U.S. military forced Indians into areas west of the Mississippi River, a brutal process that had special dangers for women of reproductive age and therefore for the community as a whole. During coerced marches westward, pregnant, parturient, and mothering women were under terrible physical stress and also unable to observe cultural rituals and traditional practices associated with health and well-being. Consequently, many women and their infants did not survive. One missionary reported, "Troops frequently forced women in labor to continue [marching] until they collapsed and delivered" surrounded by soldiers.[17]

Trying to forestall such atrocities by drawing on their maternal authority, Cherokee women led Native resistance against removal. They stood against the government's demand that the Cherokee trade their ancestral lands for alien tracts far away, arguing, "The land was given to us by the Great Spirit above ... to raise our children upon, and to make support for our rising generations." Tens of thousands of Native people were removed to the west anyway, and when they arrived, men far outnumbered women. In the new settings, women's health and their lives were threatened by sexual assaults by white men, deadly diseases, insufficient food, and poverty. Consequently, the reproductive potential of Native communities was devastated. Far from regretting this development, elite whites approved the sentiment of Charles Francis Adams, Jr., the descendant of presidents and a leading industrialist, who declared that official policies and their antinatalist outcomes "saved the Anglo-Saxon stock from being a nation of half-breeds."[18]

By the time of the Civil War, more than two centuries of white lawmakers had drawn dramatic distinctions between the reproductive bodies of white women and others and had assigned profoundly different values to these bodies by race. White authorities used the locus of life to define the source of racial identity and civic value. While laws, policies, and brutal practices degraded enslaved and Native women, they ennobled free white women in contrast. According to law and cultural norms, the white mother was the fundamental creative symbol of the white nation: dependent but dignified, innocent and pious but wise, a person of deep sentiment but also judicious. She was tethered to the home while shaping the destiny of the nation by raising citizen-sons and future mothers of the Republic. Prescriptively, and in distinction to the African American mother, the white mother could, due to her whiteness, choose her husband and the father of her children. Her whiteness allowed her to manage and protect her own family. Her embodied, intimate whiteness—her alleged "chaste" sexuality, together with her fecund reproductive capacity—amounted to the nation's most precious resource.[19]

The nineteenth-century laws against contraception and abortion expressed the importance of the white mother's role in making the white nation and the government's interest in protecting her fertility. They were also expressions of legislators' concern that white women might be shirking their duties. Before independence and for the first half century afterward (and decades longer for some states), contraception and early abortion were entirely legal. A woman could, for example, legally seek termination of her pregnancy if she did so before she had reported "quickening" (that is, told someone that she'd felt the fetus move within her). Indeed, many white women believed the rhetoric of the American Revolution, the ways it exulted the "free individual," liberty, and "inalienable rights." Many white women heard within this rhetoric a corollary that African American women knew excluded most of them: that "freedom" could include the right to manage their own bodies, including their fertility.

As women went about trying to limit their fertility and their pregnancies, states moved to put a stop to this behavior. Beginning in the 1820s, physicians interested in professionalizing their status as well as controlling the lucrative domains of gynecology and obstetrics worked successfully with members of state legislatures to stamp out women's traditional prerogative to ask midwives or physicians to "restore their menses"—that is, to terminate their pregnancies. By the end of the nineteenth century, all states had criminalized abortion.

The federal Comstock Law (1873) gave officials the right to conduct surveillance of letters and packages passing through the U.S. postal service. Deploying this power, the post office system could ensure that its services weren't being used to transport "obscene" materials, especially contraceptives. Together, these legislative efforts constrained women's opportunities to learn about contraceptive options and ultimately blocked many from handling their fertility as they thought best. The Comstock Law put control of pregnancy and matters constituting gynecological and obstetric medicine legally in the hands of physicians alone.

Some historians have underemphasized a key justification for laws criminalizing contraception and abortion in the nineteenth century: to make sure that white women brought their pregnancies to term and so gave birth to all the white children necessary for populating the white nation.[20]

After the Civil War, most African American women, the majority of whom lived in the South, did not have the cash to pay for the new commercial contraceptives or for the services of professional obstetricians, few of whom served newly freed African American communities in any case. Most women probably continued to use traditional herbal preparations to control fertility, and most continued to seek out "granny midwives" in their communities to perform abortions and oversee birthing.

The economic and health-care options of African Americans in the South were not about to stabilize or expand, despite new opportunities in the one-decade-long Reconstruction period after the war. During Reconstruction, Black men could vote; many formerly enslaved persons were elected to office; and the rule of law described a new regime in which this population would be incorporated as full citizens into the polity. But after a scant decade of various kinds of progress in this direction, political deals to resolve the presidential election of 1876 destroyed many of the possibilities and promises of the Reconstruction period and empowered "Redeemer" governments determined to reinstate full white supremacy in all its forms.

Indeed, when Redeemer governments seized power throughout the South after 1876, their officials spent the next thirty years reversing the actions of Reconstruction governments and nullifying the postwar amendments to the Constitution that ended slavery (Thirteenth) and guaranteed citizenship status and voting rights for formerly enslaved men (Fourteenth and Fifteenth). The overthrow of Reconstruction legally reaffirmed white supremacy in the South. Legislatures passed laws that enforced the involuntary labor of African Americans.[21] Tolerating white violence against formerly enslaved people, they rebuilt what historian Eric Foner has described as a "unique combination of legal and extralegal coercions" amounting to a "seamless web of oppression." In 1883, eighteen years after the ratification of the Thirteenth Amendment, the Supreme Court found the Reconstruction-era

Civil Rights Act unconstitutional. One government official wrote that the time was over when Blacks could be the "special favorite of the laws." By the 1890s, full racial segregation characterized Southern society.

In many states, Redeemer governments, targeted institutions that had served formerly enslaved persons: They ended public funding for hospitals, ensuring their collapse. They dismantled public school systems. Most thoroughly consequential, Redeemer governments made sure that the federal government could not deploy its powers in the South to safeguard the welfare and rights of African Americans or curtail any manifestations of white supremacy. Local "campaigns of violence" targeted formerly enslaved people and their communities. Altogether, these programs directly threatened the health, the welfare, and the reproductive dignity and safety of African American women and their communities.[22]

At the same time that formerly enslaved African Americans were losing access to the various forms of freedom that emancipation and the post–Civil War amendments had promised, white upper-middle-class reformers such as Jane Addams, Florence Kelley, and the sisters Grace and Edith Abbott, along with some state policy makers, focused for the first time on using public policy to meet the needs of poor white mothers. Underscoring the rigidity and "natural" logic of the racial divide, they crafted and promoted state-run programs to protect "deserving" and "virtuous" mothers, mostly white widows. The new mothers' pension programs recognized the value of mothers who met certain cultural, racial, and so-called moral standards.

State programs usually did not support women of color, implicitly defining them as "unfit" due to their color, their poverty, and their alleged moral failings. According to theories of white supremacy, these women were highly unlikely or incapable of producing "fit" citizens. Moreover, they were rarely targets of law enforcement when they sought abortion. Especially now that their fertility no longer represented profit for whites, their bodies were not worth policing, a brutally ironic illustration of what it means to be "beneath the law." [23]

Many African American women looking for sexual safety and reproductive dignity moved north between 1910 and 1930 as part of the first phase of the Great Migration, when more than six million African Americans left the South for the Northeast, the Midwest, and the West. For women, leaving the South meant, in part, moving away from sexually predatory white men who rarely faced legal sanctions when they attacked women of color. Moving away from the South meant leaving the everyday violence of white supremacy and protecting their children from the degradations of Southern apartheid, even as they faced different types of racism and sexism in these new locales. When African American women and their families made new homes in urban centers, they often found better access to contraception and African American abortion providers. [24]

Fertility and motherhood continued to be sources of danger for Native women as well. A government agent to the Shoshone tribe in the 1880s explained that the problem was biological. If Indian children were to be raised to become proper Americans, he observed, they must be taken away from their families because the capacity to raise "civilized" children was "not in their mothers' milk." The federal government pressed Native mothers to send their children to boarding schools with curricula designed to suppress tribal languages and cultural practices and to promote patriotic U.S. citizenship. Those allowed to keep their children were pressed to embrace "scientific motherhood": that is, to cast off their traditional child-rearing practices in favor of European American methods.[25]

Many Native parents resisted as hard as they could when federal agents came to take their children away, and in response, agents withheld food rations and called in agency police. An agent to the Mescalero Apache described what parents faced:

> Everything in the way of persuasion and argument having failed, it became necessary to visit the camps unexpectedly with a detachment of police, and seize such children as were proper and take them away to school willing or unwilling. Some hurried their children off to the mountains or hid them away in camps, and the police had to chase and capture them like so many wild rabbits. This unusual proceeding created quite an outcry. The men were sullen and muttering, the women loud in their lamentations and the children almost out their wits with fright.[26]

The sale of enslaved African American children away from their families and the removal of Indian children from theirs are horrifying examples of how some women—and only some— have historically faced official, legal obstacles to the right to be mothers of children they bear.

Even as massive immigration from Asia and Europe substantially met the labor requirements of many employers, the state still turned to population policy to distinguish between the value of women's reproductive bodies by race, class, and ethnicity. For example, the government became increasingly involved in setting standards for mothering in the late nineteenth and early twentieth centuries. Immigration and welfare officials pursued cultural and political initiatives that designated hundreds of thousands of girls and women as unfit to be mothers and as unfit to produce new American citizens. Under the Chinese Exclusion Act of 1882, the wives of Chinese laboring men were prevented from immigrating to the United States. The impacts of the law (and its 1875 predecessor, the Page Act) were dramatic. In 1880, females constituted 3.6 percent of the Chinese population in the United States; in 1920, 12.6 percent; and in 1940, still only 30 percent. Gendered immigration restriction, along with antimiscegenation laws, ensured that Chinese men could not legally have sex in the United States and that few ethnic Chinese babies would be born here. Therefore, hardly any Chinese babies would be granted birthright citizenship.[27]

In addition to these government efforts, other official projects ranked the value of mothers. Textbooks and assimilationist school curricula overrode the norms and authority of immigrant parents (as well as Native parents), and various programs supported effective criminalization of premarital childbearing for the poorest and most vulnerable young white women. Laws and policies provided for institutionalizing these young women and sending their children to "orphan farms." These kinds of efforts reinvigorated the qualifications for "republican motherhood," ennobling mothers who were not subject to these degradations while disqualifying the ones who were.

The best evidence shows that, in the face of these kinds of laws and policies—and in the context of urbanization and industrialization—women everywhere were more determined than ever to limit their fertility, however they could. Even under a regime that continued to criminalize abortion and contraception, the average number of children born to white women declined from 4.4 to 2.1 between 1880 and 1940, while the decline for African American women was even more dramatic: from 7.5 to 3.0 during that same period.[28]

MODERN AMERICA AND
REPRODUCTIVE "QUALITY"

The early twentieth century has been known as the Jim Crow era, a time when white officials compensated for the end of racial slavery by building or reinforcing multiple structures of racial exclusion and separation—an apartheid system—in all regions of the country. Local, state, and federal governments and courts validated racial segregation of neighborhoods and institutions including schools, hospitals, movie theaters, hotels, libraries, restaurants, parks, and swimming pools. Employment was governed by the principles of racial segregation as well: through the 1950s, people of color were disproportionately—and sometimes exclusively—hired only as agricultural and domestic laborers, or for jobs in segregated settings. And very consequentially for reproduction, legislatures and courts used the law to enforce the sexual separation of the races, making interracial sex and procreation a crime in many states.[29]

At the beginning of the twentieth century, a number of prominent social scientists used the new "science" of eugenics to revitalize older theories of white supremacy and justify Jim Crow practices of racial separation. Eugenics claimed that the human population was perfectible. Public policies and medical practices could be used to promote the reproduction of the "best examples" of humanity and eradicate "negative expressions" of human life. This second category included persons with psychological, physical, and cognitive disabilities and nonwhites. Working with eugenicists, politicians and policy makers created laws that criminalized interracial sex and permitted sterilization for "racial betterment." Beginning in 1907 in Indiana, state laws encouraged sterilization of "socially inadequate persons," a vast map of humanity that pinpointed "promiscuous" women, the "feeblem-inded," some habitual criminals, and others. President Theodore Roosevelt, a eugenicist, strenuously exhorted white Americans to avoid committing "race suicide," a calamity that would befall the country if white women did not reproduce often enough to maintain the demographic advantage of "the race." These kinds of laws and official pronouncements defined racial difference and racial hierarchy as primary goals of the government.[30]

Politicians and policy makers pursued reproductive goals in a number of ways. Here we will introduce several of the ways, including immigration policy, reproductive policy, and policies addressing support for poor mothers and their children. In each area, experts developed policies and programs that depended on regulating reproduction to promote racial exclusion, racial dif-ference, and racial separation.

Following the Page Act (1875) and the Chinese Exclusion Act (1882), the United States continued for decades to enact immigra-tion legislation that would protect the white identity of the United States. In 1911, the Dillingham Commission published a forty-one-volume report, which among other things, condemned the "quality" of Eastern and Southern European immigrants arriving in America and recommended racial quotas to control which persons could enter the country. Eight years later, the most comprehensive exclusion act thus far created an "Asiatic barred zone," which effectively stopped immigration from India.

The Immigration Act of 1924, also called the National Origins Act, which would remain the law of the land with some modifica-tions until 1965, aimed to radically reduce non-Nordic immigrants and thereby curtail the number of "inferior" children born in the United States as American citizens. The law required visas and photographs for all immigrants, which represented a significant expense especially for Mexicans, who had previously been able to cross the border casually. As part of this act, Congress mandated a "scientific" study of the origins of the population as of 1920 to use as a guide for future allowable quotas by nationality and ethnicity. Subdivision d of Section 11 of the act excluded from "inhabitants of the United States in 1920," among others, Asians and their descendants, descendants of "slave immigrants," and "American aborigines." These laws had profound impacts on the color and ethnicity of the population. For example, before the 1924 law, about 150 Chinese women a year were allowed to enter the country; between 1924 and 1930, none were allowed.[31] All of these immigration restrictions had enormous impacts on the color and the ethnic origins of the babies who would be born in the United States, far into the future.

Second, eugenicists supported public policies that promoted contraception and sterilization as strategies for enhancing national strength, public health, and a better (white) "race." Suppressing fertility, temporarily or permanently, they argued, would diminish poverty and could stabilize a society staggering under the impacts of urbanization, industrialization, migration, and immigration and, most pointedly, could protect the interests of the industrialists and others members of the ruling elite. When Margaret Sanger, the most prominent early advocate of contraception in the United States, promoted the term "birth control" in 1914, she was opportunistically appealing to the era's commitment to "rational," eugenically minded, efficient solutions to social problems, not just to a woman's right to control her own body.

But Sanger was also responding to millions of women of all races and classes who wanted or desperately needed to manage their fertility, and she became a force in helping women meet that need. Indeed, millions found ways to curb their fertility, especially during the Great Depression of the 1930s. Women were extraordinarily resourceful, getting information and supplies from a variety of new sources. They gathered in labor union settings and in maternity and infant centers for African Americans in the South. In Oklahoma, a coalition of fourteen Black women's clubs underwrote a clinic. In San Francisco, schoolteacher Jane Kwong Lee took Chinese women to the Planned Parenthood clinic, she said, so they could get birth control before they got pregnant. Women opened their homes to door-to-door contraceptive salesmen. Many purchased preparations at five-and-dime stores, ordered "preventatives" from the Sears and Roebuck catalog, and responded to magazine advertisements.[32]

Nevertheless, many authorities ranked their political interests in population control and male authority over the interests of women. When the American Medical Association endorsed birth control as a "proper sexual practice," the organization insisted that doctors retain authority over women's access. Public health officials developed birth control clinics for poor African Americans only partly as a service to women. The key goal was to serve "the public good" by reducing Black fertility. The American Birth Control League and the American Eugenic Society sponsored contraceptives for relief clients as an antinatalist project that would help the country out of the Depression while improving the quality of the population. Notably, long before the government decriminalized female contraceptives, it provided condoms to soldiers during World War I and also listed condoms as "approved prophylactics" in the 1930s, to protect uniformed men against venereal diseases. Using the principle of "public health," the government itself promoted a strategy for separating sex and pregnancy, at least for men.[33]

Various court decisions in the 1930s removed all federal bans on birth control but did not address state bans. In fact, bans or not, birth control along with abortion had become basic requirements of many women determined to manage their bodies safely.[34] We know about these requirements, in part, because experts at the time estimated that between 25 and 40 percent of all pregnancies were terminated by abortion during the Depression. Women who could pay a physician or a midwife encountered few complications, even in this era before antibiotics and even though abortions were often performed in secret, poorly equipped venues. Those who resorted to self-abortion did not fare so well. More than three-quarters ran into serious trouble—infections and death.[35] These women typically lived in either the most rural parts of the country or in the poorest urban areas. They were likely to have had the fewest resources, including money, information, and access to professional medical care. Here we can see again that no matter what the law said, no matter whether a woman had the money to pay or not, millions were deeply determined, in a time of special desperation, to manage their fertility as they saw fit, even when the risk was great.

Sterilization—permanent birth control—was not merely formally allowable by law during the Depression, but it was actively pursued as a public health measure, especially after the Supreme Court had affirmed the right of officials to carry out these operations for eugenical purposes.[36] In fact, the 1930s saw the highest rates of sterilization in the greatest number of states since 1907, when Indiana passed the first sterilization law. In some states, such as Virginia, where the second-highest number (after California) of sterilizations took place between 1932 and 1941, poor people were terrified, with good reason, by the threat of the new laws and the public's enthusiasm for them. One Virginia official said, "The state sterilization authority raided whole families of 'misfit' [white] mountaineers." The official reported that events like these left "everyone who was drawing welfare ... [sure] they were going to have it done on them.... They were hiding all through these mountains, and the sheriff and his men had to go up after them ... and ran them down to Staunton [Western State Hospital] so they could sterilize them."[37]

Demonstrating the limits of the value of "whiteness," policy makers and others claimed that (white) "relief babies" *caused* the great poverty of the Depression era and deepened it, in the same way that many Republicans blamed poor people for the 2008 mortgage crisis, the Great Recession. Both are examples of politicians and others shielding elite financial leaders and the impacts of their decisions by pointing fingers at the least powerful people in the country.[38] Attacks on poor women of all races and ethnicities—and their children—functioned both as commentary on the unfitness of poor women and as a critique of New Deal programs developed to help them. Many politicians and others, including liberals, marked reproductive control as an important remedy for everything that ailed the country. Nationwide, the number of public clinics dispensing contraceptives, pregnancy and maternity care jumped from 145 in 1932 to 357 in 1937.[39] These clinics tied the sexuality and fertility of poor women to public institutions, services, and scrutiny, and they aimed to suppress the reproduction of the poor. They also dispensed crucial information and materials to poor women trying to manage their own fertility. In the meantime, groups as diverse as the New Jersey League of Women Voters, the 1930 White House Conference on Children and Health, and various religious organizations, as well as scores of prominent academics, supported terminating the reproductive capacity of a broad category of "unfit" persons as one strategy for saving America's cherished democracy myth.[40]

The development of federal programs to aid poor mothers and their children was a third policy area that promoted racial exclusion, racial difference, and racial separation while legitimately addressing the needs of some women, generally white women. The Sheppard-Towner Act of 1921, which established the first federally funded social welfare program in the United States, was born, in part, of the Progressive impulse to standardize and Americanize care for children in the era of massive immigration. Policy makers were also determined to rationalize public health programs and bring infant mortality rates into line with those of other industrialized countries. White feminist activists fervently supported this legislation (while the American Medical Association opposed it as "socialistic") because it provided services such as infant and maternity care for the poor and pre- and postpartum education for pregnant women. Some states permitted inferior services to women of color under this program, while, as we have seen, a number of states that sponsored mothers' pension programs limited recipients to "worthy," effectively white, widows and their children. This persistent feature of public programs gave special value to white mothers and their families while devaluing the maternity and the children of others.

Again in 1935, when the government initiated Aid to Dependent Children (ADC) as part of the Social Security Act, the program excluded children of "immoral" unmarried mothers and most women of color. The latter were neatly excluded in part because, to keep the support of Southern politicians, President Franklin Roosevelt agreed to categorically exclude agricultural and domestic workers from benefits, an exclusion that covered the only kinds of jobs most African American women could get in an apartheid labor system.[41] White mothers received help if they promised they would stay home and take care of their children, even during the labor-hungry years of World War II. But women of color were forced to go to work no matter their maternal responsibilities.[42] One reads the racist, antinatalist, population-control intentions of the framers of ADC in subsequent iterations of welfare policy up to the present time.[43]

All of these developments during the Progressive Era, the Great Depression, and the New Deal raised fundamental questions about interactions between sex, citizenship, and race. Congress and state legislatures passed laws that determined the character of the population, the structures of communities, the quality of municipal services, and the availability of credit. These included the "repatriation" of Mexican immigrants brought to the United States for agricultural labor and now forced to return to a country many hardly knew; restrictive immigration controls; and fierce enforcement of segregation, naturalization, and antimiscegenation laws. These laws used reproduction to regulate who could live in the United States, who could become a citizen, who could live where, who could be "white," who could love and have sex with whom, who could marry, who could be born. These laws structured the reproductive lives—and even the physical appearance and the "race"—of people living in America. And they attempted in various ways to associate citizenship with whiteness. Accomplishing this racial goal relied on pursuing policies and encouraging cultural expressions that devalued the inescapable condition of being nonwhite.

RIGHTS, RESTRAINTS, AND REACTION
AFTER WORLD WAR II

Women of color had always labored to sustain their families and communities, either as forced or low-wage workers. But social norms increasingly defined white women, especially "respectable" married women with children, as noneconomic actors. Nevertheless, during and after World War II, as during the Depression, white women's employment outside of the home surged, leading to a steadily growing demand for birth control. Given this huge demand, contraceptives were no longer the enemy of respectability, at least in the case of married women. Medical schools offered contraceptive training, and as we've seen, the number of public clinics grew quickly in this era.

But still the culture transmitted terribly contradictory messages about women's sexuality, fertility, and maternity—messages still structured deeply by race. After the Depression ended, white women were pressed to have many children, to create a large population for the "greatest democracy the world had known" and to undergird the supremacy of the free world and the consumer basis of the free market. Fecund white women of the growing middle class were beneficiaries of cultural approval and various kinds of tax benefits. White women who did not reproduce or did not reproduce enough, who put work before motherhood, or had an abortion, or who got pregnant without having a husband were targets of harsh disapproval.[44]

At the same time, public policies discouraged and punished the childbearing of women of color. The Supreme Court's *Brown v. Board of Education* decision in 1954 provided an occasion for new expressions of white hostility to African American children because many white parents did not want to see these youngsters in school with their own. The centerpiece of the complaint was an old charge: African American women and other women of color were hypersexual. They did not have the intellectual or the moral resources to be good mothers raising future citizens. Lacking these qualities, they did not qualify as rights-bearing persons. At the outset of the civil rights movement, many whites charged that women of color (most of whom still earned pitiful salaries within the apartheid labor system) lacked the economic resources to be legitimate mothers. As poor persons, so the charge went, they would give birth to welfare recipients and worse, but not to the consumers that the American economy was increasingly dependent on.[45]

Similarly, as immigration restrictions relaxed in the 1960s, immigrant women had to struggle to assert their authority and legitimacy as mothers and to insist on their basic right to have children. A particularly tragic outcome of this era was that the rise of new, more humane public policies addressing the needs of poor mothers and their children stimulated a virulent and lasting backlash. Paradoxically, the civil rights movement articulated the dignity of persons whose lives then became the public policy symbol of unbearable equality for decades to come.[46]

From the 1950s forward, female sexuality and fertility were arguably the most potent and symbolic lightning rods in the domestic policy arena. Laws and policies governing civil rights, racial equality, citizenship qualifications, women's status, and other fundamental conditions of American life were hammered out on the terrain of female fertility. Added to this, fertility became a potent flashpoint in the policy arena at a moment in the early 1960s when many academics and public officials became interested in the concept of a worldwide "population bomb." Typically, these experts warned of the dangers of the bomb's

American manifestation: the supersaturated ghetto that had to be "contained" for the safety and the future of the country's democratic institutions. Proponents of containment cited the especially high birth rates of "Negroes," who "reproduced beyond the capacity of the economy to handle," naming escalating welfare costs, overcrowded urban schools, urban crime, and other ills linked to the impacts of the Great Migration.[47] These experts ignored the apartheid labor system, poor educational systems in poor neighborhoods, and lack of quality medical care as causes of poverty. Instead, relying on post-slavery-era racist charges, they pointed to the "excessive" fertility of "irresponsible females," who persisted in having "unwanted babies" that cost the taxpayers too much.

White resentment about public provision for poor mothers continued for the rest of the century to be a major political issue. So did a state's right to assert its own authority to limit or block welfare benefits, against the authority of the federal government to require them. The fact was, ADC, later called Aid to Families with Dependent Children and then Temporary Assistance for Needy Families provided poor mothers only enough money to keep them desperately poor and did not provide comprehensive child-care services or facilitate effective job training or employment that paid well. These programs and the ways they were administered did not shield poor mothers from stigma or from public contempt for their "dependency." In fact, welfare opponents pointed to public assistance to justify new antinatalist public policies that discouraged poor women from having children or punished them when they did. States often gave African American, Mexican-origin, and Native women the smallest benefits and for a long while resisted making payments in cash, claiming that women of color were too irresponsible to manage money. Especially in regions with larger populations of color, welfare programs distributed surplus commodities and rent vouchers instead.

Policy makers, politicians, and welfare officials typically used the term "illegitimate" to define poor children, as if the government itself disregarded their humanity. Many states used public policy to define mothers as illegitimate, too. Rules permitted welfare-department surveillance of a mother's house, typically targeting households of women of color. Staff were directed to take note, and even to barge in, when a male visitor was present. The point was to entrap women who were, extraordinarily, forbidden by so-called man-in-the-house rules to have sexual relations and to have additional children while they received public benefits. This system operated on the premise that sex-while-poor was against the law, and the punishment was loss of benefits. (Some state legislatures tried to pass laws that mandated sterilization or even imprisonment for this "crime.") Once again, sexuality and fertility and maternity became sources of danger and degradation for poor women.

Poor women typically did not want more children than their middle-class counterparts wanted. Studies at the time showed that poor women reported they had more children than they desired only because they didn't know how *not* to get pregnant. Scholars, welfare administrators, public health physicians, and others who looked into this matter directly found that poor women were absolutely eager for birth control. A North Carolina welfare official said that when his office sent "homemakers" out into the community, knocking on doors, asking the woman of the house if she wanted to "learn something about this subject," no one "ever had one door slammed in [her] face." In Chicago, for example, the number of patients, most of them poor, who sought birth control at Planned Parenthood clinics doubled in the first nine months of 1962.[48]

A report from Detroit a few years later, after the civil rights–era rebellion of the summer of 1967, showed a stunning commitment among the poor to contraception. Dr. Gary London, a physician attached to the Office of Economic Opportunity, reported, "We have a family planning program, funded by OEO, which is situated in the heart of the riot area. On the block where that building is situated, all the buildings on the block were burned and gutted [during the urban rebellion in July 1967], except for two. When the smoke cleared there, they found two unburned buildings. One was the Negro church ... the other was the family planning center."[49]

Also in the mid-1960s, the Amalgamated Laundry Workers, representing many African American women and in part responding to these workers' demands, launched a free birth control program through its health center.[50] Even the Southern Christian Leadership Conference, belying the common wisdom that African American men were uniformly opposed to birth control for religious, political, and masculinist reasons, issued a publication at this time entitled "To Make Family Planning Available to the Southern Negro through Education, Motivation, and Implementation of Available Services."[51]

Many poor women, organizing welfare-rights groups and women's health organizations in the 1960s and 1970s had, themselves, received welfare under degrading conditions. When they founded the National Welfare Rights Organization and other groups, they emphatically defined themselves as rights-bearing persons and legitimate mothers of legitimate children. Most profoundly, they insisted on their right, despite their poverty, to be mothers, and they maintained that their status as mothers qualified them as citizens deserving social provision. These claims would later form the backbone of the reproductive justice movement.[52]

The war on motherhood in the 1960s and 1970s excluded several categories of women from legitimate motherhood, along with poor, unwed women of color. Commentators of many political persuasions accused white feminists—women who claimed "too much" power for themselves—of turning their backs on childbearing. These accusations were aimed even at women who were, in fact, mothers but had outside jobs too, and women who advocated for reproductive rights. In the 1950s and 1960s, psychiatrists, social workers, teachers, religious leaders, and other community authorities had disqualified white females who got pregnant outside of marriage from legitimate motherhood. Defining white unwed motherhood as a psychological disorder, authorities promoted adoption as a mass solution for dealing with the growing number of white girls and women who had sex, got pregnant, and stayed pregnant without being married. Authorities decreed that a white unwed mother could "redeem" herself only by secretly "surrendering" her child for adoption to a properly married white couple.

Cultural and political authorities disqualified both white females and females of color without husbands from authentic motherhood, but the strategies for dealing with women in this situation were completely racialized. The white mother was pressed hard to relinquish her child; the mother of color had "no choice" but to keep hers and suffer official punishments for having given birth.[53] At the dawn of the women's rights movement, many mothers of whatever race were vulnerable to degradations associated with their sexuality and fertility. Politicians and policy makers deployed this vulnerability to achieve various public policy goals, including the reinstitutionalization of racial discrimination at the same time that the civil rights movement was taking form and achieving significant advances.[54]

Hundreds of thousands of girls and women, both whites and people of color, who wanted to avoid the horrible experiences of coerced adoption or impoverished, shamed, or unwanted pregnancy turned to abortion in the decades before decriminalization. These persons, probably more than one million a year around the country, were willing to resist the law. But they also walked a dangerous path because, after decades of ignoring abortion laws, now law enforcement authorities, eager to show how well they were "cleaning up" urban vice, began to target abortionists. District attorneys and police superintendents did not typically call upon religion or the fetus's right to life to justify their raids and crackdowns. Frequently, they did not save their surveillance and arrests for practitioners accused of harming clients or causing death. They hung their reputation for law enforcement on newspaper headlines and lurid photographs and on courtroom sensations. In these locations, the mostly white women who came to the attention of the law were accused of murdering not babies, but their own destiny: motherhood.

Beyond the courtroom, these images and events broadcast a warning to all women, or at least to the white women they focused on and featured: to rededicate themselves to proper female norms. The sensational exposés instructed women that the law (together with their sexuality and fertility) was a source of great danger (a much greater danger than the abortionist) because the law said that women were not permitted to manage their own bodies. Regarding sexuality and fertility, all women were subject, in fact, to this core condition of bondage.[55]

It is worth noting that the surviving death statistics from the decades before the legalization of abortion—numbers which are complicated to interpret since they reflect imperfect knowledge about a secret, criminal activity—provide scant evidence of high death rates from abortion before *Roe v. Wade*. Nevertheless, abortion-rights activists and others press us to remember the criminal era as a time when "back-alley butchers" botched the abortions they performed and caused no end of mayhem and death. In fact, the iconic butchers may have been most palpable as a scare tactic, constructed to distract and discourage women from going into "back alleys," outside the law, to manage their fertility.

Women of color may have had closer relations to practitioners within their communities, granny midwives and others with long-time practices who performed abortions for those they knew. These abortionists would have been protected by their own long-standing knowledge about the procedure and also by the fact police did not generally pay attention to their work. These factors may have allowed girls and women who turned to practitioners in their own neighborhoods to make decisions about pregnancy under less frightening circumstances than many whites faced.

As we've seen, repressive policies in the postwar decades were, in part, reactions to surges of citizen activism. The civil rights movement, the women's rights movement and other "liberation" activities were built on concepts of human dignity, including, in some cases, reproductive dignity. The state wobbled, sometimes supporting, sometimes defending itself against these claims, even while its power to resist claims for human dignity seemed to ebb.

One piece of reproductive technology that seemed to support sexual liberation for all women was the birth control pill, first marketed in 1960, after extensive testing, largely in programs, such as the one in Puerto Rico, that used women of color as guinea pigs, including massive sterilization campaigns.[56] In fact, even while the pill did allow millions of women substantial new control over their fertility, the policy purpose of the pill was quickly racialized. Magazines and newspapers of the day, salaciously covering the so-called sexual revolution, wrote about the birth control pill as a protective vehicle for the sex lives of (white) college girls. The media covered the so-called (black) welfare queen in exactly the same years, and just as salaciously. This female was directed to use the new pill as a social *duty*, to suppress her fertility. Elaborating on the iconic welfare queen, politicians typically portrayed all single mothers as persons of color and all persons of color as dependent on public assistance. Even and perhaps especially in the era of liberation movements, reproductive capacity and maternity continued to provide the grounds for racializing women's bodies, public policy, and the political culture to mobilize conservative resentment against progressive social change. These tactics were not just about racism and sexism; they were designed to mobilize a white electorate to maintain political and economic power.[57]

A number of important pieces of federal legislation and several Supreme Court decisions in the 1960s and early 1970s, together with the new birth control pill, enhanced the potential for women's sexual and reproductive dignity and safety. Unquestionably, these developments were stimulated by popular demands for human rights, welfare rights, and reproductive rights. The Medicaid Act of 1965 created a health care system that drew on a combination of federal and state money to provide medical services to low-income people, including pregnant and parturient women who previously had little access to costly medical care. The Supreme Court's decision in *Griswold v. Connecticut* (1965) finally fully dismantled the old Comstock Law, specifically its measures criminalizing contraception. *Griswold* defined birth control as a matter of marital "privacy." The *Roe v. Wade* decision (1973) that legalized abortion gave women individual reproductive "choice" (not "rights" or "justice") while tying their decisions to a physician's permission and other limitations.

Roe closely associated the concept of choice with a "zone of privacy" within which women could make reproductive decisions. Women of color activists began to point out in the 1970s and 1980s that only women who could afford to enter the marketplaces of choices—motherhood, abortion, and adoption, for example—had access to this zone. Women without resources could not exercise choice in the same way. For example, a poor woman might not have access to a doctor's prescription for birth control pills. She might have to decide whether to use her family's rent money or food budget to pay for an abortion. Or she simply may not have had the cash to make any such decision at all, unlike middle-class choice makers with hard cash on hand.

Women of color activists pointed out that the concept of choice masks the different economic, political, and environmental contexts in which women live their reproductive lives. Choice, they argued, disguises the ways that laws, policies, and public officials differently punish or reward the childbearing of different groups of women as well as the different degrees of access women have to health care and other resources necessary to manage sex, fertility, and maternity. In contrast, white advocates of legal and accessible contraception and abortion were often focused solely and fiercely on women's right to prevent conception and unwanted births. They typically ignored the other side of the coin: the right to reproduce and to be a mother, a crucial concern of women whose reproductive capacity and maternity had been variously degraded across American history.[58]

Ironically, after *Roe v. Wade,* some white women began to claim the right to decide whether or not to be mothers of the children they gave birth to. Many unmarried pregnant girls and women claimed the right to block parents and other authorities from making them put their "illegitimate" children up for adoption. (They also thoroughly rejected the concept of illegitimacy.) After all, the pill gave women the option to protect against pregnancy, and *Roe v. Wade* gave women the legal right to choose whether to continue a pregnancy. Shouldn't we have the right to keep the baby we give birth to, they insisted. Thus, the phenomenon of respectable white single motherhood was born, leading to the decline of domestic white adoption and the rise of searches for adoptable infants in the new international marketplace of babies. Public institutions responded to the burgeoning numbers of white single mothers; for example, in the early 1970s, new laws directed schools to develop in-building programs for pregnant and parenting teens, whereas earlier, these students would have been expelled. But still most middle-class white women did not make common cause with poor mothers of color—or even with poor white mothers—who were also struggling to assert maternal rights.

In this period characterized by progressive politics *and* old bigotry, new laws could cut in any number of directions. Notably, the Supreme Court decision *Loving v. Virginia* (1967) ended the government's long-standing power to criminalize marriage between a person identified as "white" and another identified as "colored." Forcing the law out of this terrain had substantial consequences for the ways ordinary people could think about—and experience—intimacy, race, family, reproduction, the law, and related matters—but antiwelfare policies were attacking the parental rights of women of color at the same time.

The Stonewall riots in New York City staged an immense public objection to the official policing of male sexuality. After a police raid of a Greenwich Village bar with a gay, lesbian, and transgender clientele in 1969, hundreds of protesters massed in the streets for several nights, both engaging and interrupting police aggression. The Stonewall rebellion has been credited with stimulating the public emergence of the gay rights movement as an ongoing struggle, with its own history of pursuing a full range of human rights. Within several years of Stonewall, the American Psychiatric Association and the American Psychological Association both stopped classifying homosexuality as a mental illness, moves that relieved millions of the burden of an inaccurate, unjust diagnosis linked to social degradations.[59] And yet, a generation later, in 1996, the federal Defense of Marriage Act allowed states to refuse to acknowledge the marriages of same-sex couples that had taken place in states that permitted such unions. The government validated the use of religious dicta to place restrictions not only on who a person could love and marry but also on who could be a parent and what could constitute a family.

NEW STRATEGIES OF CONTROL

Female sexuality and reproduction, still at the heart of American politics in this era, remained for decades a key policy arena for conservatives interested in rolling back human rights advances. It bears underscoring again that at the height of the civil rights movement, conservatives packaged the sexuality, reproduction, and maternity of women of color as transgressive and argued that the bad choices of these women disqualified them from being modern women and full citizens. These degradations directly harmed women, their children, and also the communities in which they lived. In these communities, all females—the mothers, the grandmothers, the sisters, the daughters, the aunts—were under official suspicion as potentially too fertile and likely targets of punishment for reproducing while poor.

In the civil rights era, programs of coercive sterilization were established in a number of hospitals serving communities of color.[60] The Indian Health Service was particularly aggressive in this arena, although it is difficult to know exactly how many sterilizations were performed under its auspices since the IHS neglected to keep complete and accurate records. A Native organization, Women of All Red Nations, has estimated that on some reservations, the rate of female sterilization was as high as 80 percent. Scholars have found that between 1968 and 1982 about 42 percent of Native women of childbearing age were sterilized compared to 15 percent of white women.[61]

African American, Puerto Rican, and Mexican immigrant women were also targets of sterilization programs. Legislators in at least thirteen states tried to pass laws that would mandate the sterilization of women for having "too many" children while receiving day-care or housing assistance, welfare, or Medicaid. In fact, poor women could not generally afford private physicians, so mostly they relied on public clinics, where they too often received treatment from staff who agreed with legislators that motherhood was an economic status: poor women had no business having children if they didn't have "enough" money. A number of studies conducted in the 1970s showed that women of color, Medicaid recipients, and women receiving welfare benefits were sterilized at much higher rates than women who did not fall into these categories. The head of obstetrics and gynecology at a public hospital in New York reported, "In most major teaching hospitals in New York City, it is the unwritten policy to do elective hysterectomies on poor black and Puerto Rican women, with minimal indications, to train residents." [62] Indeed, the Medicaid program paid for sterilizations of poor women—although not for abortions—up to 150,000 annually. [63]

We don't have documents showing how many physicians literally forced women to undergo sterilization, but this question provides a good opportunity to consider the meaning of "choice." When a poor woman arrived at a public health clinic for health care or had just delivered her baby at a public hospital and the physician, a person she probably did not know, pressed her to terminate her fertility, how much latitude did this woman have to assert her own interests? How much did her poverty and lack of education, perhaps her lack of English, and the various other stigmas arrayed against her prevent this woman from objecting to the physician's prescription, sterilization? [64] We do know that sterilization was the fastest growing method of birth control in this era. In 1970, 200,000 operations were performed; in 1980, more than 700,000, a disproportionate number of them on women of color. [65]

Ironically but predictably, at the very same time, white women had a hard time getting their doctors to agree to tie their tubes. Presumably, doctors believed the babies these women produced represented superior value to American society. A white woman typically could not be sterilized unless her reproductive output satisfied a formula devised by the medical profession: her age multiplied by the number of children she had already given birth had to equal the number 120 or greater. Plus, she needed the permission of two doctors and a psychiatrist before sterilization was approved. Only after meeting all of those conditions would the white woman have satisfied her reproductive duty. For example, if a white woman had three children, she had to wait until she was forty before even beginning to seek permission to terminate her fertility.[66]

Clearly, the experience of sterilization was profoundly different for white women and women of color. For white feminists developing their "reproductive rights" program in the late 1960s and 1970s, easy access to sterilization was an important demand. Generally, white women did not understand, and often did not try to understand, that historical and contemporary sterilization abuse of women of color meant that these women had an entirely different perspective on the issue. For women of color, the right to refuse sterilization was paramount. Even more fundamental, women of color sought to put an end to the political culture that had defined their babies as "unwanted' and made their own bodies into targets for sterilization.

By 1990, however, policy makers still pursued the sterilization option, especially now that an FDA-approved chemical agent, an implantable set of capsules called Norplant, was on the market. Norplant caused five-year periods of sterility, and after the implant was removed, infertility could persist for several additional months. At first the implant was simply offered to women—again, disproportionately to poor women, through their contact with Medicaid. Soon, though, as in earlier instances, numerous state legislatures devised measures to pressure poor women to use the contraceptive. But these new laws and policies did not require a medical determination of Norplant's safety for a given person. Legislatures also considered bills offering financial incentives to people on welfare who accepted Norplant and making acceptance a condition of receiving welfare benefits. Some states tried to make acceptance *mandatory* for women on welfare, for "inner-city" teenagers, or as a punishment for various kinds of behavior. While most teen mothers at this time were white, as were the majority of welfare recipients, these efforts targeted girls and women of color. Policy makers and public supporters of these efforts vociferously denied the racist assumptions driving the programs, claiming that their purposes were to reduce single motherhood, end poverty, and reduce the economic burdens facing the American taxpayer. They did not address how these new sterilization efforts singled out and harmed the persons and the communities they targeted.[67]

Right in the midst of these sterilization efforts, Congress passed the Hyde Amendment and has continued to reaffirm support for it every year since 1977. This is the rule that bars the use of federal funds to pay for abortions of low-income women. According to the author of the Hyde Amendment, the resourcelessness of poor women and their dependence on public health care provided an effective opportunity to pass a federal law embedding a religious objection to legal abortion.[68]

While cutting off access to abortion, the amendment's supporters frequently described poor women as "bad choice makers" and bad mothers who require reproductive restrictions on their sex life and its consequences. For many policy makers in these antiwelfare decades, an unintended pregnancy was no longer simply an "accident" but more like a crime, punishable by reduced welfare benefits or ineligibility for any assistance at all. A poor pregnant immigrant or a woman of color dealing with public officials and agencies might be sentenced (without medical consultation) to a regimen of long-acting contraceptives or prosecuted for a behavior that pregnant middle-class women could easily keep private. Using public services, a poor woman might also suffer the consequences of public policies that accommodated Catholic and other religious strictures.[69] Notably, neither the Hyde Amendment nor the criminalization of the reproductive lives of poor women has been a major issue for mainstream reproductive rights organizations in the United States until very recently after pressure from the reproductive justice movement.

However, some progressive reproductive freedom organizations, such as the Reproductive Rights National Network, the National Women's Health Network, and the National Network of Abortion Funds, have supported the campaigns against Hyde, distinguishing themselves from mainstream organizations.[70]

DEFINING REPRODUCTIVE JUSTICE

Not surprisingly, in the 1990s, after generations of sexuality- and fertility-related degradations—from slavery times throughout the twentieth century—a number of women of color spoke out together, making the case that their route to reproductive dignity did not depend on simply making good *personal choices*. These women, many associated with SisterSong, an Atlanta-based reproductive justice organization founded by Luz Rodriguez, Loretta Ross, and others, were responding to white feminists (and white-led organizations) who had, for several decades, defined "reproductive choice" as the watchword of that era, the key to life as a modern, independent woman. Looking across history, women of color activists, such as members of the National Council of Negro Women in 1973 and the National Black Women's Health Project in 1984, focused on the serious limits of choice. They underscored the lived experience of the enslaved woman who could be raped and impregnated with impunity. They pointed at the child who could be sold away from her mother or taken away and given to others to raise. They invoked the massacred Native populations. They catalogued the ways that law could mandate a woman's sterilization, could punish her for having a child, could enforce her poverty and punish her for it, could exclude her from hospitals and her children from schools and jobs, based on race. They added that laws had blocked women from immigrating to this country to join their husbands, to make families and citizens. The law could criminalize birth control and punish a woman for trying to manage her fertility. The law and other instruments of power could use this woman's body and her fertility to degrade her and her children, harm her community, and protect white supremacy in the United States. In the context of such histories, such laws and policies, what role did individual, personal choice have in safeguarding the reproductive dignity and safety of women of color?[71]

The women of color activists also pointed out that "choice," as conceived by white feminists, focused almost entirely on a woman's ability to *prevent* conception and motherhood. The activists, again pointing to their own history, objected to this singular focus on prevention. They argued that the right to have a child was as crucial to women's dignity and safety (and the dignity and safety of her community) as the right to prevent conception. The activists agreed with the mainstream reproductive rights organizations that legal, effective, and accessible contraception and abortion were crucial to women's reproductive safety and dignity, but they added that these methods of limiting reproduction did not comprise everything, or even the core conditions, that all women needed to achieve these goals.

They pointed out the limits of the U.S. legal system that could not address multiple, simultaneous vectors of oppression, and they critiqued the policy-making process that fails to address the needs of the most vulnerable populations or give them access to political power.

Once more drawing from the histories of their peoples, their families, and their communities, reproductive justice activists maintained that reproductive safety and dignity depended on having the resources to get good medical care and decent housing, to have a job that paid a living wage, to live without police harassment, to live free of racism in a physically healthy environment—all of these (and other) conditions of life were fundamental conditions for reproductive dignity and safety—*reproductive justice*—along with legal contraception and abortion. The first reproductive justice activists explained that the right to reproduce and the right not to—the right to bodily self-determination—is a basic human right, perhaps the most foundational human right. Therefore, they determined, they would begin the struggle to achieve this broadly defined human rights goal, building broad-based coalitions to move forward.

From the mid-1990s onward, an ever-expanding group of activists and organizations, most of them affiliated with an Atlanta-based umbrella group called SisterSong, built and promoted the reproductive justice framework and movement. Proclaiming that the organizations, united, could succeed by "doing collectively what we cannot do individually," the reproductive justice movement influenced activism, scholarship, and policy in a number of domains, while pressing for a broad redefinition of the constituent elements of reproductive dignity and safety.

The reproductive justice movement worked with groups fighting the effects of toxic waste on communities of color, including the negative effects on their reproductive potential and on infant and maternal health. The movement pressed the Centers for Disease Control to include women in all public health information and treatment regarding AIDS. Reproductive justice activists helped defeat several state attempts to restrict or ban abortion as well as so-called personhood legislation in Colorado. They championed the cause that led to the landmark Supreme Court decision *Lawrence v. Texas* (2003), effectively ending criminalization of same-sex sexual activity in every U.S. state and territory. Reproductive justice organizations promoted state legislation and supported legal cases validating domestic partnerships for same-sex couples, antidiscrimination measures protecting LGBT persons, and voluntary hormone therapy for incarcerated trans persons. They have given perspective and support to legislation and legal actions on behalf of pregnant women who face a variety of prosecutions and punishments based on their pregnancies. Acting collectively, reproductive justice organizations and their allies have refocused and redefined the basic elements of sexual and reproductive dignity for all.

The next three chapters will look at the conceptual, theoretical, and practical bases of reproductive justice and at ways that the reproductive justice framework has redefined three broad areas: decision making about conception, reproductive health, and parenthood. Each chapter will show how new definitions have driven politics, activism, and accomplishments in these arenas. The discussions will also address some of the major challenges ahead. Finally, the last chapter looks at how activists are pursuing reproductive justice goals around the country.

TWO

Reproductive Justice in the Twenty-First Century

This chapter explores ideas that drive reproductive justice today and speculates about how this third decade of reproductive justice activism, theorizing, and strategizing will shape reproductive justice activism and scholarship going forward. We consider the challenges, processes, and possibilities for building a human rights movement in the United States through reproductive justice activism and practice.

The chapter focuses on the origin of the reproductive justice movement and on the conceptual building blocks of reproductive justice including intersectionality, human rights, reproductive oppression, and population control. It assesses the prospects for using reproductive justice theory, strategies, and practices to build a unified, radical, and inclusive movement.

WHY DOES REPRODUCTIVE JUSTICE MATTER?

We begin with one woman's story, to illustrate how reproductive justice can change what we know about the past, how we interpret the present, and how we envision the future. We also begin with a story because we want to show how storytelling is an act of subversion and resistance. Stories help us understand how others think and make decisions. They help us understand how our human rights—and the human rights of others—are protected or violated. Storytelling is a core aspect of reproductive justice practice because attending to someone else's story invites us to shift the lens—that is, to imagine the life of another person and to reexamine our own realities and reimagine our own possibilities.

We use the metaphor of shifting lenses to signify how each person finds a unique standpoint for her own story. As an eye doctor shifts multiple lenses during an examination, asking the patient to pick out the lens that provides the sharpest perception, so each of us needs to find the correct lens through which we can "see" our own experience and its context and tell our own story. We need to identify the lens that gives us clear vision and allows us to describe our life experiences, our reproductive experiences, from where we stand. No one story (lens) can describe everyone's experience. No lens (story) is incorrect, and it takes many lenses to provide a full range of possibilities. No single lens can work for all. To embrace the vision of reproductive justice, one must embrace polyvocality—many voices telling their stories that together may be woven into a unified movement for human rights.

A great deal of what we know about life comes from the way we store and organize our memories of lived experience and how we make them into stories. What we know about life can also be expressed in the complexities of our silences, which can express many meanings. We may be silent because we don't trust others with our truths. Our stoical silence may represent a survival strategy, not acquiescence. Vulnerable people may recognize the dangers of telling their truths individually, no matter how much they are dying inside. So we often work together for strength and safety. In the 1970s, the women's movement, for example, used storytelling in groups—what was called "consciousness-raising" then—to interrupt cycles of gendered silencing and oppression. Enslaved people also used stories—in the form of orally transmitted narratives or singing with their peers, in a group—as a safe way to express truths about racial oppression and the brutality of slavery.

Storytelling helped create the national coalition SisterSong Women of Color Reproductive Justice Collective in 1997. Sister-Song, the leading proponent of the concept reproductive justice in the United States and abroad, adopted the motto "Doing collectively what we cannot do individually" to reflect its members' conviction that our collective power is based on and derived from our power to tell our own stories.[1] We break the conspiracy of silence when we move from silence into speech. We make speech our revolutionary gesture: we tell our own stories and determine what they mean. We pay attention to Black feminist writer Zora Neal Hurston, who wryly remarked, "If you are silent about your pain, they'll kill you and say you enjoyed it."[2]

At this historical moment, narratives have become a key strategy for making social justice claims to change the world. Social justice groups all over the world are using stories to explain—and claim—their power to "build a bridge across our fears of what has never been before," in the words of Black feminist Audre Lorde.[3] Stories make our individual and community survival more likely, especially when we tell subversive stories about resisting oppression. First, women told their stories about being raped and battered in the early 1970s, and then they launched a global movement to end violence against women. Reproductive justice helps break our silences to ask many questions about knowledge and beliefs, about the nature of society, about who benefits and who is harmed. We break our silences to ask why lethal inequalities persist. We trust in the power of personal and cultural biographies.

The Political Is Personal: A Reproductive Justice Story

Imagine you're a young woman in college on a scholarship in her first semester, because great grades helped you graduate at sixteen. You're majoring in chemistry, eventually headed to medical school. You've met someone who might be your future husband, a first-year law student who teaches you how to drive, and helps you improve your already good study habits. He patiently explains how to conquer both precalculus and pinochle. A thousand miles from home, you're enjoying both your first "adult" relationship and the freedom and responsibility of going to college.

By the second semester, you've had sex with him three times. Of course you're a little worried, because you didn't use condoms each time. You're not old enough to get other birth control without your conservative parents' permission.

And then it happens. Your period is two weeks late. Your mind seizes on a frenzied set of oh-my-god questions: "OMG! What will my family say? OMG! Can I stay in school? OMG! Can I tell my boyfriend and will he freak out? OMG! I only work part-time; will I lose my job? OMG! I believe in abortion, but what if he doesn't? OMG! What will I do?"

This young woman does not even know for sure that she is pregnant, but she will soon realize that the answers to her OMG questions determine whether or not she's ready to become a mother. If she has the economic, emotional, and moral support of her family and partner, maybe she will continue the pregnancy.

If she doesn't, maybe she will seek an abortion for what might have been a wanted pregnancy under other circumstances.

Nearly every woman who has unprotected sex with a man and is scared by a late period has faced these OMG panics. Many women confront these difficult situations that pro-choice/pro-life abortion debates rarely mention. Not every unplanned pregnancy is unwanted, and not every wanted pregnancy leads to a birth. The OMG questions involving education, financial security, family relationships, and the partner's reaction are far upstream from the "to be or not to be" question of motherhood. The pro-choice side is primarily concerned about legality, safety, and access. The pro-life side emphasizes morality, religion, and the potential life of the unborn child. Sometimes pro-life advocates scorn a woman's reasons for seeking an abortion, finding them much less important than considerations of a potential human life. At the same time, some pro-choicers question a woman's decision to continue a pregnancy by judging this person as unfit to parent. They may claim she already has too many kids, she is too poor, she has a bad contraceptive history. Both sides fail to understand that the answers to the OMG questions are the actual logic chain that a woman goes through when she is deciding to continue or end a pregnancy.

Of course, not every pregnant woman is in total control of her decisions. She may be mentally disabled. She may be physically disabled, unable to marshal the necessary resources to have a real choice. He may be a transman rejected by a health care provider. Or she may live on a Native American reservation with access only to health care provided by the Indian Health Service, which prohibits abortions. Or, in the eyes of the law, she may simply be too young to have an abortion, even though she is not too young to become a mother. To understand and respond to stories like these, we needed reproductive justice.

BIRTHING AND DEFINING REPRODUCTIVE JUSTICE

[We are] participating in the creation of yet another culture, a new story to explain the world and our participation in it, a new value system with images and symbols that connect us to each other and to the planet.
　—Gloria Anzaldúa[4]

I—Loretta—had experiences that were like the ones that this first-year college student had. They were part of my Black feminist journey. I was that young woman with the OMG panic in 1970. Twenty-four years later, I helped create the reproductive justice framework with eleven other Black women meeting in Chicago in 1994 at a larger pro-choice conference advocating for health care reform.[5] The meeting was organized by the Illinois Pro-Choice Alliance and the Ms. Foundation for Women. At the time, the Clinton administration's plan for health care reform avoided the issue of reproductive health care, especially abortion, an attempt to placate Republican opponents.

After the first day of the conference, the twelve of us gathered to discuss Bill Clinton's transparent and overly optimistic attempt to appease implacably hostile Republicans, an attempt which didn't make sense to us. We didn't trust that the administration would feint to the right and then move left. If health care reform did not explicitly prioritize women's needs, how could we support it? We felt we were being thrown under the bus by our purported allies.

To begin with, we absolutely recognized that reproductive health care is the main reason many women first visit a doctor. After menstruation, our *second* most unforgettable memory of becoming a woman is often the cranked-up cold speculum during our first pelvic exam. Those stirrups, together with the speculum, basically say, "Welcome to womanhood!" Too many girls and women still receive that message under conditions that feel sexist. And the conditions feel sexist in part because health care is meted out or withheld according to a regime of male-controlled political calculations regarding what medical services our society—and women, in particular—need and deserve.

We objected first of all to the fact that the Clinton health reform efforts in the early 1990s, efforts that ultimately failed, pandered to Republicans. But second, we objected to the ways that their proposals isolated reproductive rights issues from other social justice issues (the OMG questions) for vulnerable people. The proposals on the table did not make connections between the decision to become a mother—or not—and extremely relevant issues such as economics, immigration, and incarceration. Third, the twelve Black women at the pro-choice conference in 1994 collectively questioned the primacy of abortion, but not its necessity. We placed *ourselves* in the center of our analysis and made the case that while abortion was a crucial resource for us, we also needed health care, education, jobs, day care, and the right to motherhood. Taking this position was a powerful example of *centering,* placing oneself in the center of the lens in order to discover new ways of describing reality from a particular standpoint. These fresh perspectives—so different from the endless and debilitating debates that focused exclusively on abortion—radically shifted our thinking and launched the concept of reproductive justice by splicing together the equation of *reproductive rights + social justice = reproductive justice.*

Reproductive justice is not difficult to define or remember. It has three primary values: (1) the right *not* to have a child; (2) the right to *have* a child; and (3) the right to *parent* children in safe and healthy environments. In addition, reproductive justice demands sexual autonomy and gender freedom for every human being. The problem is not defining reproductive justice but achieving it.

Our group of twelve, an informal alliance we called Women of African Descent for Reproductive Justice, decided to launch an ad campaign to challenge the Clinton administration's strategy and to get the attention of Washington policy makers. We crafted a national statement for Black women regarding our demands for health care reform. Six weeks after the Chicago meeting, we raised the funds to place a full-page signature ad in both the *Washington Post* and *Roll Call* (a publication that serves all the people who work in Congress and on Capitol Hill) on August 16, 1994, under the more media-friendly name Black Women on Health Care Reform. Almost 850 African American women joined, including professor Angela Davis, novelist Alice Walker, and supermodel Veronica Webb.[6]

Our group created the concept of reproductive justice and a nascent movement out of our need to develop a response to a public policy proposal for health care reform that, as it stood, failed to meet the needs of women. As Black women, we shared a unique standpoint that expressed how the reproductive privileges of some women depended on the reproductive disciplining of other women in ways that did not challenge racism or other vehicles of inequality. This new reproductive justice perspective began to explain how all people experience their reproductive capacity according to multiple intersecting factors including their class, race, gender, sexuality, status of their health, and access to health care.

In 1994 we had no idea we were literally at the forefront of a new movement that would revolutionize reproductive political activism in the United States. Yet at the end of the twentieth century, reproductive justice offered new visions of self-determination, collective unity, and liberatory practices. Reproductive justice was a breathtaking and innovative theoretical breakthrough that changed the way that mainstream and grassroots groups in the United States and abroad thought about reproductive politics.

After the original reproductive justice conceptualization, other women of color—particularly members of SisterSong—expanded and deepened our analysis of reproduction and human rights, based on a wide-ranging set of intellectual influences and foundations, particularly Black feminist theories of intersectionality and identity politics, as we will explain.

In 2003, the SisterSong Women of Color Reproductive Health Collective organized its first national conference and featured a plenary and workshop on reproductive justice.[7] SisterSong challenged the speakers to address these questions: What is reproductive justice? Could it serve as a new way for women of color to address reproductive injustices? Could it be used to build a movement by and for women of color to address reproductive politics in the United States? The six hundred participants at SisterSong's conference enthusiastically supported this revolutionary concept. Reproductive justice began to march from the margins to the center of reproductive activism to protect the human rights of all women.

At the 2003 conference, the Feminist Majority Foundation, NARAL Pro-Choice America, the National Organization for

Women (NOW), and the Planned Parenthood Federation of America asked SisterSong to help organize a national march for women's rights to take place in Washington, DC, in 2004. After some negotiation, members of SisterSong and other women of color, particularly members of the National Latina Institute for Reproductive Health, the Black Women's Health Imperative, and the National Asian Pacific American Women's Forum, agreed to help organize the April 25, 2004, March for Women's Lives, which reportedly became the largest protest in U.S. history with 1.15 million participants. NARAL and Planned Parenthood originally wanted to call the event the March for Freedom of Choice, focusing exclusively on abortion and birth control. But women of color insisted that the name be changed to the March for Women's Lives, a more inclusive name,[8] and demanded that the organizers move beyond a singular focus on abortion to include other reproductive justice and human rights issues.[9] The impact of the march helped to advance the concept of reproductive justice, and in the minds of many analysts, its new reproductive justice focus helped the march achieve its unprecedented size. The National Organization for Women became the first mainstream women's organization to use the phrase "reproductive justice" when it promoted the march in a 2003 newsletter.[10]

The first book focusing on reproductive justice, *Undivided Rights: Women of Color Organize for Reproductive Justice,* was published in 2004. This book introduced the concept to an even broader activist and academic public, particularly students and young people. The book detailed the histories of Native American, Asian Pacific Islander, Latina, and African American activists working in local and national community-based organizations devoted to reproductive health, sexual autonomy, and human rights.[11]

The book told a vibrant history that was largely unknown to the general public, but after these events in 2003 and 2004, the recognition of women of color as a growing power base within U.S. reproductive politics accelerated. This was an important shift because up until that time, women of color were largely seen as *objects* of reproductive control by family planners, elected officials, demographers, and eugenicists. The development of the reproductive justice framework forcefully demonstrated the *agency* of women color and the power of our movement to produce new theories, new knowledge, and new forms of activism that could alter the American political and economic landscape.

A groundbreaking essay, "A New Vision for Reproductive Justice," in 2005 by Asian Communities for Reproductive Justice (now Forward Together) argued that advocacy and policy work must center the lens on the most vulnerable people in part to get politicians to stop sacrificing members of this group as a strategy for achieving quick wins that, in fact, intensify long-term oppression.[12] The essay analyzed the differences between the reproductive health, reproductive rights, and reproductive justice frameworks, a particularly insightful and original contribution.

The essay showed how these three conceptual structures together provide a complementary and comprehensive response to reproductive oppression as well as a proactive vision articulating what we are fighting for and suggestions for how to build a new movement to advance women's human rights:[13]

> *Reproductive Health* is a framework that looks at service delivery and addresses the reproductive health needs of individual women. It focuses on the lack of health care, services, and information, including research and health data. Within the reproductive health structure, the goals

are to improve and expand health-care services, research, and access, and particularly to improve and expand preventative services.

Reproductive Rights is a legal and advocacy-based model that is concerned with protecting individual women's legal right to reproductive health care services, particularly abortion (often called the pro-choice movement). It addresses the lack of legal protection and weak enforcement of laws to protect individual women's reproductive choices regarding health care services. The goals are to have legal protection for all individuals and to claim these protections as rights under the U.S. Constitution.

Reproductive Justice is a movement-building and organizing framework that identifies how reproductive oppression is the result of the intersection of multiple oppressions and is inherently connected to the struggle for social justice and human rights. Reproductive justice argues that social institutions, the environment, economics, and culture affect each woman's reproductive life. Reproductive justice activists invoke the global human rights system as the relevant legal framework using treaties, [and] standards, [while] moving beyond the U.S. Constitution.

Each of these frameworks has strengths and limitations; together they form the matrix of reproductive activism for the twenty-first century. Reproductive justice calls for an integrated analysis, a holistic vision, and comprehensive strategies that push against structural conditions that control our communities by regulating our bodies, our sexuality, our labor, and our reproduction. Reproductive justice demands that we work across social justice movements to build a united struggle for universal human rights in a way that includes everyone. It enables us to pursue a vision that will protect and determine our complete physical, mental, spiritual, political, economic, and social well-being. In order to turn reproductive justice into action, we must develop new leaders, organize young people, and educate existing community leaders about reproductive justice. How will we know when we win? According to ACRJ's "New Vision" statement:

> Reproductive Justice is achieved when women, girls, and individuals have the social, economic, and political power and resources to make healthy decisions about our bodies, sexuality and reproduction for ourselves, our families, and our communities.[14]

Since 1994 when the term "reproductive justice" began to eclipse pro-choice language as the primary way many activists talked about reproductive politics, the transition frequently produced tensions. Some people thought the reproductive justice framework had been created to counter the pro-choice framework, a mistaken impression that assumed that white women, not Black women, were at the center of our lens in Chicago. Some people were skeptical about this new framework, worrying that it improperly minimized the focus on abortion or, too often, avoided mentioning abortion altogether. Other skeptics thought reproductive justice was too broad a concept and a claim. By bringing together the right to have children and the right to parent them in safe and healthy environments, these skeptics claimed, reproductive justice included *everything,* even the kitchen sink. Women of color pushed back, pointing out that both historically and in contemporary America, ubiquitous and persistent white supremacy and population control efforts have clarified that the motherhood rights of all women are not equally valued and neither are all children. Some critics doubted the efficacy of the human rights framework, since most Americans associate the term "human rights" with other countries, nations where the torture of political prisoners is commonplace. Some larger organizations in the movement simply saw reproductive justice as an intriguing phrase applicable to women of color but largely irrelevant to their own constituencies.

But despite these concerns, the reproductive justice concept and the movement surged forward. Today, many women of color and their allies are producing a prodigious body of work on reproductive justice in the United States and internationally. For example, in 2014 the social development minister of South Africa, Bathabile Dlamini, announced that reproductive justice was the conceptual framework she used to determine health policies for her nation.[15] The New York City Department of Health and Mental Hygiene has adopted the reproductive justice perspective to inform and guide all of its work in its Bureau of Maternal, Infant, and Reproductive Health, which will surely be a model for other municipal health departments around the country. This global explosion of reproductive justice activism and its fertile scholarship have sparked a radical provocation and an interruption of narrow, repetitive, and unproductive debates on abortion.

We think of reproductive justice as an open source code that people have used to pursue fresh critical thinking regarding power and powerlessness. The results of this analysis are only beginning to emerge. As musician, activist, and scholar Bernice Johnson Reagon said, "Most of the things that you do, if you do them right, are for people who live long after you are long forgotten. That will only happen if you give it away."[16] Women of color offered reproductive justice to the feminist world as an important contribution to political and social analysis of reproductive politics. In the process, they successfully transformed reproductive activism at the beginning of the twenty-first century.

One key to the success of reproductive justice is that this framework infers a universality that has previously eluded the women's movement, while avoiding essentialism. That is, reproductive justice does not insist that one set of meanings or experiences describes the experiences of all people. On the contrary, reproductive justice insists that no particular reproductive experience is superior to or more authentic than other experiences. Reproductive justice is universally applicable because every human being has the same human rights, a foundational reproductive justice principle. While reproductive justice was created by women of color, its precepts apply not only to women of color. But only women of color created a theoretical breakthrough in this arena that is universally relevant.

The reproductive justice framework begins with the proposition that while every human being has the same human rights, not everyone is oppressed the same way, or at the same time, or by the same forces. Nevertheless, the experiences of oppression and struggling against oppression are constants in human experience. Most of us have had or will have the experience of being unjustly degraded and rendered powerless by another individual or by an institution, often because of our personal characteristics such as gender, race, class, religion, or sexual orientation.

Reproductive justice incorporates "standpoint theory" and its concept of shifting lenses to understand these matters. This concept helps us interrogate a host of injustices that may seem tangential to reproductive health, rights, and justice—for example, gentrification, environmental degradation, incarceration, migration, and militarization. Reproductive justice looks at how these issues intersect with each other and how, at various points of intersection, they affect the reproductive bodies of women and individuals.

INTERSECTIONALITY: DO DIFFERENCES DIVIDE?

Several decades ago, women of color invented ways to describe how gender is structured through race and class and to show how women are targeted for multiple forms of oppression simultaneously. For example, every human being has multiple identities based on race, gender, class, religion, ability, immigration status, and other characteristics. Naming and owning all of these identities, and understanding how they interact simultaneously to create unique individual experiences was a difficult undertaking. In 1989 critical legal theorist Kimberlé Williams Crenshaw named the concept "intersectionality" to illustrate how racial and gender oppression interact in the lives of Black women. She used a traffic metaphor: Black women stand at the intersection of Race and Gender Streets, vulnerable to injury from cars traveling along either axis. Crenshaw explained that neither race nor gender by itself could capture the particular experiences of Black women.[17] Only when we imagine the *intersection* of race and gender can we imagine the needs and perspectives of African American women. Without this perspective, their situations are unseen, neglected, and misunderstood. Lacking an intersectional perspective, African American women do not have the vocabulary or the conceptual spaces for addressing the harms they suffer, especially because our legal structures are not designed to account for multiple forms of simultaneous oppression. Intersectionality has become one of the most significant Black feminist contributions to feminist theory and practice.

Crenshaw drew on a long legacy of the objections of women of color to social and cultural constructions of "woman" that included only white women. For example, Sojourner Truth's declaration "Ain't I a woman?" foreshadowed Black theorist and activist Frances Beal's 1969 concept of "multiple oppressions." In 1970 Toni Cade (Bambara) expressed a key dilemma: the English language does not adequately offer a way to describe the multiple locations in which individuals actually exist.[18] Consequently, she argued, we either have to rediscover ourselves within the limited vocabularies that do exist or create new words and meanings to describe the realities we see. The deeply influential 1977 Combahee River Collective's statement by Black feminists including Barbara Smith, Demita Frazier, and Beverly Smith, introduced the term "identity politics" and argued that racial and sexual discrimination, homophobia, and classism were "multifaceted and interconnected."[19] In *This Bridge Called My Back,* Chicana activists, theorists, and writers Cherríe Moraga and Gloria Anzaldúa wrote about the linkages of class, race, sexuality, and feminism in a way that explored the concept of intersectionality nearly a decade before Crenshaw named it. This family lineage provided a strong platform for launching a new theoretical framework offering all human beings a chance to explore their own intersecting identities and to resist being forced into a one-dimensional box.

Reproductive justice is based on the understanding that the impacts of race, class, gender, and sexual identity oppressions are not additive but integrative. For each individual and each community, the effects of these impacts will be different, but they share some of the basic characteristics of intersectionality: universality, simultaneity, and interdependence. Intersectionality powerfully addresses human rights violations and helps us move away from single-issue and top-down approaches. It provides an avenue for cross-issue alliances to achieve systemic, institutional changes because systems of oppression overlap and interact with each other. For example, a Dominican homeless transwoman may be simultaneously affected by poverty, gentrification, transphobia, sexism, racism, and xenophobia (that is, hatred of immigrants). These oppressive forces do not emerge or act independently of each other; they depend on each other, they feed on each other, and they gain strength from each other: they are integrative. Solutions based on an intersectional analysis require a holistic approach, not a linear approach that distorts our realities. A homeless woman's problems will not be effectively addressed, for example, by giving her a bed in a temporary shelter or even permanent housing. If we use a holistic, intersectional approach, we ask, why is this woman homeless in the first place? We attempt to address the multiple root causes of her situation and not simply pay attention to the immediate, presenting symptoms.

The concept of intersectionality has evolved to describe a system of advantages and disadvantages dependent on markers of difference. The result is not an account of identity but an explanation of power disparities. Sometimes *identity politics*—making claims for recognition and resources based on, for example, race or sexual orientation—can overwhelm efforts to build a human rights movement. Indeed, differences can be a platform for positive creative change, or they can build barriers that separate people into bitter, competitive camps.

When activists assume that only those with whom they share particular identities are acceptable, safe, or credible, they are promoting a mechanical "angel/devil" practice of radical struggle, creating a false binary. This kind of "purity politics" foments criticism, shaming, and silencing—and turns naturally occurring political disagreements into excuses for dismissing the voices of others. Purity politics harms the chance, as Toni Cade Bambara put it, to "make revolution irresistible." [20] In the reproductive justice movement, we always need to emphasize that using difference as a weapon is contrary to our framework. Using difference as a weapon thwarts the transformative and radical solidarity of reproductive justice as people become "identity bullies." No one wins in the Oppression Olympics. In order to achieve reproductive justice, we need a united human rights movement that includes all persons and their voices.[21]

On the other hand, identity politics can be a positive force. As people explore their multidimensional identities, they sometimes seek a "safe space" with others like them, a space in which to explore the meanings and power of these joyfully ambiguous realizations. They want and deserve a nurturing space in which to decide who they are and how they want the world to recognize who they are. This is the essence of identity politics, to help create that womb-like safe space where one is fed, nurtured, and encouraged to grow.

But when people mistake the collective movement for a womb—that is, a very safe place—they sometimes become fierce language disciplinarians or boundary-watchers who experience their lack of safety outside the womb as a form of violence. When this happens, a human rights movement—in this case, the movement for reproductive justice—is harmed. It may be a hard lesson, but the road to human rights is not necessarily a protected space. Over and over we've seen that antioppression work does not necessarily guarantee or provide a safe space free from painful triggers. If being oppressed is dangerous, why would anyone assume that fighting oppression—the toxic forces of capitalism, homophobia, racism, sexism, ableism, transphobia, nativism—can take place in a safe space? Did the sit-in activists in the civil rights movement experience safety? Do the antiviolence feminists who confront rapists and batterers expect safety? Do the Dreamers who are fighting for respect and legal rights as immigrants live in safe spaces? Are fast-food workers fighting for the $15-an-hour minimum wage too afraid of being fired to protest? In short, coalition work is often scary and challenging. Indeed, Bernice Johnson Reagon warned that coalition work "is the most dangerous work you can do.... Some people will come to a coalition and they rate the success of the coalition on whether they feel good when they get there. They are not looking for a coalition; they are looking for a home!"[22] The reproductive justice framework is defined by coalition politics and cannot achieve its human rights goals without building coalitions.

Reproductive justice activists are also challenged by the difficulties of making their claim for justice at a time when many Americans, including many politicians, claim that all racial problems in the United States have already been resolved. The Black Lives Matter campaign—a powerful public articulation since 2013, when the murderer of Trayvon Martin, a Black teenager in Florida, was found not guilty—calls attention to the modern, slow-moving, genocidal legacy of slavery in the twenty-first century. But notably, some liberal activists have tried to convert "Black Lives Matter" into the slogan "All Lives Matter," overlooking and misunderstanding the purpose of the original campaign. "Black Lives Matter" signifies that *not all lives have mattered* in the United States. "Black Lives Matter" names the lives that have not mattered and directly and forcefully asserts the inherent worth of Black lives.

In the same way, Black feminist intellectual-activists who created the interrelated concepts of *identity politics, intersectionality,* and *reproductive justice* are on guard, on their own behalf and on behalf of others, against being rendered invisible by what we can call "misogynoir erasures." "Misogynoir" is a term coined by queer Black feminist scholar Moya Bailey to name anti-Black misogyny, the space where race and gender intersect in the hatred and contempt for Black women. Bailey's term defines the terrain upon which the campaign for the dignity and safety of Black women's lives is waged.[23]

Human rights activists stand behind these truths because they express the fundamental human rights commitment to foreground the lived experiences of those most vulnerable to danger from settler colonialism, racism, sexism, homophobia, transphobia, classism, xenophobia, Islamophobia, and Christian nationalism.[24] The lived experiences of these most vulnerable persons, groups, and communities cannot be folded into the "American fabric" and forced to disappear.

Predicting and reflecting the turn toward intersectionality, poet and essayist Audre Lorde affirmed: "It is not those differences between us that are separating us. It is rather our refusal to recognize those differences and to examine the distortions that result from our misnaming them and their effects upon human behavior and expectation."[25] It takes all of our differences to make our movement whole; differences become barriers that break us into fragments only if we let them.

HUMAN RIGHTS VS. THE U.S. LEGAL SYSTEM

After the reproductive justice framework situated our analyses of reproductive politics within the human rights framework, we found we could have new kinds of conversations and develop new opportunities. Our maxim became both foundational and aspirational: *Reproductive justice is the application of the concept of intersectionality to reproductive politics in order to achieve human rights.*

Reproductive justice is a restatement of women's human rights in the United States and globally. Reproductive justice reintegrates human rights and civil rights and looks to the international human rights framework as a sturdy moral, political, and legal structure through which reproductive justice goals may eventually be accomplished.

One of the ways the U.S. Constitution is limited is that the legal system it produces focuses on *intentions,* not *effects.* The Supreme Court has held that if a law disproportionately burdens a class—even if the disparate impact is credibly caused by discrimination—it is not constitutionally suspicious and is likely to be upheld.[26] It is only when a law is unequivocally determined to have been motivated by discriminatory intent that its constitutionality is seriously in question. Thus, if a woman who is employed by the federal or a state government is paid less than her similarly situated male counterparts, she must prove that the government intentionally discriminated against her to produce this disparate outcome. The fact that all other women also receive less compensation for the same jobs as men is not sufficient; if she cannot prove intent, she will most likely lose her case. Harm has to be done with purpose. This denial of justice may sound familiar to rape survivors.

Women have also been harmed by the Supreme Court's interpretation of the Constitution as it visits and revisits *Roe v. Wade* in ways that have all but voided the decision, validating a variety of state-imposed restrictions that render geography and private economic resources the greatest determinants of abortion rights.

Over and over, state legislatures have trumped the Constitution, severely narrowing access to the right to privacy that the Court inferred in the Constitution. Women with money or private health insurance may choose to have an abortion within the guidelines of various state restrictions. But women who cannot afford to pay for their health care (such as those on Medicaid) or those whose health care is provided by the federal government (women in the military, on Indian reservations, or in the Peace Corps), are prohibited from using their health care insurance anywhere to pay for an abortion.

These federal restrictions were enacted by the Hyde Amendment, originally adopted by Congress in 1976 and upheld by the Supreme Court in *Harris v. McRae* (1980). The Court's majority in *Harris* decided that a women's "freedom of choice," as established by *Roe v. Wade*, did not require the government to pay when a poor woman wanted to "avail herself of the full range of [her constitutionally] protected choices." In *Harris* the Court said that poverty did not constitute a "suspect classification," so a poor woman did not deserve or could not demand special consideration for public funds to pay for an abortion she could otherwise not afford. This decision blatantly illustrated the limits of the paper-thin "privacy" protection articulated in *Roe*, with its words that had seemed to promise women a guaranteed Constitutional right to decide about their own reproductive lives. In fact, antiabortion politicians in many states behave as if they were physicians. They ignore the guarantee of choice. They ignore privacy guarantees. They ignore everything but their own political agendas when they pass thousands of laws using spurious "science" to mandate pelvic examinations, force ultrasounds, require parental consent, privilege wholly unscientific claims of fetal "pain" over women's rights, and mandate so-called waiting periods and irrelevant restrictions and requirements on abortion clinics and physicians—all of which create massive obstacles to women's access and create health risks for women forced to negotiate so many obstacles that they end up getting abortions later in their pregnancy.

The construction of obstacles that amount to attacks—manifestations of what is often called "the war on women"—discriminate not only against women seeking abortion health care but against all women because these laws and regulations imagine women as insufficiently mature and intelligent to make their own decisions about their own bodies.

The fact is that, although the government intrudes on and effectively stifles women's private reproductive decisions, it *enables* private decisions in other domains all the time by regulating their safety, accessibility, and affordability. For example, if you make the private decision to travel in a plane, the government plays a major a role in enabling you to implement your private decision. First, it regulates the airline industry to ensure that the plane is *safe* and does not plummet from the sky because of shoddy maintenance. Second, it ensures that the airports are *accessible,* distributed reasonably, according to the needs of regional populations. Third, the government regulates airfares to keep them *affordable,* ensuring that competition keeps fares down and that airlines cannot make unreasonable profits from smaller markets in which there are few airline options. Safe, accessible, affordable—that's what we expect from a responsible government dedicated to protecting the enabling conditions for its citizens on the move. So why is abortion exempted from that protection simply because of the objections of a religious minority?

Between the lines, but still very legibly, the Hyde Amendment and state laws express these religious objections, even though legislators often deny religious intent and always deny any intent to cause women harm. Famously, the author of the Hyde Amendment, Representative Henry Hyde (R-IL), a Catholic who objected to abortion on religious grounds, described his agenda this way: "I certainly would like to prevent if I could legally, anybody having an abortion, a rich woman, a middle-class woman, or a poor woman. Unfortunately, the only vehicle available is the HEW Medicaid bill." [27] Decades later, still ignoring this country's foundational commitment to the separation of church and state when it comes to women's reproductive capacity, the Supreme Court continues to accommodate religious objections while denying any intent to harm women. Its decision in *Burwell v. Hobby Lobby* (2014) establishes the right of corporations with owners who oppose fertility control on religious grounds to refuse to pay for insurance coverage of contraception. [28]

In contrast, our northern neighbor, Canada, focusing on real-life impacts, recognized in the 1980s that denying abortion and birth control coverage is a form of sex discrimination, and decided that the government has no legal justification for discriminating against women.

These failures in the United States to protect people (women, people of color, gender variant people, and people with disabilities, among others) from denial of basic health services and thus from discrimination propelled creators of the reproductive justice framework to explore the usefulness of the international human rights system of laws and treaties as an avenue of relief from such injustices. We posit that undergirding reproductive justice and intersectionality with the current eight categories of human rights creates a powerful impact, important to everyone's life. These categories have developed and expanded since the original affirmation of the Universal Declaration of Human

Rights (UDHR) by the United Nations on December 10, 1948, now known as Human Rights Day. The goals following the categories illustrate some, but not all, the ways these rights may be applied:

Civil rights: nondiscrimination, equality

Political rights: voting, freedom of speech, right to assembly

Economic rights: living wages, workers' rights, fair economy for 99% of Americans

Social rights: health care, food, shelter, education, welfare, social security

Cultural rights: freedom of/from religion, freedom of language, freedom of dress

Environmental rights: clean air, water, and land; no toxic neighborhoods; no GMOs

Developmental rights: control and develop own natural resources

Sexual rights: right to have or not have children, right to marry and when, same-sex rights, transgender rights, right to birth control and abortion, right to sexual pleasure, and to define families.

While these eight categories are firmly established in the international arena through treaties and laws, new categories will likely be added over time, just as environmental, developmental, and sexual rights were added after 1948, as social movements and anticolonial struggles demanded these rights.[29]

Long before the acrimonious debates on abortion in the latter part of the twentieth century, the United Nations articulated a commonsense recognition that only persons who are already born can claim human rights. In fact, the first article of the UDHR states: "All human beings *are born* free and equal in dignity and rights" (emphasis added).[30] Thus, the UDHR does not confer human rights on those who have not yet been born, but the declaration does demand that the rights of people already born are respected and protected. This includes, of course, people capable of giving birth. Human rights as established by the UDHR are not negotiable; they are inalienable, indivisible, and universal—the birthright of all human beings. To achieve our human rights, reproductive justice activists seek reproductive justice for ourselves, our families, and our communities.

Reproductive justice activists also emphasize the dialectical, or interactive, relationship between individual and group rights. The rights of a group must be protected in order for individuals to exercise their human rights. We can understand the relationship between individual and collective human rights by thinking about how human rights are used to address public health issues like HIV/AIDS and other global pandemics. Dázon Dixon Diallo of the reproductive justice organization SisterLove, considering the safety of individuals within the larger society, points out: "We're not only fighting a virus; we're fighting the conditions that allow it to proliferate.... We need to look at public health issues from within a human rights framework."[31]

Similarly, human rights and reproductive justice activists protest the practice of pressing women in communities that lack basic health care to adopt dangerous contraceptives or to use contraceptive devices that may not be safe for a particular woman. Sometimes clinic workers use feminist language to encourage women to suppress their fertility, explaining that controlling their bodies is a fundamental condition for improving women's status. Nevertheless, clinic workers around the world—and also in the United States—are often trained to prioritize population control goals even above women's empowerment. A holistic human rights approach asks why these communities lack adequate health care systems in the first place and posits that when women have educational and economic opportunities, no coercive family planning methods are necessary to persuade women to have fewer children.

The global human rights system offers the most powerful and likely pathway through which the goals of reproductive justice may be achieved. If reproductive justice activism confines itself to attempting to realize intersectionality within the U.S. legal system, the result would offer a much less radical and comprehensive challenge to the status quo. Some partial adopters of the reproductive justice framework may focus almost exclusively on the process of intersectionality—the work that allows individuals to claim their full identity—rather than on the outcome of actually achieving human rights protections. This may be problematic, because there is a real intrinsic loss in the deradicalization of the potential of the reproductive justice framework if it is divorced from its foundation in the human rights system. Special conditions based on identity markers of difference create special needs. For example, all people giving birth are entitled to safe, dignified, and compassionate health care. Incarcerated people also deserve not to be shackled during childbirth. These are not special rights; these are special needs determined by conditions in prisons that violate the human rights of pregnant people. To meet human needs, intersectionality is the process; human rights are the goal.

For example, under the United States Constitution, many issues which should be considered matters of human rights are left up to the individual states to legislate and adjudicate—to limit, to forbid, or to provide. These issues include some matters regarding access to and funding of educational opportunities, food availability, and qualifications for public assistance and basic human services such as housing, reproductive health (especially access to abortion), and many environmental protections. Reproductive justice activists believe that human rights should not depend on geography; that is, individuals should not be denied or provided with basic human rights according to their state of residence. Although the United States has often refused to ratify or objected to many provisions of various international human rights–related treaties, it has signed the Universal Declaration of Human Rights, but this declaration does not have the force of law. International treaties turn intentions into law, and Article 6 of the U.S. Constitution defines treaty ratification as having the same force as a federal law. For this reason, conservatives in the Senate repeatedly refuse to ratify many human rights treaties because doing so would overturn countless instances of legal injustice.[32] Reproductive justice activists point out that since the United States has signed the UDHR and other human rights treaties, individual states cannot pursue discriminatory policies that deny their residents basic human rights.

The U.S. government, like a number of other governments, is reluctant to limit its power; thus, the U.S. Senate has ratified only three of the dozens of human rights treaties it has reviewed in the past sixty years. A common argument since the founding of the United Nations in 1946 is that treaty ratification would alter the balance of power between the federal government and the states.[33] Elected representatives in the Senate have often been nervous about limiting states' rights and federal overrides of state laws, a fear also related to hostility to the civil rights movement and Southern states' resistance to racial desegregation when the federal government had to use force to achieve integration. Those who oppose treaties are also justifiably fearful that granting human rights to people and communities could be costly in various ways. If universal high-quality education—a human right—were provided to everyone in the United States, for example, corporations and the wealthiest Americans would likely have to pay higher taxes. Banks and other lenders who profit from student loans would lose a massive income stream if higher education did not require thousands of young people to take out enormous loans. Universal high-quality education would also produce a more informed and sophisticated electorate, a threat for politicians who depend on a poorly informed voting public.

Treaties that countries sign under the aegis of the United Nations and other international agreements signed between countries make much of modern life possible. For example, we enjoy relatively seamless planet-wide communications, air travel, and postage systems because of treaties that encourage countries to cooperate to the benefit of all humanity. Imagine the dangerous chaos that would result if each country established its own air traffic control system without cooperating with the rest of the world.[34]

We recognize that these treaties are the products of national boundaries, entities that have historically been unstable, defined by colonialism, and that may in the future disappear. Indeed, in our own time, capital, environmental issues, and, in effect, corporations are stateless. Why, then, should human rights depend on national borders? Why, then, should human rights not be universal? There is, however, little chance that national boundaries will dissolve anytime soon. For the foreseeable future, nation-states will be the dominant form of geographical and political human organization. And the human rights framework offers the best moral, political, and legal strategy for respecting persons and communities and for pressuring governments to live up to their obligations.

We recognize that the United States has both failed to ratify many human rights treaties and has not adequately enforced many of the provisions of those it has ratified. For example, the United States ratified the International Convention Against Torture in 1994 but then proceeded to ignore it, torturing prisoners incarcerated at the U.S. military detention camp in Guantánamo Bay, Cuba. This hypocrisy may increase skepticism about the power of the human rights system to stop violations by the United States, especially violations that occur within the United States. It also feeds skepticism about the commitment of the United States to human rights generally.

The task of achieving human rights-based reproductive justice in the United States is complicated, but reproductive justice activists are not deterred. We remember that on March 31, 1968, four days before his assassination, Dr. Martin Luther King, Jr. pointed out the need for a human rights revolution in the United States. The media's simplistic accounts of Dr. King tell us that he had a dream. What gets lost is that he had a plan: that we should build a united human rights movement in this country, a movement that will hold our government accountable to the promises of human freedom. Our task in the twenty-first century is to dedicate this century to human rights and to end the ceaseless wars that waste our human capital. We have the right to be more than providers of cannon fodder—our children—for the next military entanglements overseas, projects that may increase certain U.S. corporate profits, whatever else they accomplish or fail to accomplish. For our purposes now, we will draw on the human rights framework—and all that it promises—to both claim and struggle for reproductive safety and dignity for all persons.

RACE AND REPRODUCTIVE OPPRESSION

As we've seen, the impulse to police sexuality and reproduction has been a constant across the history of the United States. Politicians and policy makers have used this form of social control to achieve various purposes involving various individuals and groups, including controlling the destiny of entire communities. Today we see the renewal of a subtle form of negative eugenics, a desire to halt or diminish the reproduction of some groups while encouraging the reproduction of others. Certainly, state legislatures are committed to the policing of gender and race, in part through the proliferation of antiabortion laws.

Reproductive justice activists draw sharp attention to the United Nations Convention on the Prevention and Punishment of the Crime of Genocide, a document that articulates this point: reproductive oppression constitutes genocide because it can be characterized as "imposing measures intended to prevent births within the group, and forcibly transferring children of the group to another group." [35] In 2014, Justice NOW, a California advocacy group for women in prison, won legislation that prohibited the state of California from illegally sterilizing incarcerated women—nearly forty years after the federal government issued guidelines prohibiting such sterilizations. [36] Justice NOW collected evidence that hundreds of women had been illegally sterilized through coercive and duplicitous means, violating both federal and state prohibitions against such practices.

The UN definition of genocide also includes forcibly transferring children from a community, such as federal officials did, over many decades, when they forced Native American parents to surrender their children to be placed into boarding schools. The white Christians who ran the schools aimed to strip these children of their Indian culture and imbue them with European American culture and assimilate them as "whites" into U.S. society.[37] Legal scholar Dorothy Roberts has shown how the foster care system, another structure for separating children from their families and communities, has targeted African Americans, constituting another practice akin to genocide as it destroys the basic social units of a people.[38]

These kinds of population-control efforts are human rights violations exactly because they violate principles of self-determination as well as harm the livelihoods, health, and safety of communities. Forward Together, the multiracial progressive organization, defined "reproductive oppression" this way in 2005: "Reproductive oppression is the control and exploitation of women, girls, and individuals through our bodies, sexuality, [labor,] and reproduction. The regulation of women and individuals thus becomes a powerful strategic pathway to controlling entire communities. It involves systems of oppression that are based on race, ability, class, gender, sexuality, age, and immigration status."[39]

Some have asked whether the state of California intended reproductive genocide, or was it accidentally achieved on the path to controlling fertile incarcerated females? Are anti-immigrant policies that deport parents away from their children merely upholding the immigration law, or are these policies designed to destroy families? Are Black children, such as twelve-year-old Tamir Rice shot by police in Cleveland in 2014, and eighteen-year-old Michael Brown, shot by police in Ferguson, Missouri, in the same year, accidentally killed to preserve law and order, or is military-style policing targeted towards communities of color? The fact remains that state and nonstate actors target primarily women of color—and our children—for oppressive reproductive measures, and these take many forms that are not traditionally recognized in the pro-choice/pro-life debates.

Reproductive oppression is also implemented with policies that criminalize pregnancy by targeting and prosecuting certain women for behaviors that they would not be prosecuted for if they were not pregnant; by withholding medical care such as drug treatment from pregnant women; by mandating a five-year residency period before immigrants can access Medicaid-covered prenatal and other health care; by excluding near-poor female citizens from Medicaid benefits; by sustaining immigration restrictions; by preventing LGBTQ individuals from parenting (for example, in Mississippi, where gay couples are barred from adopting children); and by coercing pregnant incarcerated women to have abortions. These oppressions reflect the lethality of inequality and are associated with a number of degradations, including lowered life expectancies, high infant mortality rates, disrupted families in which mothers and fathers are deported away from their minor children, and denial of basic and emergency health care for transwomen and transmen. Most of these forms of reproductive oppression are mandated by state policies, the effects of which harm poor women most severely. Some forms of reproductive oppression or violence occur on an individual level as well: for example, when a woman asks a man to use a condom and he does not, or when a person attempts to control someone else's decisions about abortion or childbirth.

Jessica Yee Danforth of the Native Youth Sexual Health Network defines environmental conditions that cause harm to residents and workers as "environmental violence."[40] This analysis echoes the findings of midwife Katsi Cook, who investigated toxins accumulated in the breast milk of Indigenous women who ate fish from a river on a reservation in New York after the river had been poisoned by corporations. Cook, who defined women as "the first environment" for babies, started the Mother's Milk Project in 1985 to protest such practices by unregulated corporate polluters, actions that profoundly harmed the gestational environments and maternal and other food supplies of Indigenous communities.[41] Here the intersection of layers of bias against Indigenous people, unrestrained corporate power, lack of economic resources to defend the community, women's vulnerability due to their reproductive capacity, and mothers' ultimate incapacity to protect the future of their community—represented by the bodies and the health of their babies—among other forces, all together demonstrate the importance of the reproductive justice framework.

The reproductive justice analysis illustrates that political and medical officials have enacted population-control-related reproductive oppressions upon white women as well as women of color. As we've seen, authorities have targeted poor white women for sterilization while forbidding sterilization for middle-class white women unless they met an arbitrary mathematical standard. We've seen that between the 1940s and *Roe v. Wade* in 1973, unmarried white women who had babies were often institutionalized in maternity homes or otherwise hidden away by their families and forced to give up their babies for adoption to properly married white, middle-class people. Research by the U.S. Department of Health and Human Services has shown that about 2.6 million women, mostly white, relinquished their babies under these circumstances between 1951 and 1975.[42] Each of these and other reproductive oppressions visited upon white women expressed at its core a eugenical purpose, an attempt to make sure that the *right* white women were having as many white babies as possible and that these children were being raised in the *right* white families.

While the reproductive oppression of white women has differed in detail and scope from oppressions faced by women of color, all women are vulnerable to state control because every government throughout history has depended on the reproductive capacity of those who can give birth for achieving key national goals, such as producing a white country, creating a no-cost (enslaved) or low-cost labor force, and producing sufficient population for military forces. These reproductive controls have also aimed to achieve key cultural goals such as enforcing female subordination and enforcing standards of racial normativity. Across history, governments and private actors such as corporations or individuals have promoted laws and policies to achieve these goals, designing laws and policies to impact the reproductive capacity of different groups of women differently, depending on race, ethnicity, class, citizenship, and other characteristics.[43]

Women who cannot give birth—transwomen, older women, and surgically sterilized women, as well as those who are biologically infertile—are vulnerable to control and degradation because of their perceived incapacity or barrenness. Also subject to reproductive oppression are those who social workers, policy makers, or physicians classify as unable to manage their sexual or reproductive decisions responsibly, such as women with mental or physical disabilities. Clearly, women occupy intersectional categories, the life of any one woman being defined by multiple categories. In fact, because context matters and is ever-changing, no two oppressions are the same, and for the targeted woman, no axis of oppression stays constant over time. For example, parents may decide to sterilize their disabled child before she has reached the age of consent, a coercive and life-changing act that could express society's disinclination to allow that particular body to reproduce. But we can imagine if a similarly disabled child, unsterilized, grows into a woman who is the sole inheritor of wealth that can only be secured and transmitted within the family, that family may overlook the same disability and press the woman hard to have children, possibly using assisted reproductive technologies, her own wishes notwithstanding.

In the twenty-first century, some doctors are calling for an easing of sterilization guidelines, the rules that were hard-won in the 1970s by the Committee to End Sterilization Abuse in New York City, the National Welfare Rights Organization, and other organizations.[44] These groups argued that even with the right to abortion established by *Roe v. Wade,* thousands of women were still vulnerable to reproductive oppression and abuse when they were sterilized against their will. The first famous and catalyzing of these cases was that of a young white girl, Carrie Buck, who, in 1927, was sterilized because the authorities claimed that with an "incompetent" mother (read "poor"), Carrie, would also be incompetent.[45] The best solution, they argued, was to terminate her reproductive capacity, a claim validated by the Supreme Court decision *Buck v. Bell.*[46] Forty-five years later, another sterilization case centered on fourteen- and twelve-year-old African American sisters in Alabama, Minnie Lee and Mary Alice Relf. This time many were shocked because the events took place in the civil rights era and the same year that the Supreme Court decided *Roe v. Wade.* In this case, the girls' mother, a sharecropper denied literacy education all her life, was, like Carrie Buck's mother, unable to protect her daughters from medical authorities. Officials targeted Minnie Lee and

Mary Alice because they were poor and Black, defined them as "mentally incompetent," placed them on a long-acting contraceptive, then sterilized them, all without meaningful evidence that they were sexually active or intellectually impaired.[47]

In the same years, a group of Mexican-origin women accused a group of doctors at the Los Angeles Country Hospital of sterilizing them without their full understanding or consent.[48] Indeed, this charge was consistent with a study of doctors' attitudes, published in the January 1972 issue of *Family Planning Digest,* showing that among ob-gyn physicians, 94 percent "favored compulsory sterilization" or other punishments, including deportation, for poor women who had babies despite their poverty. Today, the physicians who want to roll back protections for women in danger of sterilization abuse say that the guidelines are an inconvenience when they are preparing to provide "voluntary" sterilizations to Medicaid patients.[49]

But instead of demanding the removal of guidelines that protect vulnerable women who are pressured in so many ways not to reproduce, progressive doctors inconvenienced by the guidelines should ask why such obstacles exist, and if, without the sterilization guidelines, vulnerable people will be adequately protected. Will dismantling the guidelines actually serve the long-term interests of all women? Some doctors and many other Americans may think about sterilization and the question "Who should be a mother?" within a particular and persistent context contoured by white supremacy and class bias. A key tactic for building the anti-welfare movement during the administration of President Ronald Reagan in the 1980s was to claim that motherhood should be a class privilege reserved only for women who can afford children. This claim has been stunningly successful on a number of levels, including dividing women against each other, setting financial qualifications and class hierarchies regarding who deserves to be a mother and who does not. Most harmful, the politics of "legitimate" and "illegitimate" mothers has created real difficulties in building coalitions among women of different races and classes in which they could work together for a national day-care policy, for example, or for birth justice, a subset of reproductive justice. Birth justice is the right to give birth with whom, where, when, and how a person chooses. These divisions and their consequences underscore a key contribution of the reproductive justice framework that seeks to move people from contemplating only their own experiences to understanding the root causes of reproductive injustices and how they affect us all.

NEOLIBERALISM AND WOMEN'S REPRODUCTIVE LIVES

As we've seen, racial slavery and white supremacy structured the laws, practices, and values associated with reproduction in North America and then in the United States. Together, the legal and moral apparatus supporting racial slavery and white supremacy defined which women possessed wombs that represented profit for whites and which women had the right to be mothers of the children they bore. The legal and moral apparatus dictated whose babies were born free and whose were born enslaved. And this apparatus regulated which babies had market value and which ones had value as white citizens. After the end of the slavery regime, when the United States developed an economy based on industrial manufacturing, principles governing reproduction evolved and changed shape. But law and policy continued to ascribe and enforce variable, racialized values regarding women's reproductive bodies and their children.

Since approximately the last third of the twentieth century, reproductive politics has developed within the context of neoliberalism, an economic-political system that prevails today in the United States and continues to produce unequal access to reproductive dignity and safety. We will consider here how neoliberalism continues to generate valuations of mothers, children, individuals, and communities depending on their race and class. First, though, we must ask, what is neoliberalism? Why did the cluster of ideas and policies that make up neoliberalism become so potent in the United States? And how does neoliberalism perpetuate and intensify reproductive harms?

Neoliberalism expresses a worldview that many elites—politicians and those who fund political campaigns, along with those who benefit from the government's business-friendly legislation and regulations—subscribe to. This worldview champions personal freedom and free-market principles. In practice, this means that neoliberals promote the idea that while the size and scope of government should be severely restrained in almost all other ways, government (or the state) should properly have a major role in creating a good environment for business and guaranteeing the health of financial systems and institutions, such as investment banks. Neoliberals believe that government should support business interests, in part by passing laws and regulations, tax and subsidy policies that help corporations and entrepreneurs maximize and protect profits.

David Harvey, a leading scholar of neoliberalism, explains how politicians and other elites who draw on these commitments have produced "corporate welfare [programs] … at federal, state, and local levels [that] amount to a vast redirection of public moneys for corporate benefit."[50] Harvey underscores that neoliberals define the state's chief purposes as protecting

individual rights, protecting the rights of private property owners, and protecting entrepreneurial freedoms. Pursuing these
goals since the 1970s, elites have worked to construct a state that
exists to ensure "corporate welfare," not the people's welfare.
Here, we will pay attention to how, in the absence of a government that prioritizes the people's welfare, the reproductive lives
of women and individuals in the United States, their children
and their communities, have been harmed.

But before enumerating some of these harms, we will briefly
sketch out why neoliberalism arose in the last third of the twentieth century and consider how proponents of neoliberalism cat-
alyzed support for an ideology that seems to benefit only rich
people. After all, in the forty years before the rise of neoliberalism in the 1970s, the government had focused considerable effort
on New Deal and civil rights–era programs to extend public
benefits and equal opportunity to a larger proportion of the
population. ·

We can begin by citing the well-known fact that by the late
1960s, the U.S. economy was no longer growing at rates that had
characterized the postwar decades. There were a number of
overlapping reasons for this development. Unemployment and
inflation rates were high; business profits were in negative territory. The war against Viet Nam was draining billions of dollars
away from civil society. Manufacturing costs were high in the
United States compared to countries with low-paid, nonunion-
ized workers who did not receive benefits. Factory owners, eager
to take advantage of cheap labor in other nations, began to close
down operations here and move off-shore, exacerbating U.S.
unemployment. The oil crisis of the 1970s, in which gas prices
shot to record highs because of the manipulation of supply by
governments in the Middle East, also spurred the sieving of jobs

out of the United States. All of these factors and others led to falling tax revenues and cuts in federal aid—to schools, hospitals, and other public services—just when society's civil rights–era interest in social and economic justice seemed to be calling for more generously funded public programs and for more, not less, equality.[51]

Elites—again, we are using this term to refer to many politicians and corporate and entrepreneurial business leaders, among others—were horrified by what they saw as out-of-control social upheaval in the 1960s and early 1970s.[52] They abhorred challenges to the stability and structural foundations of society: the claims for racial and gender equality, the legitimacy of ethnic identities, sexual freedom, the rights of disabled persons, and other such claims, all of which threatened to cost money, to redistribute wealth, and to boost the political clout of groups previously lacking power. Elites were determined to revitalize the steady, healthy profits, year by year, that had sustained the upper class since the birth of the nation, and they were especially determined to neutralize challenges to their own power as a class.

As David Harvey and others have pointed out, elites would surely have had a difficult time convincing ordinary Americans that they should vote for particular candidates and support particular policies simply because doing so would sustain the power of the rich. Instead elites who were allied with the Republican Party made "individual freedom" against "big government" their rallying cry, using these tropes to stand for white resistance to the claims of the African American freedom movement, marrying racial resentment to business deregulation. Republican elites and Southern white Democrats in the process of morphing into Republicans used this language to appeal to individuals and groups that made up the so-called silent majority, a conservative social movement later called the Moral Majority and the Christian Right.

The government pursued racial justice through affirmative action programs, the Civil Rights Act of 1964, the Voting Rights Act of 1965, and other legislation and judicial decisions. But at the same time Middle Americans (that is, economically and culturally stressed whites) associated their own economic vulnerability in a time of high unemployment and falling federal aid with the government's support for "special rights" for people of color and with family-threatening guarantees for women, such as "equal rights" with men and legal access to contraception and abortion, even for unmarried girls and women. Indeed, as we noted earlier, unprecedented numbers of unmarried white girls and women were also at this time beginning to claim their right to be mothers of the children they gave birth to, even without a husband. And many women demanded entrance to professional and graduate training programs, took jobs while they had young children at home, and insisted on equal pay and on day-care centers for their children and other public services, all developments that enraged the Moral Majority.[53] In short, business elites devoted to capital accumulation, financial innovation (the "financialization of everything"), and class privilege made a peculiar and enduring political alliance with economically and culturally vulnerable whites hostile to racial and gender equality and devoted to religious traditions that justified their resistance to social change. The ideology of white supremacy was discredited, but the institutionalization of white privilege continued.

In the quarter century between the election of Richard Nixon in 1968 and the end of George H. W. Bush's administration in 1993, the Republicans won every presidential election except one, and under their leadership, Wall Street bankers and financial power-houses came to control social policy. Little changed in subsequent decades once the neoliberal worldview took hold, even when Democrats controlled the government. Neoliberal policy initiatives included curbing the power of unions and destroying worker protections via presidential appointments of antilabor individuals to the National Labor Relations Board and the Equal Employment Opportunities Commission, cutting welfare benefits and then ending "welfare as we know it," cutting public supports for education at all levels while building the world's biggest prison system and then privatizing a significant part of the system—that is, making incarceration into a profit-making business. Presidents in this era regularly appointed probusiness jurists to the Supreme Court who guided majority decisions that weakened democratic processes. *Shelby County v. Holder* in 2013 gutted key provisions of the 1965 Voting Rights Act and concentrated political power in the hands of the rich. *Citizens United v. Federal Election Commission* in 2012 allowed corporations and labor unions to give unlimited amounts of money to political campaigns, which, in practice means that many presidential candidates are substantially funded by billionaires. Most consequential of all, in the decades since business- and finance-friendly law and policy has been ascendant, wealth has been dramatically redistributed upward.

Finally, we can consider two examples that indicate what the embrace of neoliberal economics, racial politics, and policy has to do with women's reproductive lives. First, let's consider the consequences of adopting the concept of choice as the key requirement for a modern woman, a person who is supposed to take responsibility for her life, including her sexual and reproductive life. In the early 1970s, at the dawn of the era of neoliberalism and the commercialization and commodification of everything, abortion-rights advocates selected the less-threatening shopping concept "choice" over the harder-edged political term "rights" to signify what women need. "Choice" was palatable in part because it directly associated sexual women with an approved female activity, consumerism: a woman seeking to control her fertility could enter into a marketplace of options and select the one she liked best. This association suggested that every woman possesses the wherewithal—the money and legal terrain—to enter into that marketplace of options and to pay for whatever option she selected: contraception, abortion, or motherhood. Clearly, many women lack the cash to pay for these choices, including motherhood, and thus face what might be called choiceless choices. One thinks, for example, of the "choice"—and the OMG questions—facing a pregnant person who wants to have a child but who lacks adequate housing and a secure job.

Another problem with "choice" is that this market concept strongly refers to the preferences of the individual and suggests that each woman makes her own reproductive choices freely, unimpeded by considerations of family and community. In addition to economic matters, a person deciding whether to get pregnant, to stay pregnant, or to be a mother might be pressed by family values, religious beliefs, work or educational responsibilities, and access to appropriate medical care, day care, and many other necessary resources. Having or not having access to proper resources, including family and community supports, fundamentally shapes the meaning of choice. It also underscores the truth that reproduction is a biological event and also a social (family and community-based) event, and that the concept of individual choice cannot capture the context in which persons do or do not become parents.

Racism and states' rights arguments also played an important role, because some abortion advocates believed they could split conservative opponents by appealing to a libertarian, antigovernment framework. The same opponents of federally ordered desegregation could be persuaded to oppose government intervention in abortion decisions, according to some analysts, giving rise to the pro-choice, antigovernment framework in defense of abortion rights.[54] On the other hand, abortion opponents systematically linked up with anti–civil rights, antigay, and antiunion forces to build a conservative political base for electoral power.[55]

When politicians, policy makers, and others assess some persons as lacking the wherewithal to properly enter the marketplace of reproductive options, particularly when they judge those who choose to become mothers, their judgments are often swift and cruel. Brutally disqualifying poor persons from commercial transactions, including child-rearing, politicians and social commentators have claimed that such persons have no business being parents. Such persons who get pregnant and stay pregnant are thus bad choice makers. In contrast, the same commentators have defined middle-class women, iconically white, as good choice makers, persons whose wealth and other resources make their decision to reproduce a rational, responsible choice. Here we see the neoliberal mantra, often unspoken, always legible: motherhood is properly a (white) class privilege in America. In addition to fueling class prejudice in the United States, this economistic, neoliberal view of reproductive choice making divides women against each other, as we noted earlier, and seriously undermines the possibilities for people working together, across race and class, for human rights and social policies that would support the reproductive lives, childbearing, and child rearing of all.

Having shown how neoliberalism has infected the crucial domain of language, we will next sketch out the impacts of neoliberal ideas on the reproductive bodies of incarcerated women. Throughout this chapter and others, we see how neoliberal ideas and the polices they dictate specifically and especially target and harm the reproductive experiences of poor persons.

Beginning in the 1970s and coinciding with reduced public funding for education and health and welfare services, and at the same time that real wages (the purchasing power of a person's paycheck) began to stagnate and decline, the number of persons incarcerated in the United States began to explode, harming families and communities around the country, particularly communities of color.[56] Resisting the civil rights movement's claim of human dignity for all persons, many politicians and policy makers disassociated jails and prisons from the project of rehabilitation and turned to these institutions as the architecture for a new prison-industrial complex, housing for a disposable population excluded from the marketplace of economic opportunities. The inmates in the new system were disproportionately poor people of color, many who had committed nonviolent crimes, many of whom had substance abuse problems and mental health problems prior to incarceration. For example, imprisoning people for failing to pay debts and civil penalties has been resurrected as a public policy is some states. Most of these people, no matter the length of their sentences, would be permanently barred from participating as full citizens forever because they had served time.[57]

For the first time, a growing number of women were incarcerated, too, from 11,200 nationally in the late 1970s to about 111,300 by 2013, an increase of nearly 900 percent. A substantially disproportionate percentage of these women were also people of color and poor.[58] The use of prisons as warehouses for persons defined as disposable and valueless (the implicit, economistic, neoliberal subtext) is reflected in the quality of the health care, including reproductive health care, provided to incarcerated women. The Correctional Association of New York has found that penal institutions generally establish no procedures for overseeing reproductive health care; their written policies are not comprehensive and do not meet established standards regarding either care or evaluation. The women who enter prison pregnant—one in twenty-five to thirty-three at federal prisons—receive substandard medical care during their pregnancies and regularly face serious delays in receiving the care a pregnant woman requires. Most states do not require nutritional counseling or appropriate nutrition for pregnant women, screening, or treatment for women with high risk pregnancies, or HIV testing. Not surprisingly, the failure to meet nationally recognized standards for reproductive prenatal care results in poor health outcomes for the children born to incarcerated women. That these kinds of practices prevail around the country suggests that politicians and policy makers assess this terrain as likely to bring a poor return on investment. Thus, they withhold public funds and disregard the consequences.

Furthermore, prisons pursue policies that actively degrade pregnant and parenting women.[59] Federal prisons ended the shackling of pregnant women in 2008, but many state prisons allow shackling during pregnancy and birthing, often even in states where the practice has been outlawed, and despite the fact that restraints make it difficult for doctors to assess the condition of the mother and the fetus and to know if emergency intervention is necessary. Sixty-two percent of women in state prisons and 56 percent of women in federal prisons are mothers. The siting of prisons at great distance from the communities from which most incarcerated mothers are taken, burdensome prison visiting policies, the lack of nursery programs in most state prisons, and the lack of other programs that promote the parent-child bond again reflect the lack of value accorded the reproductive lives and the children of the women caught in the carceral net. These policies and practices also reflect the state's willingness to rupture and even sever the relationships between these mothers and their children.

Reiterating (and adapting) a key idea that we began with, we must note that the application of neoliberal concepts to the reproductive lives of women has the joint, simultaneous effect of ennobling the reproductive capacity and motherhood of free, white, wealthier women and degrading the reproductive capacity and motherhood of all others. The one outcome structures and depends on the other.

POPULATION CONTROL AND WHITE SUPREMACY

Proponents of zero population growth call for fewer bodies on the planet, and the labor force in the United States is contracting in response to a number of developments, including technological innovations. What are the implications here for population politics? As we've seen, historically and now in contemporary life, many politicians, public figures, and others continue to promote white supremacy and anti-immigrant politics. This strain of population politics depends on "alarming" information about the demographic transformation of the United States: by 2044, whites will constitute a minority of the country's total population.[60] The film *Demographic Winter: The Decline of the Human Family* is popular among those who worry about such facts. The film, created to look like a documentary, combines right-wing Christian morality and ultraconservative ideology to make the argument that birth control, the sexual revolution, gay marriage, and declining white fertility constitute a set of sins that will cause the collapse of Western civilization.[61] The clear message is that white people must devote themselves to reproducing their own if the United States is to preserve its position of supreme global power. Indeed, Black feminist theorist bell hooks writes that "the very concept of white supremacy relies on 'the perpetuation of a white race,' and it is in the interest of continued racist domination of the planet that the bodies of all women are controlled."[62]

It is important to underscore that white supremacy is an ideology—a set of ideas—used to promote unequal laws, practices, and social outcomes, such as differential, racially structured access to power. "White supremacy" is not a fact of genetics or an accurate description of either a race of people or the hierarchy of all races. Not all white people are white supremacists, and not all white supremacists are white. Clearly, many people in the United States defined as white are disgusted by the tactics of the formal white supremacist movement and by its ideology. After all, President Obama received 39 percent of the white vote in 2012.[63]

Moreover, conservatives of color have proved that supporters of white supremacy do not have to be white. For example, Black conservative neurosurgeon Ben Carson often articulates white supremacist notions, such as "Obamacare is the worst thing that has happened to this country since slavery," a statement that simultaneously trivializes slavery and histrionically condemns and racializes the Affordable Care Act.[64] Carson ignores the fact that millions of Americans gained health care coverage they could not previously afford. He, like Black antiabortion activists such as Ryan Bomberger and Alveda King with their billboard campaigns claiming to save Black babies from abortion, uses his racial status to condemn Black people generally and Black women in particular.[65]

All white people do not benefit from white supremacy in the same way because class, religion, gender, sexual orientation, and gender identity, among other characteristics, create access to different degrees of privilege. These differences of degree cause some white people to deny that they are beneficiaries of white privilege. Some people hear "privileged whites" (instead of "white privilege"), and since they are acutely conscious of their lack of privilege relative to the elites of society, perhaps especially relative to rich, well-educated people of color. The argument here is that, despite differential access to resources among whites, all whites benefit from white supremacy relative to people of color. For example, wealthy people of color may be ideologically indistinguishable from wealthy white people. They may buy the same luxury watches and even share the same beaches at luxury resorts. But core racial vulnerabilities will dog them. After all, Oprah Winfrey, Condoleezza Rice, and President Obama have all described their personal experiences of "shopping while Black"—that is, having been treated by store clerks as individuals unlikely to be able to afford the merchandise and therefore likely to steal. In these and thousands of other cases, white supremacy trumped class. In a decidedly nonluxury, mixed-class commercial environment, we saw the impact of white supremacy when, in June 2015, a group of security personnel at CVS drugstores in New York filed a federal lawsuit complaining that their supervisors regularly instructed them to trail Black and Latino shoppers because they were likely shoplifters.[66]

While the mainstream pro-choice movement ignores the impacts of white supremacy, including its powerful role in reproductive oppression, the reproductive justice movement draws attention to the fact that many white Americans think of women of color as hyperfertile and define their children as "unwanted," "excessive," a threat to the body politic, a dysfunctional feature of the education system, a source of economic chaos, environmental degradation, and a criminal underclass. On the other hand, white women are pressed to reconsider their decision to forego reproduction altogether or have a small family because the demographic, racial fate of the country is potentially in their wombs.[67]

Conservative governors tie their political credentials and their chances for success to cutting state funding for public education, a budget decision that targets and has the biggest impact on children, many of them children of color living in poor neighborhoods with the lowest property taxes and the most poorly funded schools. These governors and the state legislatures they work with have also been devoted to reducing public funds for housing and food aid, job training, municipal services, and day care and to denying any hike in the minimum wage. All of these commitments inflict the worst harms on communities of color and shape the context in which women make reproductive decisions. What does it mean to have choice in this environment? No wonder long-acting reversible contraceptives (LARCs) appear to many girls and women as their only choice. With scant job opportunities, few living-wage jobs, and severely slashed public services, childbearing feels much more like a class privilege than a choice.[68]

At the same time that the context for reproductive choice turns so sour, the same state legislatures and politicians, mostly white, deepen and complicate the problem for low-income people of color even further when they strictly limit or cancel entirely all access to sex education, abortion, and birth control.

Once again, we must observe that politicians and policy makers who enact these policies seem to be indulging in the fantasy that they can define sex itself as a class privilege, a human activity appropriate only for those who can privately pay for sex education, contraception, abortion, and motherhood. The fantasy must rest on the proposition that if the resources supporting reproduction and parenthood are out of reach for low-income people, disproportionately people of color, and are available only to higher-income whites, then only they, the sex-enabled, the higher-income whites, will have babies, forestalling the demographic transition to white minority status.

Reproductive justice is a resource for analyzing these contemporary forms of white supremacy, including the racialized politics of conservative Tea Party activists who claim that the United States is a "post-racial society." [69] Tea Party members and others argue that the persistent evidence of white privilege—for example, the racial demographics of income disparity and wealth accumulation, of access to high-quality health care and the Internet, of rates of home ownership by race, and of rates of incarceration and police abuse—has nothing to do with race. [70] Reproductive justice activists are allowed to be optimists, but we are not allowed to be dangerously naïve about white supremacy.

MOVEMENT BUILDING THROUGH REPRODUCTIVE JUSTICE

Now that we had a name, some of the fragmented pieces began to fall together—who we were, what we were, how we had evolved. We began to get glimpses of what we might eventually become.

—Gloria Anzaldúa, *Borderlands* [71]

Reproductive justice is essentially a framework about power. It allows us to analyze the intersectional forces arrayed to deny us our human rights, and it also enables us to determine how to work together across barriers to accrue the power we need to achieve and protect our human rights. As individuals, we cannot change the systemic reproductive injustices we face. We must work together in solid alliances that put our own lives in the center of the lens through which we theorize, strategize, and organize.

As an action strategy for movement building, reproductive justice requires working across social justice issues, bringing diverse issues and people together and revealing differences and commonalities using the human rights framework. Reproductive justice offers the human rights movement an opportunity to build a movement of solidarity in which differences are strengths, not liabilities. As an activist practice, reproductive justice has integrated multiple issues and brought together constituencies that are multiracial, multigenerational, multigendered, and multiclass, across a range of gender identities, to help build a more powerful human rights movement in the United States.

Black feminist scholar Barbara Smith asserts that this type of solidarity through human rights is based not on expediency—that is, simply an interest in getting something done. It is based on our actual need for each other.[72] Cherríe Moraga pointed out in *This Bridge Called My Back* that women of color are not a natural affinity group but are people who come together across sometimes painful differences to survive white supremacy. Moraga challenged us to come to terms with our own suffering, understand how we are different from each other, and acknowledge that differences are relational.[73] We are not merely allies; we are co-conspirators.

> By shifting the reproductive rights paradigm—from one focused on abortion to one that focuses on the shared values at the heart of a range of interrelated reproductive, social, and family justice issues—we can speak to and engage millions of potential new advocates and activists.
>
> —Lynn Paltrow, National Advocates for Pregnant Women[74]

Reproductive justice offers a compelling and defensible framework for empowering women and individuals to create healthier families and sustainable communities. The reproductive justice analysis helped transform reproductive health, a futile public debate focused almost entirely on abortion, into a public discussion that deals with a full range of reproductive health, rights, and justice issues. Using this framework, organizations like SisterSong, New Voices Pittsburgh, Justice NOW, Forward Together, California Latinas for Reproductive Justice, Native Youth Sexual Health Network, SisterLove, COLOR, National Advocates for Pregnant Women, SPARK Reproductive Justice NOW, and many others have built communities of new activist voices working to expand the base and connect to other social justice movements.

Notably, in the second decade of reproductive justice activism, a large number of mainstream organizations partially embraced the reproductive justice framework. For example, after the 2004 March for Women's Lives, NARAL Pro-Choice America and the Religious Coalition for Reproductive Choice invited SisterSong to offer trainings on reproductive justice. In 2005, progressives in Planned Parenthood Federation of America (PPFA) sponsored its first reproductive justice conference entitled "Reproductive Justice for All," at Smith College. Law Students for Choice became Law Students for Reproductive

Justice in 2007.[75] Sometimes mainstream organizations or ordinary people are confused about the relationship between pro-choice politics and reproductive justice. Is reproductive justice in tension with choice politics, or does its theory and activism rest on an entirely different basis? Is reproductive justice an attempt to make peace within the pro-choice and pro-life framework? It is important to underscore here that reproductive justice is neither an oppositional nor a peacemaking framework. It is an emergent radical theory that reframes the problem.

Reproductive justice offers the chance to explore whether a conversation created by women of color can be recentered around white women without reprivileging whiteness. Given the history of some forms of white feminism as predominantly concerned with a specific set of single-issue, nonintersectional practices, can white feminists adopt a reproductive justice approach without deradicalizing and flattening out the rich, deeply textured reproductive justice analysis? Can radical and mainstream white women appreciate the elasticity and inclusiveness of reproductive justice without reinscribing white supremacy?

Recent events make these questions feel important. One such event occurred when antiabortionists placed a personhood initiative on the Mississippi ballot in 2011 in order to make abortion illegal by declaring that life begins at conception. At the same time, anti–civil rights conservatives placed an initiative on the ballot that would limit voting rights, disenfranchising many poor people, African Americans, immigrants, students, and women. The initiative to limit voting aimed to lock in the leadership of politicians devoted to racist and male-dominant politics and policies for years to come, including policies that would increasingly limit women's access to reproductive health care, oppose the expansion of Medicaid to include medical insurance for the near-poor, and continue to attack the Affordable Care Act. Leading pro-choice organizations flocked to Mississippi to fight the antiabortion initiative, but the largest mainstream groups chose not to fight the anti-voting-rights initiative at the same time, even though the millions of dollars they raised for their campaigns may have covered a fight against both initiatives. When the personhood initiative was defeated, most feminists celebrated their victory. But human rights activists, including many people of color, lost the voting-rights initiative. African American women working in Mississippi and throughout the South were profoundly disappointed that some mainstream feminists failed to understand the intersection between women's rights and voting rights.[76] This failure demonstrated how single-issue feminism could be used to perpetuate white supremacy and thwart human rights, even in the twenty-first century.

Women of color have had to push our allies into a deeper, more intersectional analysis committed to fighting all forms of oppression, not just antiabortion legislation. Reproductive justice advocates perceive a real risk of deracializing and deradicalizing reproductive justice issues in order to appeal to people who are not as fiercely committed to fighting white supremacy. They may insist on conflating their struggles with other marginalized people (for example, claiming that sexism is the same as racism or that transphobia is the same as racism) while replicating racism and misogynoir (erasure of Black women) within their own organizations.

In the process of making the reproductive justice framework effective in the world, we have shifted from individual resistance to proactive organizing with a new vision for political engagement. This shift transcends siloed single-issue identity politics. Rather, it connects multi-issue, multiracial, and polyvocal movements across borders, incorporates multiple and variable identities, and interrogates the structures below the surfaces of our sufferings. The shared values we can unearth, name, and celebrate have the potential to create solutions. We especially aim to create a culture of caring that can transform U.S. society through social justice activism.

> In our world, divide and conquer must become define
> and empower.
> —Audre Lorde[77]

The reproductive justice movement has connected many activists across progressive movements, including many new activists, through shared core values. It has changed the public discourse on reproductive health and rights issues in the United States by connecting to broader progressive movements. Collectively, we are pressing our ideas into public policies that address the structural and systemic issues that contribute to reproductive oppression. We seek to achieve institutional and public accountability for the conditions in our communities that compromise our ability to possess our human rights. Women-of-color organizations that work on a variety of issues, such as HIV/AIDS, midwifery, abortion rights, health disparities, abstinence, teen pregnancy, breast cancer, environmental justice, police brutality, and immigrants' rights, among others, are working together in the spaces created by reproductive justice. While members of each group work on their own focused matters, addressing developments and goals in a specific community, the shared values and analyses of reproductive justice align work in unprecedented ways, producing great synergies and possibilities.

At the same time, the justice framework itself—economic justice, racial justice, prevention justice, health justice, climate justice, environmental justice, food justice, transjustice, restorative justice—is shifting away from the linear equality framework. This focus on an intersectional conceptualization of justice exposes why and how simple demands for equality are inadequate. For example, do we want incarcerated women to be treated the same as incarcerated men, or do we want to end the prison industrial complex altogether?

To some degree each of these new movements is shifting its analysis toward the global human rights framework. Will this shift finally facilitate common human rights grounding for all justice movements and offer a shared vision and set of practices? While this process is barely under way and cannot as yet be measured, those committed to bringing human rights home to the United States are excited about the prospect for movement building that this development seems to promise. The reproductive justice movement, with its distinct commitment to personal storytelling, can help create a culture of collaboration among human rights activists, enabling us to organize with people who think differently about issues or who focus on different issues but who agree to work together to achieve human rights goals. As a transformative framework, reproductive justice can revolutionize our approach to reproductive politics.

THREE

Managing Fertility

The reproductive justice framework has two especially power-ful ideas at its center: first, that access to comprehensive health care, including reproductive health care, is a human right, and second, that neither this nor any other human right can achieve the status of a right if it doesn't apply to all people. Reproductive justice does not simply call for including poverty in debates about abortion or insist on including the plight of immigrants as especially vulnerable people who encounter unfair restrictions when they seek health care. When the reproductive justice per-spective draws sharp attention to the social context in which individuals live and make their personal decisions, it aims not for simple inclusiveness but for changing the rules of the game.

No other movement devoted to reproductive rights has been built on these ideas. No other reproductive rights movement intertwines individual and collective human rights and asserts them both as entitlements based on the humanity of individuals. The white women who struggled for legal contraception in the early decades of the twentieth century and built the first birth control and family planning organizations had a number of goals. They wanted to save the lives of poor women who died from too many pregnancies and from self-abortion. They wanted to distribute contraceptive devices as part of an effort to reduce the birthrate of poor immigrants and African Americans and to produce a more "eugenic" population. And they wanted to secure the ability of better-off, educated women like themselves to go to their private doctors for contraceptive services. They wanted to legalize contraception so that all of these goals could be reached.

African American women who supported birth control in this period had similar but distinct goals. They were invested in the politics of "racial uplift"—the belief that the Black community could best enter the middle class if women had control over their fertility so that they could take advantage of the limited educational and economic opportunities they had access to. They also wanted to resist the eugenical impulses of the time by asserting agency over their own reproduction and at the same time deny the racist charge that African Americans were a genetically inferior population. By the early 1900s Black women had been making significant gains in controlling their fertility by marrying late and having fewer children, even before the campaign for legal birth control began.[1] Many of the early activists, both African American and white, believed that being able to manage one's fertility—being able to choose whether, when, and how often to get pregnant and have a child—was a hallmark of middle-class status and a key to middle-class security. The middle-class white women whose resources and whiteness protected them against the intrusion of public authorities into their private lives also believed that the right to have children—as many or as few as they wanted—was nobody's business but their own. And they knew that their white children were unequivocally welcomed into American society as valuable citizens. Working on behalf of themselves and others, they defined the problem and the solution as the ability to limit childbearing.

When the Supreme Court legalized contraception for married couples in its *Griswold v. Connecticut* decision (1965), contraception was defined as a "privacy right," a definition that was entirely consistent with the long effort by white family-planning advocates to make birth control the private business of married women. Indeed, the *Griswold* decision suited the lives of middle-class women because its privacy right was appropriate for a woman with access to a physician who would fit her for a diaphragm or, after 1960, write her a prescription for birth control pills. Now she could purchase these services legally and privately, without government interference. But achieving this privacy right—having what amounted to the "negative right" to be left alone—was not likely to help women without those resources. If you didn't have a private doctor, if you were poor, if you were African American, Mexican American, or Puerto Rican and the target of various forms of racism including population-control measures, then reproductive rights required much more clearly defined guarantees or "positive rights," beginning with a safe and healthy place to live with your family in a community free of the impacts of chronic racism, a living-wage job, and access to comprehensive public health services, including, if you chose, contraception.

Neither the text of the *Griswold* decision nor the mainstream leaders of the movement for legal birth control raised concerns about the historical and contemporary structures of oppression that limited or barred poor women, especially poor women of color, from access to reproductive health care, including contraceptive choices, while pressing many to terminate their fertility. Lawmakers and most activists did not challenge *Griswold* on the grounds that the decision did not establish any positive right for women—that is, that it did not say that the government was obliged to provide all women with contraceptive information and materials as part of public health services. With merely a negative right to be left alone, significant numbers of girls and women could not afford health care, much less a diaphragm or the pill. Many remained unable to manage their fertility. Contraception remained for many fertile persons simply another unattainable class privilege.

Eight years after *Griswold,* the Supreme Court's *Roe v. Wade* decision added legal abortion (with conditions) to the reproductive choices women could make. Once again, the court relied on privacy as its justification, now extending women's right to be left alone by the government. Certainly, after *Roe* many white women with resources could pay their rent, avoid coerced adoption, avoid adverse health consequences of too many pregnancies, stay in college, finish their degree, and advance in their career because the law did not force them to carry an unwanted pregnancy. But, at the same time, the *Roe* decision, like *Griswold,* interpreted the Constitution as not requiring the government to establish women's positive rights to reproductive health care. The decision also carefully balanced the new abortion right against the government's "interest" in fetal life and the physician's authority over women's pregnancies, leaving gaping holes in the capacity of many women to make their own decisions. After *Roe,* privacy, liberty, and equality—and reproductive rights—the goals of second-wave feminism, remained conditional, dependent upon a woman's access to money and other resources.

THE LIMITS OF CHOICE

In the decades following *Roe,* mainstream reproductive rights and feminist organizations did not effectively predict or object to the limits of the *Roe* decision, especially the ways its dependence on a negative right did not protect women who needed guaranteed access to information and services, not official neglect. The mainstream liberal women's movement celebrated choice as the defining achievement of modern women. Many aspects of the *Roe* decision were debated within activist feminist communities, but over time, choice was typically portrayed as the modern woman's personal key to the ownership and control of her own body. The term signified women's new freedom as individuals to have nonprocreative sex and children by choice. But "choice" turned out to be a flimflam mantra more suited to describing a commercial transaction (as in "Italian Beef, the Better Choice") than to providing the foundation for female dignity or the signal condition of modern womanhood for all. *Roe v. Wade* and its legalization of choice had guaranteed nothing to women who could not pay for reproductive options. These women remained dangerously vulnerable. After *Roe,* many poor women of color suffered coerced sterilization, were denied public assistance if they had one "too many" children, and were targeted for other methods of population control. The anti–civil rights, anti-welfare political culture depended, after *Roe,* on the symbol of the hyperfertile woman of color as toxic reproducer, as a female unfit for rights or choices.

In the meantime, mainstream second-wave feminists, mostly white women, many with promising futures, valorized *Roe v. Wade*—and the law, generally—as crucial to women's liberation. Feminist activists called for judicial decisions and new legislation establishing the government's commitment to positive rights for women, such as laws protecting women's pursuit of educational and career goals and financial autonomy and measures to protect victims of rape, domestic violence, sexual harassment, and employment discrimination. At the same time, white feminists demanded to be *free* of laws that refused women reproductive autonomy. This dual view of the law—as both friend and enemy—did not stimulate most white feminists to reexamine their own ideas about the power and the limits of Constitutional law. Few white feminists pointed out the weaknesses of negative rights for redressing injustice. Again, the major reproductive rights organizations did not devote themselves to repudiating racialized and class-biased attitudes about fertility and legitimate motherhood or promoting strategies for making sure that access to contraception and abortion achieved the status of rights for all.

In the decades since the flowering of the reproductive justice perspective, analysts of *Roe* have pointed out that neither this Supreme Court decision nor many liberal white feminists, generally, criticized the government for tolerating or promoting social conditions that denied so many people reproductive health information and services. In contrast, reproductive justice advocates call for "enabling conditions," that is, the network of opportunities, support, and services that would allow all women to meaningfully exercise the abortion right in a context that supports reproductive health, economic justice, motherhood, and the well-being and safety of individuals and their communities.

Constantly pressed to protect legal abortion from many directions, the reproductive rights movement has stuck with a single-issue pro-choice position for decades. Scholar-activist Andrea Smith argues that this position "not only does not serve women of color but actually promotes structures of oppression which keep women of color from having real choices or healthy lives." For example, many women are constrained to make a choice among dangerous or potentially dangerous contraceptives, hardly a *choice*, even though it may be "the best of even worse choices."[2] Legal scholar Robin West points out that the singular focus on choice can eclipse and thus effectively legitimate the coercive sex that might have caused a pregnancy. Similarly, the focus on choice eclipses and thus at least tacitly legitimates the "profoundly inadequate social welfare network and hence the excessive economic burdens placed on poor women [seeking abortions] and women who decide to parent."[3]

The right to make an individual, private choice may be exactly what many people need when they face an unwanted pregnancy, but individuals with lower incomes may not benefit from this "right" as much as their higher-income counterparts. For example, being able to plan or schedule the birth of a child may not benefit a lower-income person in the same ways that it does people with higher incomes in part because poor people may have less control over whether they have a job, where they work, and for which hours of the week so "their job security does not benefit as much from contraceptive access." The obstacles that people with lower incomes face with regard to steady, reliable employment make it even more important, of course, that they have equal and affordable access to contraceptives, while acknowledging that access to such contraceptives is not a panacea for the lack of educational or employment opportunities that can actually help them escape poverty.[4]

The reproductive justice perspective stresses that when the need for abortion services is isolated from all other social justice issues and identified simply as a "choice," we ignore all the conditions and circumstances that influence a person's decision whether or not to have a child. In making the decision, she likely thinks about her access to economic justice—that is, to a living wage and affordable housing and child care, as well as to a healthy environment. If she is an immigrant, is she eligible for health insurance and other human rights? Is her life shaped by the nation's reliance on mass incarceration and militarism in ways that are important to her decision?[5] Reproductive justice activist Tannia Esparza directs our attention beyond the individual rights that "choice" signifies and explains that "whole people, whole families, whole communities" are the relevant elements. From where the decision maker stands, the calculation about affording an abortion includes assessing

> whether a gender nonconforming person can feel safe from the threat of discrimination or violence while accessing gendered care; whether a person has a clinic nearby or whether they have to travel a significant distance; whether there's an immigrant checkpoint along the way; what access to transportation looks like; the economic impact for the person who does not have paid sick leave of taking several days off due to long-distance travel and waiting periods; whether the clinic is wheelchair accessible and on and on.[6]

Clearly, the liberal commitment to individual rights—to "choice," which often refers simply to a woman's preferences and makes reproductive matters seem like consumer or lifestyle issues—doesn't incorporate these kinds of considerations. Choice, privacy, freedom from interference, and personal autonomy are all necessary for all women to achieve reproductive justice, but they are also completely insufficient. These components of reproductive rights do not actually guarantee women's access to those rights in a society where sexism, racism, economic exploitation, and bias against immigrants flourish. Invoking individual rights or even constitutional protections of those rights does not accomplish what could, in fact, be accomplished through altered power relations, including the shifting of resources to people who currently lack them.[7]

Sociologist Barbara Gurr explains that when we bring all of these matters to bear on a pregnant person's situation, we can begin to see a particular individual in the context of "social, economic, and political structures and histories" as well as *within her own community*. Understanding a reproductive health decision, such as the decision to use contraception or to get an abortion in these real-life terms "expands local, national, and transnational conceptualizations of reproductive health as a human right."[8]

THE LIMITS OF CONSTITUTIONAL LAW

Reproductive justice activists point out that up until now, the reproductive rights movement has relied heavily on litigation to achieve its goals and to protect what has been achieved. But reproductive justice analysts point out that taking these matters to U.S. courts has not secured women's reproductive autonomy. Legal scholar Cynthia Soohoo explains some of the problems of relying on litigation strategies. "The reproductive rights movement," Soohoo writes, "has marginalized issues that cannot be expressed in the existing legal framework, for example, issues involving the impacts on women when they can't obtain full or even adequate reproductive health care." Plus, when the movement focuses its activities on litigation, its "leadership is concentrated in the legal elite rather than in communities."[9] In addition, Soohoo and others point to the problem that in the courtroom, lawyers and judges speak of rights and justice, invoking these concepts as if they have the objective legal power to protect the individual. Again, we see how abstract ideas—rights, justice—can eclipse lived experience and obscure the actual results of litigation. For example, a court's decision may establish a right that is too expensive for many people or otherwise inaccessible. Or the Supreme Court may decide, as it did in *Burwell v. Hobby Lobby* (2014), that certain employers may omit contraception from their employees' health insurance plan without consideration of the harm that this may cause employees.[10] Litigation that relies on deciding the meanings of abstract ideas also tends to leave out consideration of the social environment in which a person lives, even though health is a profoundly social phenomenon.

What's more, the litigation process in a conservative political climate tends to promote the idea that the government and its actions are the only source of injustice and that court-created rights are the most powerful tool for protecting individuals from "irrational state-involvement in our private lives." Here we see a simplistic and misleading duality. The private realm is constructed as vulnerable and virtuous. The public realm—government, democracy, group activism—looks like a negative force and dangerous. Part of the distortion here is the implication that the private realm—the corporate world, for example—is never a source of harm or oppression, compared to the government.[11]

One of the allures of the law is that it appears to provide definitive decisions, especially when a case is decided by the Supreme Court. *Griswold v. Connecticut, Roe v. Wade, Harris v. McRae* (which we will discuss in the next part of this chapter), *Burwell v. Hobby Lobby,* and many other decisions have shaped reproductive lives and have appeared to settle matters such as whether or not abortion is legal. But, in fact, the Supreme Court has not provided stability or security regarding reproductive law and policy. Beginning in the 1960s with the *Griswold* decision, the court recognized various reproductive rights that subsequent Supreme Courts—and other judicial and legislative bodies—have repudiated or squeezed almost to death.

Robin West argues counterintuitively that rights are generally not a source of power or dignity for everyone but are, in fact, "the coin of the realm of the relatively entitled and will likely always remain so," making the establishment of a new right a "relatively conservative" accomplishment. She explains that rights primarily protect property, profits, contracts, and the current power structure far more powerfully than they protect the basic needs of vulnerable people. Further, when we look to courts to ensure basic human rights, we are assuming that courts are the key, perhaps the only, source of "the language of moral principle, reasoned discourse, and civil dialogue." West argues that this assumption assigns a lesser value to democratically expressed moral principles and implies a second-class status for reasoned discourse and civil dialogue that emanates from political activism.[12]

Proponents of reproductive justice support this idea but go further, arguing that the most effective pathways to reproductive autonomy and dignity are community-based organizing, coalitions of social justice organizations, activist alliances across race and class, and other democratic initiatives. In contrast to the belief that courts *create* rights, reproductive justice activists believe that human rights are natural, inherent, and inalienable because of one's status as a human being. Human rights are first most powerfully expressed as moral commitments, then political structures and opportunities, and then as legal demands on the judicial system. For example, reproductive human rights start with the acknowledgment that a person has an inherent human right to control her own body and then seeks to use the political process to express this right and the judicial process to protect this right. Reproductive justice challenges the paradigm that starts with the judicial system, because activists believe that the law is only as good as social justice movements make it be. Laws don't create movements; movements create laws.

ENDURING IMPACTS OF
THE HYDE AMENDMENT

As we noted in chapter 1, the Hyde Amendment is the rule that bars the use of federal Medicaid funds to pay for abortion. The amendment, renewed by Congress every year since 1976, is an anti-abortion provision that targets low-income people. Rep. Henry Hyde (R-IL), who wrote the amendment in 1976, explained that on religious grounds, he hated abortion. By refusing support to poor women who depended on public health care, he explained that he could reduce the number of abortions in the United States. In 1980, a Supreme Court decision, *Harris v. McRae,* upheld the constitutionality of the Hyde Amendment. The court's majority agreed that the federal government did not create a woman's poverty and therefore was not responsible for alleviating it. When one considers the laws, policies, and Supreme Court decisions (all emanations of the federal government) that enforced slavery, segregation, and the second-class citizenship of women and institutionalized anti-immigrant policies, white supremacy, and ultimately poverty, this is a hard proposition to accept. Nevertheless, Justice Potter Stewart, who wrote the majority opinion remarked, "although government may not place obstacles in the path of a woman's exercise of her freedom of choice, it need not remove those not of its own creation: indigency falls in the latter category."[13]

With these words, Justice Stewart clarified and encoded the core difference between negative rights—the government's obligation to create no obstacles (and, later, no "undue burdens") to freedom of choice—and positive rights—the government's responsibility for responding to the needs of pregnant women, including being able to exercise (that is, to pay for) their constitutional right to abortion as established by *Roe v. Wade.* Seven years after *Roe,* the *Harris* decision reaffirmed the government's responsibility only for the former, leaving us with what Robin West calls "a *property right* in pregnancy and a *contract right* to purchase the means to end a pregnancy." Indeed, the court noted, "It simply does not follow that a woman's freedom of choice carries with it constitutional entitlement to the financial resources to avail herself of the full range of protected choices."[14]

Given the wide-ranging and ballooning impacts of the Hyde Amendment, we can conclude that this measure was about a lot more than whether the government was obliged to pay for a poor woman's abortion. First, we can think back to one of the key powerful ideas giving life to reproductive justice: that no right can achieve the status of a right if it doesn't apply to all people—and to its corollary: that no right is secure if it is not secure for everybody. When Hyde diminished the rights of poor women, the rights of all women were bound to be diminished too, both in principle and in practical ways. Soon after the Hyde Amendment and *Harris v. McRae* opened the door to using government programs to force women to make particular reproductive decisions, Congress voted to extend the amendment's restrictions to many other groups of people who rely on the federal government for health care and who may be rich, poor, or in between: military personnel and their dependents, Peace Corps volunteers, federal prisoners, people who receive care from the Indian Health Service, federal employees and their dependents, disabled women enrolled in Medicaid, teenagers receiving care through the Children's Health Insurance Program, and others. The Hyde Amendment began by targeting poor women, but the amendment's claim that the government could make a "value judgment favoring childbirth over abortion" and could allocate funds accordingly justified restricting the "choices" of all women through the imposition of waiting periods, state-directed counseling, parental notification rules, and other constraints.[15]

Furthermore, Hyde reopened the old 1870s Comstock door, allowing private religious beliefs to structure public reproductive law and policy. That is, Hyde and the steady stream of legislation and judicial decisions that followed have accommodated the religious beliefs of some elected and nonelected officials who have religious objections to abortion. While freedom of religion is a human right, so is freedom *from* religion. Reproductive justice proponents argue that when elected leaders impose their private religious views on a pluralistic, multireligious society like the United States, this is not only a violation of the separation of church and state but a human rights violation as well because someone else's religious views should not control what a person decides to do with her own body. Today a legal medical procedure that an estimated three in ten women in the United States will have by the time they are forty-five is substantially governed for all women, no matter their own religious beliefs or their socioeconomic status, by the religious inclinations of innumerable politicians and judges.[16]

The Hyde Amendment has shaped the reproductive lives of millions more than its original target group of Medicaid recipi-

ents, but at the same time, it enforces difference and defines privilege. As the late activist-scholar and lawyer Rhonda Copelon
reflected, "The divergence between the right to abortion and the
reality of access transformed abortion from a privacy right into a
privilege." This divergence effectively insists on different degrees
of reproductive autonomy for different groups of people, depending on race and class. Poor pregnant people, disproportionately
poor people of color, seeking abortions but lacking the money to
pay for them can be coerced because of their poverty to carry to
term. This central outcome of Hyde revitalizes the position that
people with lower incomes do not deserve reproductive autonomy. In practical terms, Hyde can even be understood as an
astonishing warning: With abortion established as a class privilege, so is sex itself since any person who can get pregnant from
sex might get pregnant. If you can't afford to be pregnant, if
you can't afford to have a child under the Hyde regime, don't
have sex.[17]

Hyde reinvigorated other aspects of enforced difference,
including old eugenic regulations at the heart of housing, health
care, and reproductive laws and policies, such as those that punished unmarried women for having children by excluding them
from public housing.[18] Hyde gave new legitimacy to old ideolo-
gies of biological-racial inferiority—and superiority—as these
categories defined who had the right to reproductive self-determination and who did not. Unsurprisingly in this political context, the women who "deserved" reproductive self-determination—those with economic resources—did not identify with
the ones who did not. In general, in the decades after Hyde and
Harris, many white middle-class women still would not, or at
least did not, fight against the new restrictions that targeted
poor women. Their reticence arguably made it easier for Hyde

and other new restrictions to take hold, and as Copelon put it, to harm "the security of the right to abortion, the funding of abortions, [and] the Bill of Rights, itself."[19]

Sociologist Joane Nagel explains that these sorts of policies and divisions are rooted in "a kind of ... cartography" that "charts the ethnic landscape by tracing lines in the geographic, legal, cultural, social, economic, political, or sexual sand." Ultimately, this mapping is a product of the state's interest in achieving "a collective national identity that assigns different values to different bodies, reflecting and producing different reproductive experiences." The Hyde Amendment has been an indelible and pointed location on this map, marking "the beginning of a long line of regulations that have, in effect, created and maintained a two-tiered system of women's reproductive health and women's rights." The Affordable Care Act, with its Hyde-influenced restrictions, joined Medicaid as the basis of health care for millions of Americans and created an ever-growing proportion of the population without access to abortion and without the reproductive autonomy that continues to be available to many better-off individuals. Class difference is salient here even as abortion services are "severed and isolated" from other health services and become a potential challenge for all persons to access.[20]

Having set a standard for legislating and adjudicating difference and privilege, Hyde also modeled tactics for targeting poor women, especially poor women of color, poor immigrants, incarcerated women, and other relatively defenseless individuals. In the 1970s and 1980s, Hyde, together with the Aid to Families with Dependent Children (AFDC) program, stymied people with low incomes, discouraging them from having abortions and also from having children. This double whammy sounds like a paradox, but note the consistent core: poor persons are by definition poor choice makers. Defining this group by its poverty, policy makers are not against rendering its members "choiceless," without access to abortions, and not against marking them as not-mothers. In fact, as we noted earlier, public policies frequently treat "the poor" as if they are simply too resourceless to have the right to engage in heterosexual sex because it might cause pregnancy.

Today, as earlier, when women and individuals in these groups do have sex and get pregnant, they are likely to rely on public health care services and thus to be directly affected by abortion-funding restrictions. Today, they are likely to be regarded as undeserving mothers and denied welfare benefits altogether under the rules of AFDC's successor program, Temporary Assistance to Needy Families (TANF). They are likely to be unemployed or to have jobs that do not pay a living wage, and they are fairly likely to be desperately poor. If they are immigrants who have been in the country, even legally, for less than five years, they are likely to be ineligible for public health care altogether.[21]

The bodies and fertility of people in these groups continue to be objects of public concern, public policy, and public opinion, including public excoriation and a vast range of exclusions. In McAllen, Texas, for example, officials have limited the kinds of identification that low-income undocumented immigrants can present to officials in order to get birth certificates for their newborns. This is a backdoor maneuver to deny proof of citizenship to these infants, a direct assault on the Fourteenth Amendment's provision of birthright citizenship. In this scheme, public policy defines poor people as producers of babies who are unworthy of the status granted to all other persons born on U.S. soil since the mid-nineteenth century.[22]

The infamous 2011 anti-abortion billboard campaign in New York City, another descendant and extension of the Hyde Amendment, publicly proclaimed, "The most dangerous place for an African American is in the womb" of African American mothers, after proclaiming on other billboards in 2010 in Atlanta that "Black children are an endangered species." The billboards, mounted in Black neighborhoods of U.S. cities, have targeted Black women, characterizing them as undeserving of reproductive autonomy and implying that they are "mechanisms of oppression," destroying their own communities by killing off the next generation.[23] In fact, Black women often make a rational decision to terminate a pregnancy because of the impact of white supremacist policies on fertile individuals and their communities: lack of health insurance, chronic health problems, poverty, and other realities of life that afflict communities of color and make childbearing and child rearing a hazard. The politics of antiabortion groups—deploying misogynoir to "protect" Black fetuses, including passing laws to forbid abortion "on the basis of race"—amount to legislatively mandated discrimination against women and individuals of color. Clearly, inequality is behind the high abortion rates in communities of color, not self-genocide.[24]

Another anti-abortion strategy is to accuse Asian American women in the United States of aborting female embryos. As a result of this charge, states have passed laws banning sex-selective abortions based on the myth that cultural pressures are coercing Asian American women to pursue a preference for male children.[25] These laws do not identify a specific source of the pressure but generally blame "Asian cultures" and express the problem in racist and xenophobic terms, so that the predominantly white antiabortion movement claims to be saving Asian

American women from their own community, suggesting that white men are saving Asian women from Asian men who, along with abortion providers, force women to have abortions against their will and against their better interests.

By claiming to save African American and Asian American women from themselves, the antiabortion movement attempts to use race and ethnicity to weaken the abortion rights movement. Antiabortion activists believe they can legislate against the *motives* of women seeking abortions, a plan of attack that is unprecedented in abortion rights law. Previously, doctors were not forced to inquire about women's motives for seeking an abortion as a condition for medical care.[26] Women of color fighting this race- and sex-directed attack against abortion rights quickly pointed out how legislating rules against motives into law could harm all women, not just women of color.

Also clearly, the lived experience of women and individuals appears to be of little or no concern to the policy makers and judges responsible for Hyde and the other laws and policies that extend Hyde's legacy. So we must look at this lived experience in order to understand the degrading and dangerous impacts of these official acts. When a low-income person makes a decision to have an abortion, her federal health insurance, Medicaid, will not pay for it. So to pay for the abortion she may have to make the brutal decision to use money meant to pay for basic necessities, such as heat and water and rent and food for herself and her children. And the time it takes to raise money for an abortion often means that this person will have an abortion later in her pregnancy, when the procedure becomes less medically routine and more expensive. The officials who make law and policy do not compute the ways that her poverty and the state's refusal to provide comprehensive health care rob the woman of dignity and physical safety and are likely to deepen her poverty and lack of options.[27]

We can look at the lived experiences of low-income, incarcerated individuals of color to see how pregnancy became an occasion for criminalizing them, for blaming them for their own poverty, and for racism. First of all, the War on Drugs has underwritten the explosion of the U.S. carceral system. This official adoption of a militaristic position—a war—against addicted persons expresses a brutal policy commitment to criminalize social problems such as poverty and illness. The "war" has explicitly defined prisons, instead of, say, schools and economic policy, as the key venue for addressing social problems. Robin West, Michelle Alexander, Andrea Smith and others have named the impulse behind this decision; Andrea Smith sums it up: "Given the disproportionate impact of criminalization on communities of color, support for criminalization as public policy... also implicitly supports racism."[28]

Authorized by the War on Drugs, law enforcement officials push pregnant drug-dependent individuals from communities of color. These persons often lack health services, including drug-treatment services, or are able to seek help only from public agencies, where they can end up under arrest, unlike pregnant drug-dependent middle-class women with access to private doctors and private drug-treatment facilities. In addition, the people who have built and support the prison-industrial complex have invested massive national resources in an institution of population control targeting communities of color in the United States, locking up individuals from these communities for significant portions of the fertile periods of their lives, as well as making it more difficult for formerly incarcerated persons to support children after their release.[29]

Finally, we need to look more closely at how, in recent years, the principles of the Hyde Amendment have been enlarged upon and extended, adding restrictions to the lived experience of millions of people beyond the amendment's original targets. To begin with, the Hyde Amendment modeled and validated the use of politics, not medicine, to make health policy. Today in almost every state, as well as in Congress, politicians and judges are "practicing medicine," assuming a kind of totalistic medical authority over the reproductive lives of individuals. Hyde paved the way for modern politics to trump medical judgment and also to eclipse individual rights. Many experts have taken the position that the Affordable Care Act (ACA) represented "the largest expansion of abortion funding restrictions since the [Hyde] Amendment went into effect in 1977."[30]

But even before the ACA went into effect, antiabortion politicians enacted states laws that restrict coverage of abortion in insurance plans purchased through state exchanges. Since 2010, ten states have restricted insurance coverage of abortion in all private plans written in the state, including those that are offered through ACA-established health insurance exchanges. Twenty-five states have restricted coverage in plans offered through health insurance exchanges. Some states have found new, "creative" ways to adapt Hyde's tactic of restricted funding so that abortion services become inaccessible to an ever-growing number of individuals. Arizona, for example, prohibits public funding of medical training for abortion and prevents taxpayers from taking charitable deductions on their state taxes for contributions to reproductive health organizations. Ohio prohibits abortions in public hospitals. Many states have defunded Planned Parenthood, an organization that provides basic health care services including Pap smears, breast exams, and contraceptive services to nearly three million people in the United States annually.[31]

The insights and intentions of Henry Hyde and his colleagues regarding religious accommodation have been vastly extended. Hyde demonstrated that the most effective way to insert religious beliefs into public policy was by developing restrictions that targeted poor individuals, particularly poor people of color. Hyde's insight was keen. He understood that he could depend on public hostility to "reproductive freedom" for poor women to pave the way to broader restrictions. Indeed, his successors have extended the reach of religious-based objections to the lives of *all* women. Supreme Court approval of challenges to insurance coverage for contraception on religious grounds, laws mandating that women view a real-time ultrasound image of their fetus prior to consenting to an abortion, and many additional initiatives—these are all hard signs that the Hyde Amendment's legacy of expressing religious beliefs through restrictive law and policy is robust and growing bolder. Many of the insurance plans in the state exchanges contain very narrow and stringent exceptions for coverage. And most of these are more restrictive than the Hyde Amendment's exceptions that allow abortion in the cases of rape, incest, and a pregnancy that would endanger the life of the mother. The restrictions are so harsh that insurance experts predict that soon most insurers simply won't cover abortion at all on the exchanges and that eventually private insurers will follow suit.

Public policies make poverty the most "unjustified" reason to get an abortion, no matter a person's medical needs. Studies have found that "the majority of women with government health care were denied coverage for medically necessary abortions [while] most women with private health care insurance had abortion coverage." But since the ACA is blurring the lines between private and public health care, the situation will surely deteriorate for many more people.[32]

"MARKED FOR MANAGEMENT"

As we saw in chapter 1, women's bodies have been "marked for management" throughout U.S. history.[33] Barbara Gurr argues that a country's leaders consider reproductive bodies responsible for creating or disrupting a "unified national identity," so courts, legislatures, political leaders, corporations, and business owners, among others, have continuously had a stake in crafting policies and practices to manage reproductive "output."[34] Reproductive justice draws attention to the ways that the state and other entities create unequal power relations, in this case highlighting the ways that different groups of people are marked for reproductive management differently. Reproductive justice analysis allows us to understand that some fertile people are disciplined for pregnancies or for exercising reproductive autonomy, while others are honored for the same things. The human rights focus at the core of reproductive justice analysis presses us to pay attention to the fact that social inequalities linked to race, immigrant status, disability, class, gender, and sexuality mark certain bodies as healthy and fit for reproduction and mark others as unhealthy and unfit. Under this regime, reproductive health services and health care are not strictly medical issues but social, political, and religious issues.[35]

Legal scholars Jill Adams and Jessica Arons point out the importance of the principle of government neutrality with respect to constitutional rights and as a safeguard against marking particular groups of people as deserving or undeserving of benefits. Neutrality, they write, means that "the government may not place its thumb on the scale in the exercise of those rights." The government may not mark one group of persons for benefits but deny those same benefits to another group "for reasons that are constitutionally insufficient." Adams and Arons show how *Harris v. McRae,* the Supreme Court decision that validated the Hyde Amendment, did not honor this principle of neutrality when it allowed the state to make "a value judgment favoring childbirth over abortion" after *Roe v. Wade* established abortion as a fundamental right. By giving the government the right to place its thumb on one side of this scale, the state could "cut off coverage for abortion care precisely in order to further the state's interest in protecting potential human life—i.e., in order to discourage poor women from exercising their fundamental right to choose."[36] Here the court validates both government bias and the use of poor women to carry out its bias. Reproductive justice analyses highlight biases that rely on the absence of government neutrality when the government marks fertile bodies for management.

In the United States, state governments are actively marking who is inside and who is outside the domain of reproductive health benefits, as, by the end of 2016, nearly twenty state legislatures have refused to expand Medicaid coverage under the Affordable Care Act and some have set income qualifications for coverage so low that many poor people cannot meet them. For example in 2014 in Texas, to qualify for Medicaid, working parents of dependent children had to have an annual income below 25 percent of the federal poverty level. That means that a family of three had to have an income no higher than $3,958 and a family of five no higher than $6,892. In addition, Medicaid is the largest source of funding for contraception and accounts for

75 percent of all public spending for family planning. But the states that refused to accept funding provided by the Affordable Care Act to expand Medicaid denied low-income persons contraception and other health services.[37] These kinds of state-level decisions discriminate against women by denying them a service that only they need. This act constitutes government-authorized sex discrimination, that should be a violation of the Constitution. When state legislators vote for these access restrictions, they know that the health of many people is likely to be harmed, and still they vote while keeping their thumbs on one side of the balance, "arguably ... with the intent to inflict harm for a discriminatory purpose."[38] At the very least, legislators in many statehouses have a concept of the purposes of contraception—as a means of preventing abortion, as a threat to the traditional family—that has nothing to do with reproductive freedom or the efforts of women and individuals to achieve personal autonomy, equal access, and financial security for their families, as well as reduce stress on their communities.[39]

These Medicaid restrictions have coexisted, of course, with state abortion restrictions. Studies have shown that a person who lives in a state with stringent abortion restrictions is almost certain to be living in a state that restricts support for pregnant and parenting individuals. Not surprisingly, the extent to which a state restricts support to these persons determines how well parents and their children are doing in that state. For example, Oklahoma has the highest number of restrictions on abortion access and the worst state record for women's and children's well-being. In Texas, a state that has a 19 percent higher cervical cancer rate than the national average, legislators recently proposed a budget that cut funding for breast and cervical cancer screening for low-income women.[40]

In the face of these kinds of state restrictions, many individuals seek to terminate their fertility through sterilization. We can understand the pressures that lead people to undergo this operation in part by identifying groups most likely to terminate their fertility: Black women and Latinas, people living below 150 percent of the federal poverty level, women with less than a college education, and people who are publicly insured or uninsured. All of these groups largely comprise people who are most vulnerable to targeted, harmful health-care restrictions devised by state legislatures. In some states, however, sterilization, while a relief, activates new rounds of restrictions. Since 2011, for example, poor people in Texas who rely on public services have found that once they terminate their fertility, they are no longer eligible for reduced rates for breast exams and Pap tests, benefits available only to fertile women.[41]

When state laws and policies mark certain people—the poor, immigrants, people of color, and others—for reproductive "management," denying them reproductive dignity and basic reproductive health services, such persons may end up having children who they may or may not have intended to give birth to. Having given birth, many face the reality that they have a newborn but no paid leave from work. Consequently, many parents have to leave their jobs to care for a new baby, deepening their poverty, undermining their family's security, placing additional stress on their communities. A 2015 study demonstrating the links between reproductive justice and economic justice concludes that "anyone who wishes to advance the economic security of women and their families will not be able to do so effectively without integrating access to reproductive health care into a proactive policy agenda to achieve economic equality for women." Key to this effort must be suspending the deeply entrenched project of marking vulnerable people for reproductive management.[42]

The government's lack of neutrality regarding which people get access to which reproductive health services and benefits has been a model for private businesses and other entities. In the more than forty-five states that don't have mandated paid maternity leave for employees, this matter is left to the discretion of the employer, most of whom do not offer the benefit. About half of American workers may get *unpaid* leave from the Family and Medical Leave Act because they work for companies that have fifty or more employees. Among the other half, typically only high earners receive some maternity leave. In fact, only 12 percent of U.S. private sector workers have access to paid family leave through their employer.[43]

A growing number of private businesses, such as drugstores that employ pharmacists who won't dispense contraception, mark the reproductive lives of people geographically, among other ways. Six states—Arizona, Arkansas, Georgia, Idaho, Mississippi, and South Dakota—have laws or regulations that specifically allow pharmacies or pharmacists to refuse to dispense contraceptives for religious or moral reasons and do not require that pharmacists refer people to other drugstores or transfer prescriptions.[44] Employers continue to fire pregnant women when they announce their pregnancies, even though the federal Pregnancy Discrimination Act prohibits this. In 2015, Republicans in the U.S. House of Representatives introduced the First Amendment Defense Act, which would protect employers who fire single mothers because, on religious grounds, they believe that "sexual relations are properly reserved to ... marriage."[45] The less money a person has, the harder it is to travel to another pharmacy to get a prescription filled or to fight for employment rights, so hundreds of thousands of people cannot escape the effects of these policies and practices.

Physicians and other nongovernmental entities continue to mark individuals with certain disabilities for sexual and reproductive discrimination. Many people report that their healthcare providers transmit negative attitudes about their reproductive capacities by not asking about their sexual lives and neglecting to ask about or assess their reproductive health—for example, by failing to perform full, regular pelvic exams. Because their needs are denied or ignored, persons with disabilities may have little access to mobility devices, public transportation, medical offices with handicap accommodations, and health care generally. They may lack access to computers and to information and have little contact with other people in similar situations. They may be uncomfortable communicating about sexuality and its outcomes, including reproduction, because their bodies are stigmatized and marked with taboos against the association of disabled persons, sex, and reproduction.[46]

MARKING IMMIGRANTS

Policy makers and others heavily mark the reproductive lives of immigrants for management, even though protections against discrimination are embedded in the Universal Declaration of Human Rights, numerous international and regional human rights treaties, and the U.S. Constitution. These instruments feature protections of the rights to life and health, equality, privacy, information, education, and freedom from discrimination, violence, and torture. Nevertheless, in the United States, immigrants are regularly subject to discrimination associated with reproduction, what one recent study called "widespread violations against women's rights to life and health, nondiscrimination and equality, autonomy in reproductive decision-making and freedom from ill-treatment." Activists and scholars have noted that the government might have a special duty to protect the rights of people who "experience multiple and intersecting forms of discrimination on the basis of their race, ethnicity, class, gender, and immigration status."[47] But instead, the government permits and commits violations against immigrants. Key causes and outcomes of these forms of discrimination—nativism, structural racism, and economic inequality—explain the very high rates of reproductive and sexual health disparities among both people of color and immigrants.

When the government marks immigrants for inferior health-care services or no services, the landscape is grim: lack of health insurance, lack of access to primary care and consistent, trusted providers, and the pervasive chronic stress that comes with poverty and brutal and incoherent immigration policies. Many live in areas with few medical facilities and travel long distances for health-care services, despite having no car and inadequate public transportation options. When they reach a health-care provider, that person may not be culturally respectful or able to communicate in a linguistically familiar way. Women and individuals who need reproductive health care cannot make decisions in their own best interests if they are part of whole communities of people facing the same violations: chronic exposure to racism, poverty, and pervasive anti-immigrant sentiment.[48]

Reproductive and other health-care restrictions aimed at immigrants can be so harsh that they bear special attention here. To begin with, undocumented immigrants are ineligible for all medical insurance programs, surely a human rights issue. Documented immigrants in most states are eligible for Medicaid only after a five-year waiting period. The state of Texas refuses to provide coverage to immigrants who came to the United States lawfully after 1996, even when they have completed the five-year waiting period. This means that a pregnant immigrant in Texas is ineligible to receive contraceptive services and devices, prenatal and postpartum care, testing and treatment for HIV and other sexually transmitted diseases, and breast and cervical cancer screening, diagnosis, and treatment services. In 2002, the federal Department of Health and Human Services began to allow states to use federal funds to extend prenatal services to pregnant immigrants regardless of their status only during the period of the pregnancy and only for pregnancy-related care. States can decide to cover all maternal health needs, but Texas declined, its legislature voting to cover medical care only for the fetus, not the pregnant person.

The Affordable Care Act incorporated most existing restrictions on coverage for immigrants. The ACA did allocate money for community health centers for underserved populations, but Congress cut the allocation by 25 percent, severely limiting new facilities and care overall. New regulations in 2012 excluded millions of young people from the benefits of health care reform, including nearly a million women of reproductive age, the vast majority of whom are Latina.[49]

The impacts of these laws and policies have been devastating. Fewer, sometimes dramatically fewer, fertile and pregnant immigrants are receiving health services every year. Without federal and state funding, many are unable to afford annual exams or contraceptive services, which are becoming more expensive every year. Many low-income immigrants are simply unable to get care because of the combination of cost, distance to a clinic, and the wait for an appointment with a specialist.

Previously, *promotoras,* persons trained as traditional community health workers in the Rio Grande Valley by Planned Parenthood to offer workshops on sexual and reproductive health, traveled from community to community, serving immigrant populations. But federal and state budget cuts and reduced funding for Title X, the nation's only federal program dedicated to providing family planning services—as well as the attacks on Planned Parenthood—have destroyed the *promotora* outreach program. Notably, Republicans in Congress have been focusing on the complete elimination of funding for Title X. Other opponents of birth control, such as religious organizations that pursued contraceptive exemptions from ACA regulations, effectively reduced low-income women's access to contraception too.[50]

One immigrant woman in the Rio Grande Valley explained what all these cuts have led to: "To pay for contraceptives [women] have to go hungry.... Either they eat or buy birth control, but not both." Another described the problem even more broadly: "We have all the information we need on reproductive health but have no access and no money. What good is information if we don't have help or access?" In the absence of contraceptives, money, and health services, many women have more pregnancies than they want and at shorter intervals, a pattern that yields more low-weight and premature babies, as well as health challenges for both women and infants. A Brownsville, Texas, woman described the dilemma for women who wanted to end this syndrome: "After four or five [children, many women] didn't want any more, but ironically, Medicaid covered childbirth but not the surgery not to have any more.... There's no help for women who choose not to have more children.... I say whether to have a child or not is a woman's right."[51]

Another bitter irony governing immigrants' lives in the Rio Grande Valley is that for women who cannot conceive, there is no access to infertility counseling and treatment, in part because the cost is too high. From every direction, low-income immigrants are marked as reproductively unequal and undeserving of the basic services that make access to reproductive autonomy, dignity, and safety possible.

In the face of so few supporting resources, many immigrants try anyway to scrape together the money to manage their reproductive lives, such as money for an abortion. Many make significant sacrifices to do so. It can take weeks for a person to raise enough cash, in which case the abortion will occur later in pregnancy, each week increasing both costs and medical risks. One study of the "choices" of low-income women revealed that to come up with money, some donated blood plasma. Others lied to family members about why they needed to borrow money. And still others sold their personal belongings. An undocumented immigrant may be fearful that seeking an abortion will trigger immigration enforcement and even deportation.[52]

Not surprisingly immigrant women, like other low-income women, are turned away from abortion clinics because they are too far along in their pregnancies, lack money, are too young, or for other reasons. A study of immigrant women who were turned away and gave birth instead of having an abortion found that they most often "have their economic fears realized."[53] Some who are eligible end up relying on public assistance; most stay mired in poverty. Moreover, many women who are turned away suffer adverse impacts on their own health, on their ability to provide for their existing children and other family members, and on their ability to succeed in the future, emotionally, educationally, and vocationally.

As we've seen, obtaining abortion care is only one of many obstacles immigrants and other low-income individuals face. But the barriers to abortion are stark. As two legal scholars have put it, "Our government has taken a group of women who have little access to health care generally, a heightened incidence of disease and injury, and an increased risk of unintended pregnancy, and then walled off abortion care." [54]

Given all of these policies and laws stacked against immigrants and other low-income persons, Laura, a *promotora* in Texas, advised the people she has served to go to Mexico for reproductive health care if they can "and get it done over there. But then," she warned, "another big barrier comes into play: violence. The violence in the border is terrible, so a woman says, 'Well, should I get my Pap smear, or do I get a bullet?'" [55]

UNINTENDED PREGNANCY, THE PREDICTABLE CONSEQUENCE

As we have seen over and over again, neglect, degradation, exclusion, and enforced hierarchies are at the heart of many official strategies for managing fertile bodies in the United States. [56] Predictably, these forms of management cause unintended pregnancy. The Guttmacher Institute has found that, "by age 45, more than half of all American women will have experienced an unintended pregnancy" (and three in ten will have had an abortion). The percentage of unintended pregnancies in the US is 51 percent, a very high rate compared to other industrialized countries. [57] The U.S. rate compares particularly badly with the rate of unintended pregnancies in developed countries worldwide, which is 40 percent. [58]

A key feature of unintended pregnancy in the United States is that the rate among low-income individuals is five times the rate for higher-income persons, a heavily racialized set of categories. Byllye Avery, health care activist and founder of the Black Women's Health Imperative, notes that white women between thirty-six and forty-nine have a median wealth of $42,600 (61 percent of the wealth of white men), while single Black women in that age range have a median wealth of $5. Unintended pregnancies are all too frequently a function of poverty and of the lack of many resources, as this chapter argues. This is an especially important point during periods of sharp economic downturns because these episodes hurt women the most. Women earn less than men, are more likely to be laid off, are less likely to be eligible for unemployment insurance or to have health insurance, and "are more likely to leave their jobs because of caregiving responsibilities, domestic violence, harassment, or stalking." And while poor, they are more likely to get unintentionally pregnant. From the reproductive justice perspective, if a person becomes unintentionally pregnant because she cannot get effective, affordable contraception, this can be considered a violation of her right to health and life, equality, and nondiscriminatory access to reproductive health care.[59]

But some influential experts still promote the idea that people have unintended pregnancies and children without being properly married and without being economically secure because they are addicted to dependency, an old, racially coded concept. Isabel Sawhill, for example, an analyst of social policy and the well-being of children and families, has for decades advocated, perhaps more gently than some, for a "public ethic that values self-sufficiency over dependency." While doubting that government programs can be the solution to the problem of poverty and unmarried childbearing among the poor, Sawhill does support some government initiatives that promote the public welfare, but only to a point: "More support for those who are drifting [into pregnancy and parenthood] is in order, but less drifting," she argues, "is also essential." She acknowledges that some public policies today make it harder to manage fertility, but she doubts that access to effective contraception is as important as "a new ethic of responsible parenthood." Sawhill revitalizes a new version of the old "dependency" taint: The poor pregnant person is no longer charged with dependency on the grounds that she's a scamming "welfare queen." Now she is charged, just as harshly, as a drifter with no values and no judgment. This person may live in a society that denies her health care, effective education, employment opportunities, and an economic safety net, but all these deficits seem less relevant to Sawhill than the poor choices that make people poor.[60]

Here we see the impact of neoliberalism. When Sawhill and others describe the reproductive body of the poor person, they describe a hub of unintended pregnancies stemming from lifestyle mistakes. They insist that each person, perhaps especially each low-income person, is responsible for her own reproductive health and autonomy. The neoliberal attitude asks us to excuse the government from responsibility for the well-being of its population and to discount or simply ignore the role of social inequalities in producing disparate reproductive outcomes, including unintended pregnancy.[61]

Instead of accusing poor persons who get pregnant by mistake of drifting or making bad lifestyle choices, we can look at the interaction of public policy and the lived experiences of fertile individuals. We can start by pointing to the positive impact of public funding and accessible contraception. When these resources are available, the statistics are startlingly good. In 2010, when public investment in family planning services was more robust than in later years, the country achieved a "13.6 billion dollar net savings from helping women avoid unintended pregnancies and a range of other negative reproductive health outcomes, such as HIV, STDs, cervical cancer, and infertility." Public funding prevented 2.2 million unintended pregnancies, which would have resulted in 1.1 million births and 760,000 abortions. Indeed, studies have shown that every dollar invested in helping women avoid unintended pregnancies saves more than five dollars in Medicaid costs that otherwise would have gone to pregnancy-related care. Funding is a human rights issue first, but it is also an economic matter.[62]

Data has long existed showing that access to effective contraceptive services is crucial to the dignity of women of all races. When the birth control pill became available in 1960, many middle-class women avoided marriage and childbearing while they prepared for careers, boosted their earning potential, increased their economic independence, and elevated their status as citizens. This effect continued over time: analysts have estimated that the pill was "responsible for nearly one-third of the narrowing of the gender wage gap [of] the 1990s."[63]

The Centers for Disease Control and the federal Office of Population Affairs have asserted that providing women the full range of contraceptive services is crucial to their lives in part because this is the best way to prevent unintended pregnancies. But today, only 47 percent of women in need of publicly supported contraceptive care are receiving it.[64] Studies that aim to explain this gap have not cited "drifting" as the reason for this lack of care. Rather, they show that financial and geographical access issues are important, as are problems with the quality and inventory of available methods and sometimes culturally insensitive attitudes on the part of clinic workers. Rather than accusing some individuals of "drifting," we can think about how the lack of information about sex, fertility, and even their own bodies—information withheld by school authorities and religious institutions—cause many people to get pregnant when they don't mean to. Also relevant are life events such as moving and relationship changes and the fact that many people describe themselves as having to focus so hard on getting by, or surviving, that contraception can take a back seat.[65]

The incidence of abortion is clearly an index of unintended pregnancy. So asking why people seek out abortion services helps us understand the meanings of "unintended." First of all, the most common reason given for abortion is arguably a profoundly responsible reason for not keeping a pregnancy: *poverty*, stemming from chronic racism, unemployment, underemployment, ineligibility for welfare, or a desire not to accept government assistance. (Most who seek abortions are already poor; over two-thirds have incomes 200 percent below the federal poverty level.) Many of these people—about one out of four who wish to end their pregnancies—cannot get an abortion because of the Hyde Amendment.[66]

Intimate partner violence (IPV) is also a common and responsible reason for deciding to get abortion. When intimate partner violence affects reproductive health decisions, reproductive justice activists call that "reproductive violence." Studies show that Black women report IPV at a rate 35 percent higher than whites, but they are less likely than whites to report the event, to seek social services, or to go to a hospital or a battered women's shelter. Experts have estimated that only one out of fifteen Black women report an incidence of IPV, typically because of distrust of law enforcement, cultural and/or religious barriers to reporting, poor access to service providers who share common cultures or experiences, and other reasons. A lack of economic independence causes many people to stay in abusive relationships and then to seek an abortion when they get pregnant.

Unplanned pregnancies increase women's risk for violence. In turn, violence increases women's risk for sexually transmitted diseases and HIV/AIDS. Birth-control sabotage frequently occurs when violence intersects with reproductive coercion. Many individuals report a lack of control about when sex occurs and also report that the experience does not feel safe. Reproductive violence also includes threats to children through either physical or emotional violence or removal. Obviously, interference with the decision to have an abortion or pressure to have one are both examples of reproductive violence.[67] Studies show that women who report IPV have nearly twice the odds of having a low-birth-weight baby or preterm delivery.[68]

Emergency contraception (EC) can be a good option if a woman is unwillingly pregnant, but again, this method is not always accessible. For several years after EC was approved as an over-the-counter drug by the U.S. Food and Drug Administration, for instance, the Indian Health Service did not update its policies to allow Native women, who experience sexual assault at rates more than twice that of other women, access to EC without any age limit.[69] When the promoters of the billboard campaign and neoliberal critics claim that Black women have abortions—or make other reproductive decisions—because they are selfish and do not care about the future of their communities or simply because they are "drifting," such persons show the shallowness of their knowledge of these matters, their racism, and their profound disregard for the complex lives of others.[70]

Several other reasons that people have abortions give additional dimension to the concept of "unintended." First, many, including those with low incomes, have ambitions. They want to get an education and good-paying employment and achieve all the elements of the "good life." Having a baby at the wrong time may be the single greatest obstacle to these goals, individually and all together. This is especially true in a country that lacks both paid maternity leave and a national child-care policy. Families living below the poverty line spend about one-third of their monthly income on child care. Surely, that expense alone is a major factor in defining which pregnancies cannot be managed. As we've seen, fewer than 15 percent of U.S. workers have access to any form of paid family leave. For the lowest-paid women, the figure is about 5 percent. Taking these policy deficiencies into account gives new meaning to "unintended," redefines the concept of reproductive responsibility, and clarifies the role of abortion in women's lives.[71]

Long-acting reversible contraceptives (LARCs) are emerging as an effective, if double-edged, solution for persons trying to avoid unintended pregnancy. These are methods of birth control that provide effective contraception for an extended period without requiring the user to do anything after the initial action, which can be getting an injection or having an intrauterine device (IUD) inserted or a contraceptive implanted under the skin. On the one hand, many people believe that LARCs are an economic triumph because they reduce the number of Medicaid-supported pregnancies and births and the social welfare payments that may go along with such births. The cost-benefit *is* dramatic. Studies show that if even 10 percent of birth-control-pill users switched to LARCs, total public expenditures associated with contraception and unintended pregnancies would be reduced by almost $300 million a year. Plus, we know that people who adopt one of the LARC methods stick with it, probably in part because these methods don't require daily action on the part of the user and because they may reduce menstrual bleeding, and users don't typically face the kinds of obstacles associated with accessing other methods. In addition, as Isabel Sawhill puts it rather deterministically, LARCs help "twenty-somethings" to avoid accidental births, improving their chances for reaching "an age at which stable relationships are finally possible, unencumbered by a child from a previous relationship."[72]

On the other hand, many policy analysts and people who provide contraceptive services are convinced that LARCs are the complete cure for unintended pregnancy and press their use on all fertile people who they identify as likely to have an unintended pregnancy—first and foremost, low-income women of color. They do this despite the fact that prominent studies find that few low-income women link their unintended pregnancies to a lack of contraceptives. Low-income people know that neither LARCs nor any kind of contraceptives can, all by themselves, fix the inequalities—economic, racial, educational, gender, and other—that they face and that may weaken their commitment to contraceptive use, anyway. Poor people of color, whose reproductive experiences have historically been coercively shaped by others, might well feel "targeted" when they are pressed (at rates much higher than white clients) to use LARCs, sometimes by being offered a cash incentive in exchange for having a LARC put into their bodies. Again, surely they know that such pressures reflect the service provider's conviction that the "burden of ... social change [belongs] on [certain] women's bodies and contraceptive behaviors."[73] If a person is poor, neither a college degree nor a great job opportunity that can lift her out of poverty will magically appear just because she avoided an unintended pregnancy.[74] LARCs are not the solution to racial, economic, and gender injustices. At best, they are effective long-term contraceptive choices that are not dependent on user aptitude and maintenance. This is how LARCs should be described.

The focus on LARCs as the ultimate solution for unintended pregnancies is further complicated when we pay attention to the lived experience of people who may be pressed or choose to use these methods or may be considering them. Looking at lived experience means learning about the many considerations that fertile individuals and their partners bring to making decisions about which, if any, contraception is acceptable. To make these decisions in their real lives, people weigh cultural factors, issues having to do with how often they have sex, how they feel about using a synthetic hormone, and many other matters. A person might or might not be certain about whether she wants to be pregnant or not. She may, at the same time, both want and not want to have a baby.

The reproductive justice framework underscores that individuals from particular racial and socioeconomic groups have suffered reproductive abuses throughout U.S. history and that LARCs can be used in ways that continue that history, depending on who is in charge. Thus, from a reproductive justice perspective, LARCs should be available to people who choose to use them with fully informed consent that meets human rights standards, such as accessibility, clarity, language, and cultural appropriateness. But if a person wishes to have the LARC removed or never inserted to begin with, these options must be completely available and affordable.[75]

PEOPLE, COMMUNITIES, FERTILITY: A HUMAN RIGHTS IMPERATIVE

In this final section of the chapter, we emphasize again that the essential purpose or meaning of "managing fertility" is not to reduce public expenditures or to ensure that fewer poor babies are born. As scholar and policy analyst Jenny A. Higgins puts it, "our ultimate reproductive justice endgame is to enhance the health, social well-being, and bodily integrity of all contraceptive clients." [76] This point is increasingly taken up today by international health rights and human rights bodies that are "recognizing a broader conception of rights that require states to take steps to enable individuals to exercise their fundamental rights." [77] This focus on positive rights is particularly relevant in the United States, where as we've seen, the Supreme Court requires very little from federal or state governments in this domain and repeatedly justifies rules of access that harm people and communities according to their race, ethnicity, class, and geographical location.

Human rights advocates have pointed out that all persons can have access to the highest attainable standard of health, including sexual and reproductive health only if high-quality, ethically and culturally acceptable goods and services are "available in sufficient quantity throughout the state," and if people can make decisions about reproduction in a context free of coercion or violence. Since accessibility is key, human rights advocate have spelled out its multiple, overlapping dimensions: services are accessible if they are provided in a nondiscriminatory way, if they are physically accessible, if they are economically accessible, and if information about services is accessible to begin with. [78]

Others have underscored that activism can no longer simply focus on resisting sexual and reproductive oppression. Now the human rights focus at the heart of the reproductive justice framework facilitates a full concept of what each person requires in order to achieve dignity and safety in this arena, in addition to accessible sexual and reproductive health care services. Requirements include sex education, the ability to decide whether to be sexually active, the ability to make affirmative and negative decisions about a marriage partner and a sexual partner and about whether and when to have children and how many, freedom from violence, and the ability "to pursue a satisfying, safe, and pleasurable sexual life as part of the universal human rights framework."[79]

But the reproductive justice perspective explains that it is not only the life of the individual that is harmed when she cannot achieve her own personal sexual and reproductive dignity and safety; the life of her whole community is harmed. Loretta Ross, one of the coauthors of this book, has clarified this point, arguing that the reproductive regulation, oppression, and exploitation of "women, girls, and individuals, through their bodies, sexuality, labor and reproduction [is a] powerful strategic pathway to controlling entire communities," as we saw over and over again in chapter 1, notably in the construction and maintenance of the slavery regime and then white supremacy. Clearly, when a community of persons can access the health care it requires, including sexual and reproductive health care, this is a key element and emblem of community empowerment.[80]

Focusing on the relationship between reproductive justice and economic justice helps us understand the relationship between the dignity and safety of the individual and the health of the community. To begin with, we must emphasize that when low-income people disproportionately bear the costs of public policies—such as policies that allow employers to withhold contraceptive coverage from insurance plans, that allow community-based health services to withhold emergency contraception from some individuals, or that legislate lengthy and costly waiting periods for abortion service and of course, when federal and state policies refuse financial support for one legal medical procedure—then public officials are targeting and punishing low-income people for their poverty. And the consequences of this economic inequality ripple through the communities these people live in.

We are probably all familiar with the standard antipoverty agenda that calls for affordable housing, a living wage, paid sick and family leave, child care, reliable public transportation, decent schools, and other basic services for all. But that standard agenda often leaves out affordable, accessible, quality reproductive health care, including contraception and abortion: the comprehensive package that a person relies on to respond to the circumstances of her life. By now it is clear that no effective antipoverty program can exclude the elements of reproductive justice. "After all," one prominent set of researchers argue, "the woman struggling to pay for contraception or abortion services is also the woman trying to find [and keep] a job, pay her bills, and feed her children." Whether she can meet these responsibilities also has ripple effects across her community, shaping the lives of her neighbors, her relatives, school teachers, church officials, social service providers, and others already stretching scarce resources to make a decent life for themselves and their community.[81]

Economic justice is not just about closing the income gap. Economic justice also means responding to the total lived experiences of individuals so that they have a fighting chance to thrive, to move up economically, and to contribute to the well-being of their families and communities. As we know, an individual is fertile during the same part of her life that she is getting schooling, preparing for the workforce, and then holding down a job. If this person is not able to prevent unintended pregnancy during this crucial interval of her life, she has a much greater chance of not finishing her education, not getting trained for employment, not keeping her job, and not achieving economic stability—all of which will harm her and her children and will likely stretch the already taxed resources of her community.

Some researchers have argued that the cost of mothering—again, disproportionately heavy for low-paid workers—is an especially strong argument for legal, accessible abortion. Byllye Avery has remarked provocatively, "My word to those who want to remove the right [to abortion]—they need to guarantee every woman one million dollars for each child she is forced to bear so she can have economic security to help her get some of the things she needs in order to raise a healthy child," surely an outcome that benefits the entire community.[82] As the situation now stands, over forty million women and the millions of children who depend on them are "living a single incident—a doctor's bill, a late paycheck, or a broken-down car—away from economic ruin." An unintended pregnancy is another path to the same kind of ruin, but it doesn't have to occur in the first place or to lead to economic devastation.

If instead, the person who became pregnant unintentionally had access to comprehensive reproductive health services and time off to care for herself and her family, including paid vacation and holidays, a benefit denied one-quarter of today's workforce, she might be able to manage the pregnancy. If the pregnant person had a stable work-shift schedule, denied most often to the lowest-paid workers, and if she had access to child care, a pregnancy might not spell economic devastation.[83]

If she had paid maternity leave, she could breast-feed longer, boosting the immunities of the newborn and lowering the incidence of allergies and SIDS. If she could spend more time with her child and less time at multiple low-paying worksites, she could also boost the child's development of motor and social skills. Indeed, if she had paid maternity leave, she could hold on to her job and return to it when the paid leave was complete, again reducing her chances of pregnancy-induced poverty for herself and her children and reducing the consequences of more poverty in the community. And the longer her paid maternity leave, the less likely this person would be to suffer from depression, and the more robust her own health would be after giving birth. A recent study has shown that even one additional week of maternity leave is associated with significantly lower rates of depression after having a baby. Achieving economic justice would mean providing low-income individuals the maternity benefits that public and private policies now reserve for the better-off.[84] Achieving economic justice depends on, goes hand in hand with, achieving reproductive justice.

Economic justice, together with reproductive justice, are both fundamental in order for people to have well-lived lives on the job and at home. In this view, denial of access to contraception and abortion is not simply a problem of the state's interference in people's private lives but an obstacle to the chance for "better and more integrated lives in ... families and workplaces." Surely, if these conditions of reproductive justice and economic justice—sex education, access to contraception, strong work-family policies, and a social and political commitment to equality—were a national priority, there would likely be far less unintended pregnancy in the United States and therefore less need for abortion services. One can imagine that coalitions of people with different feelings about abortion could be built around a commitment to the principles and programs of reproductive justice and economic justice. Such coalitions and other activism might be able to achieve a more enduring program of reproductive dignity and safety for all than our legal and judicial systems have achieved over the past decades.[85]

A number of the policy initiatives that this would require are laid out in the previous paragraphs, which essentially map the route to reproductive dignity and safety. But it makes sense to emphasize some of the broad principles that must pave and structure this route. First, the human right to health refers to a person's *whole body* and to that person's lived experience. Therefore, the human right to health includes the right to reproductive health, a condition that can be met only when accurate and honest information, materials, and services are distributed fairly and equitably, without geographical barriers, to all persons who require them, including immigrants. Achieving this goal requires expanding Medicaid in states that have not done so, fully funding Title X, and enacting other measures that would ensure that this right to health reaches all persons.

A corollary to the first principle is that government policies must remove *financial barriers* to reproductive health care. Even after the Affordable Care Act provided health insurance for millions of low-income persons, the act together with other legislative acts and judicial decisions still made crucial aspects of reproductive health care, specifically the management of fertility, unreachable by people who did not have enough money to live where services were available or to purchase quality services on their own. A second corollary is that government policies must remove *religious barriers* to reproductive health care because such barriers constitute violations of human rights. All reproductive-health-care-related policies and programs should obey the First Amendment's provision that state and church are separate entities. State policies that govern the management of fertility, including access to legal services, should no longer embed accommodations to some or any religious principles; otherwise, reproductive health care is not a right for all.[86]

Reproductive justice imperatives, principles, and their corollaries are all very well. But how is it possible to spread the reality of reproductive justice when so many aspects of reproductive health care are under attack, their provision more unstable and more uncertain than ever before? What can we learn from activist strategies in the past as we work to achieve reproductive justice? What new strategies can be effective in making this vision real?

We can begin by drawing on the powerful political insight of women's health movement activists in the 1970s who explained that authority over one's body and access to full-body health care are in a profoundly dynamic relationship to gender equality and to social, economic, and political empowerment. Managing fertility—suppressing it and expressing it—is at the center of full personhood. But to imagine a person as a free-standing individual, divorced from the context of her life "dishonors her lived experiences and the plight of a broader community of people."[87] To understand this crucial context, we need to pay attention to the stories that individuals tell about their lives, including their reproductive lives. We need information about how they have managed their fertility or not and about how the opportunities and obstacles that they have faced—including the ones conditioned by their families and communities—have shaped these experiences.

Cherisse Scott, founder and CEO of SisterReach, a reproductive justice organization in Tennessee, underscores the importance of context when she writes about how her organization responded to the billboard campaign that maligned Black women, excoriating them for the high abortion rate in the Black community and attempting to restrict their choices: "Our goal is to refocus the dialogue about Black women's reproductive health decisions back to the real conditions of our lives. Conditions which, if unmet, leave us vulnerable in many instances, with abortion as a choice we have been forced into." Scott goes on:

> The anti-choice billboard messages omit the context crucial to understanding why Black women oftentimes cannot or will not carry a pregnancy to term. For many women, choosing an abortion is an act of survival for herself and her family—for her unborn child, an act of mercy.... This is why we created uplifting, supportive messages about their personal decision making and autonomy. Our goal is to refocus the dialogue about our reproductive health decisions back to the real conditions of our lives.... One of our new advertisements, for example, includes a picture of a Black family with the words: "Our family's success requires: lots of love, a living wage, affordable housing, a safe environment, healthcare, reliable transportation, safe and robust schools, a chance." ... Where is the concern [of the anti-choice billboard campaigners] when we are fighting for a living wage, equal pay, health care, or comprehensive reproductive and sexual health education for our young people? If they were truly "pro-life," they would be interested in the lives of the full family before, during, and after birth.[88]

Ultimately, the antiabortion billboard campaign provides a sharp focus on how reproductive oppression is "just another way [Black] communities are under attack."[89] The Trust Black Women Partnership and SisterReach responses to the billboard campaign show that African American activists are determined to speak directly about the intricate web of barriers facing the community and how these barriers must be faced together, as an integrated system of oppression. Unlike liberal reproductive-rights feminist activism that seeks reform through legal changes, reproductive justice efforts challenge the entire system, linking all forms of oppression.

Sisters in Control Reproductive Justice, a program of Black Women for Wellness in Los Angeles, models this position, working within a broad arena, developing some goals within the political system and others outside, partnering with other reproductive justice organizations in California and throughout the nation, contributing to the work of commissions and boards—all efforts to further the community's access to reproductive justice. Miriam Zoila Pérez describes how, within various communities, reproductive justice activists have organized against population control programs, welfare caps, environmental movements that blame the community for having "too many" children, sterilization campaigns and the lack of access to contraception and abortion, abusive immigration policies, and other matters. These efforts have involved cross-movement coalitions and intersectional thinking and strategizing.[90]

A number of reproductive justice organizations point out that women of color are committed to addressing "reproductive issues through their own organizing and community-based research that [relies] on intersectional analysis to strengthen grass-roots coalitions, [rather than relying on] legal advocacy." The law, they argue has been "inadequate in recognizing the intersection of sex, poverty, race, and immigration status in its rights claims." In addition, the law relies on an "individual rights-based framework which [doesn't] address barriers to access to [services or the need to] shift resources and power to communities of color." They also point out that the law and lawyers do not acknowledge grassroots organizations as the "clients who set the movement's goals and [must] direct the lawyer toward achieving those goals."[91]

For the many decades that the reproductive rights movement has relied on the law, its focus has almost always been on the right of individuals to suppress fertility and terminate pregnancy. The ability to manage fertility in these ways has been crucial to millions of people in the United States, although fertility management has never achieved the status of a human right for all. Now we turn to an equally important nexus of human rights: the right to become pregnant, to have a child, to be a parent, and to raise that child within a safe, dignified, and healthy context. Again, individually and collectively, the elements of this grouping of human rights have not achieved the real status of *rights* since they are available to only some people, not to all. Charon Asetoyer, executive director of the Native American Women's Health Education Resource Center, a reproductive justice service provider and advocacy organization in South Dakota, explained, speaking for so many people in the United States, "In our communities, it's about the right to have children." [92]

FOUR

Reproductive Justice and the Right to Parent

The reproductive justice movement has an enormous agenda. It aims to build a world in which all children are wanted and cared for, in which supports exist for families of all sizes and configurations, and in which societies give priority to creating the conditions for people to be healthy and thrive in the United States and globally.

As we have made clear, reproduction of human bodies is not simply a biological process. Nations, political parties, religious and ethnic groups, and other entities claim a stake in reproduction—who should have sex, who should give birth, who should be born, and who should not. These claims turn an intensely private human activity into a matter of public concern, sometimes a public obsession. As a result, motherhood is not an isolated, individual experience. Motherhood is deeply politicized, both as a means to control women and a means by which women seek to gain control over their lives. Social conflicts concerning reproduction embrace a wide range of topics. The intention of this chapter is to introduce these topics and to bring them into dialogue with the activist analyses of reproductive justice.

It bears repeating that reproductive justice focuses on three basic tenets: the human right to not have a child, the human right to have a child, and the human right to parent children in safe and healthy environments. Reproductive justice is a capacious envisioning of reproductive possibilities that requires the use of intersectionality, the perspective that allows us to comprehend how race, class, ethnicity, and sexuality together construct gendered implications of motherhood and citizenship, sex and reproduction. We examine the intersections of social justice issues as they affect different human bodies in different ways and differently over time. The meanings of motherhood vary across religious, national, racial, cultural, gendered, and political boundaries that shape distinct and evolving systems of power and domination.

Reproductive justice demands that the state (that is, the government) not unduly interfere with women's reproductive decision making, but it also insists that the state has an obligation to help create the conditions for women to exercise their decisions without coercion and with social supports. In this way, reproductive justice rests on claims for both negative and positive human rights.

Reproductive justice is an interdisciplinary theory and practice that pays attention to nonbiological issues affecting reproductive bodies and parenting experiences in relation to the state and other authorities. Reproductive justice connects the dots between many social justice issues that seem unrelated to reproductive rights and to traditional views of reproductive politics. For example, reproductive justice looks at how immigration, incarceration, gentrification, and other processes and practices shape the sexual and reproductive lives of women and individuals, for example, by deepening white supremacy. Reproductive justice also focuses on the quality of schools and the availability of affordable housing because these factors shape the right to parent in safe and healthy environments. These issues do not often appear in pro-choice or anti-choice debates on abortion, but reproductive justice makes them "sites for activism and scholarship."[1]

Instead of claiming that the alleged pathologies of individuals—those who fail to adjust to a neoliberal economic system—are the source of society's ills, a reproductive justice analysis focuses on the conditions of the neighborhoods where people live and raise their children. The reproductive justice analyst looks at how economic and social systems harm lives and constrain the options both of individuals and communities. We examine the failures of public and corporate policies that create concentrated racial segregation, deindustrialization, infrastructure decay, and gentrification in order to develop critiques and consider pathways to the future that focus on achieving human rights protections.

This chapter brings questions about human rights to our consideration of the second and third major tenets of reproductive justice: the right to parent and the right to raise our children in healthy and safe environments. When we invoke the right to parent, we are not romanticizing parenthood. We are not taking a pronatalist position—that is, we are not urging the birth of many children to satisfy women's destiny or family values or religious dicta. Instead, reproductive justice maintains that all decisions about reproduction must be made by individuals and couples based on their own preferences and abilities. Reproductive justice maintains that people should be able to have the number of children they want, when they want, in the way they want to have them. Individuals must have the ability to raise their children with the social supports they need to provide safety, health, and dignity. Reproductive justice emphasizes these principles in distinction to the mainstream pro-choice movement that focuses on the right *not* to become a parent by protecting contraception and abortion rights. Since feminists of color have historically fought population-control strategies—and continue to fight these strategies, particularly the state's practice of incarcerating a disproportionate numbers of women of color—in the United States and worldwide, reproductive justice underscores the crucial and complex matter of safe and dignified parenthood.

Historically, questions about "legitimate" motherhood have begun with challenges regarding fitness: which persons, which women do politicians and ordinary people define as fit to be mothers? We have seen that women in various groups have been defined as bad mothers, lose custody of their children, and suffer arrest for parenting choices based on culturally specific standards that change over time and context. Even today, some politicians and policy makers continue to define entire categories of people as "bad" mothers because they do not reproduce within the confines of a middle-class white nuclear-family structure in conditions that are deemed "safe" by the middle-class standards that are increasingly difficult for many people to achieve. The mothers so often condemned today, unmarried when they have children, have been in fact responsible for more than 40 percent of all births in recent years, a massive group of people in America who decide to be mothers outside of an idealized tradition that may no longer be viable or desirable.[2]

Mothers of color—married or single—are more likely to be scrutinized and judged and have their babies tested for drug and alcohol abuse when they give birth in hospitals. Police and social workers are trained and prepared to expect infants of color to grow into juvenile delinquents, particularly if their mothers are among the "undeserving poor," defined that way because they receive public assistance. Authorities assume that if a woman has a low income, that fact itself is an indicator of failed motherhood, and they may blame mothers who lose children to diseases or accidents as dysfunctional persons who intentionally harm their children. In contemporary society, mothers receive a great deal of conflicting parental advice, much of it impossible for many to parents to follow—to breastfeed or not, to discipline or not, or to work or not.[3] In recent decades, government agencies and courts have terminated the motherhood status of whole categories of women and girls because they failed to meet arbitrary standards, defining them as inappropriate mothers because they were "disabled, a political activist, too young, unmarried, comatose (judge denied an abortion), divorced and had sex, too old, the wrong race, an atheist, a Native American, deaf, mentally ill, retarded [sic], seeking an abortion, lesbian, reported to speak Spanish to her child, enrolled full-time in college, a drug user, poor."[4]

Reproductive justice explains that, indeed, poverty creates poor conditions for mothering because it shortens lifespans and increases rates of infant and child mortality and lower birth weights.[5] Perhaps we ought to replace the "fitness standard" that politicians and social services bureaucrats often use with a perspective and the set of measures developed by Dr. Camara Jones, a leading public health expert. Jones analyzes the limits of individual choice and the impact of other factors in shaping reproductive options. "The social determinants of health are the contexts of our lives," she explains. "They are the determinants of health which are outside of the individual. They are beyond individual behaviors and beyond individual genetic endowment. Yet these contexts are not randomly distributed, but are instead shaped by historical injustices and by contemporary structural factors that perpetuate the historical injustices."[6]

These factors include, as we've noted before, the quality of housing and neighborhood safety and the degree of access to adequate and nutritious food, transportation, social connections, quality educational resources, and health care. When we apply a social-determinants-of-health model to analyzing reproductive politics, we can see how social and economic resources create advantages and disadvantages for parenthood based on income, education, social class, race, gender, and gender identity.

These insights can seem obvious and deeply relevant once they are in the foreground. But typically, such ideas are eclipsed, even today, by the system of white male supremacy that has historically rendered reproductive hierarchies and inequalities natural and inevitable. Indigenous feminist Andrea Smith uses the term "heteropatriarchy" to draw attention to the ways that European settlers used genocide and enslavement to colonize the United States and entrench ideas about sexuality, reproduction, and "value" that elevated whites and degraded others.[7] Even today, many politicians, policy makers, and institutions aim to "manage" or "pathologize" communities of color by constraining the sexual and reproductive destinies of entire communities.

The project of making inequality appear to be a naturally occurring development depends, in part, on accusing poor people of a hypersexuality that leads to the creation of their own poverty when they have too many children, children they cannot afford. This charge removes any responsibility for injustice and inequality from the shoulders of society and frees those who credit this charge from grappling with the complex ways that wealth and poverty are created in the United States. Clearly, the greatest determinant of wealth in the United States is being born into a family that has money. If you are born into a family without wealth, you are likely to grow up remaining poor, no matter whether you have children of your own or not.[8]

The highly charged discussions about who is fit to be a parent—who has the human right to become a parent, and how, and what happens to children once they are born—often ignore realities about birthrates and other important matters. For example, the U.S. birthrate has dipped in recent years, most strikingly because of a decline in births to immigrant women. The overall U.S. birthrate declined 8 percent from 2007 to 2010, with the birthrate for U.S.-born women decreasing 6 percent during those years, and for foreign-born women, 14 percent. The birthrate for Mexican immigrant women fell even more sharply, by 23 percent.[9] Although barely enough children are being born in the United States to replace its aging population, still many people continue to demonize mothers of color, queer parents, immigrant parents, and others they define as unfit and inappropriately "hyperfertile."[10]

REPRODUCTIVE JUSTICE
AND THE RACISM OF DOG WHISTLES

The persistence of misconceptions about birthrates and ideas about hierarchies of "value" associated with race, class, immigration status and other matters are fueled by what law professor Ian Haney López calls "dog whistle politics." He uses this term to name a specific method that allows politicians (and others) to convey their racialized opinions without ever mentioning race. These are coded appeals that cover up the racist agenda they represent in order to court white voters. Although dog whistlers have typically been conservative Republican politicians and their supporters, former president Bill Clinton, a Democrat, borrowed Republican president Ronald Reagan's concept of a "welfare queen"—historically, a highly effective dog whistle—to justify the end of welfare in 1996. That year, Clinton replaced Aid to Families with Dependent Children—a program for low-income mothers and children in place since 1935—with Temporary Assistance for Needy Families (TANF), a program providing only short-term aid for poor mothers and their children. After a family has received five years of assistance, regardless of the age of the children, regardless of the availability of childcare or the availability of jobs, no more aid can ever be granted to that family. If the family continues to be poor, Clinton's TANF program interprets that fact as a personal maternal failure, not the result of a poor economy, racism, or other structural, external factors. The new welfare program has aimed to reduce aid to the stereotypically Black, hyperfertile, lazy, and irresponsible recipient, even though the majority of recipients have always been white. Welfare reform also aimed to reduce the number of children born to such women with family caps or state-mandated limits on family support based on family size.[11]

Many white people who heard these racialized calls "to end welfare as we know it" may not have considered race as particularly relevant to their day-to-day lives. But in fact, U.S. history and culture have conditioned whites to be sharply vulnerable to racial characterizations that operate on two levels like a dog whistle: "inaudible and easily denied in one range, yet stimulating strong reactions in another," says Haney López.[12] Dog whistles are so poisonous and potent because they insinuate racial differences and divisions while denying that any such distinctions have been articulated. When a victim of racism draws attention to a dog whistle, the white speaker may deny all racist intentions and implications and instead suggest that the accuser herself is the "real racist" for calling out racism in a situation that is apparently race neutral. Coded allusions to "thugs" (referring to African American young men), to "anchor babies" (referring to children born in the United States to Mexican-citizen mothers), and to "welfare queens" are painfully obvious expressions of racism to the targets of such slurs. But because the terms themselves do not explicitly reference race, they offer deniability to the dog whistlers, who may claim racial innocence and "color blindness."

In the 2016 presidential campaign, Republican candidate Donald Trump used racism and bigotry in ways that are politically embarrassing to those who prefer subtler dog whistles. Trump sought support by tapping into an enormous vein of white rage, choosing audible wolf whistles over dog whistles. His explicit language disrespecting people of color, women, immigrants, and Muslims, a tactic eventually embraced or excused by many voters and by the Republican Party (long committed to deploying the dog whistle strategy for masking the intolerance of many of its adherents), will have consequences long after 2016. Now, apparently high-minded but racially coded expressions invoking community safety—such as "law and order," the "War on Drugs," "defending the borders," or "protecting the voting process"—have been clearly linked to racism and bigotry and also clearly sanctioned by one of the two major political parties in the United States.

These racialized attacks on poor people in African American, Latino, and Native American communities are consequential because they may justify taking money away from public education, public housing, and Medicaid expansion. The attacks may also have negative impacts on low-income white communities, where many people are also desperately trying to survive, knowing that they will not achieve the economic security of their parents or grandparents. Years of a contracting job market, flat wages, and growing income inequality have deepened economic insecurity and social instability. These factors have also led to a number of very difficult public health problems, including high levels of drug use and suicide among white men and reduced life expectancy for white women without high school degrees.[13] In recent years, individuals with fewer years of education are living shorter, sicker lives, facing higher rates of illness and higher rates of disability.[14] Less-educated women are less likely to be competitive in a diminishing labor market and more likely to become pregnant multiple times.[15] To some degree, the struggle for survival has become more color-blind.

Indeed, despite the racialized stereotype of teen pregnancy as a Black phenomenon, white teenage pregnancy rates are rising in states that mandate the toughest restrictions on sex education, birth control, and abortion access. While the national teen pregnancy rate in 2010 was 34 per 1,000 teens, the most conservative states, with the most stringent restrictions, had much higher rates—48 per 1,000 and higher, up to 76 per 1,000 in Mississippi—surely because these states resist providing the kinds of resources that would reduce teen pregnancy, concentrating instead on abstinence-only programs.[16]

Where such policies are in place, they hurt working people of all races in the absence of class, racial, and gender unity. Conservative dog whistlers convince many white people that they are the victims of an activist government that irresponsibly showers benefits on undeserving people of color and immigrants while taking advantage of the hardworking white people who "made this country great." This concept of U.S. history explains important aspects of contemporary reproductive politics, none more so than "sexual citizenship."

SEXUAL CITIZENSHIP AND
THE ECONOMICS OF MOTHERHOOD

Reproductive justice includes a radical critique of the U.S. economic system that consistently benefits wealthier people, white people, and men and confers or denies citizenship rights and obligations depending on conduct, identity, and relationships. Many people live across these categories: for example, a queer person who wants to get married and to receive medical benefits that can be assigned to the spouse of an insured employee. When the government confers (or not) the rights and obligations of citizenship according to characteristics and external criteria, old privileges and old vulnerabilities are perpetuated. People who have always benefited from class, racial, and gender injustices continue to do so. And those who have always been marginalized continue to be so. Here we will consider the concept of sexual citizenship, or the ways that the government and other authorities grant or deny sexual rights to various social groups. As we have seen, the United States has a long tradition of laws and social norms that govern what people do with their own bodies. In recent decades, authorities have been especially focused on telling poor people if and when they should have children. The punishments meted out to poor, reproducing women drive home the message that "if you can't afford to get pregnant, you can't afford to have sex," which is a fundamental violation of sexual citizenship.[17]

Feminists began promoting the concept of sexual citizenship in the 1970s as part of a conversation about the relationship between gender, sexuality, and public policy. Drawing on the Universal Declaration of Human Rights, a document that explicitly defines a human right to marry and form family units, feminists declared that women have the right to decide if and when they marry, the right to decide if and when they have children, and the right to sexual pleasure. Feminists insisted that "women's rights are human rights," and when they enumerated these sexual rights, they began the process of delineating the contours of sexual citizenship.

Reproductive justice advocates have used the human rights framework to make public claims for sexual rights and sexual citizenship, matters that are usually imagined as involving private decisions and behaviors. In 1995, at the Fourth UN World Conference on Women in Beijing, the Platform for Action provided a clear statement describing sexual rights:

> The human rights of women include their right to have control over and decide freely and responsibly on matters related to their sexuality, including sexual and reproductive health, free of coercion, discrimination and violence. Equal relationships between women and men in matters of sexual relations and reproduction, including full respect, consent and shared responsibility for the integrity of the person, require mutual respect, consent and shared responsibility for the sexual behavior and its consequences.[18]

This statement was, in part, a bold criticism of the old piety claiming that "good citizens" (especially women) have sex only for procreation and bear only the children they can afford. At this time, feminists also insisted that all immigrants, documented and undocumented, have sexual rights, as do disabled people and LGBTQ people, whose privileges of citizenship must not depend on their sexual identity, behavior, or other attributes.

Many politicians and ordinary people still disapprove of young people, poor people, people of color, single women, immigrants, and disabled people, among others, engaging in sexually pleasurable activities, especially if these activities lead to procreation. Disabled people are often singled out for sexual prohibitions and compulsory sterilization even today, long after eugenics laws have generally been repealed for vulnerable populations.[19]

More than twenty years after the Beijing conference, sexual citizenship remains elusive for individuals in many groups. While for members of gay communities, the right to marry is largely resolved, the right to fair employment and housing practices, the right to adopt a child, and the unimpeded right to express sexuality are still in flux, under local or state control, constituting far less than guarantees of full human rights.

Calls for sexual citizenship are a radical departure from the privacy arguments of abortion rights advocates. By invoking the human rights framework, reproductive justice activists are demanding *public* support for *private* actions. The U.S. Supreme Court has, over time, affirmed the same thing. In 1942, the court ruled in *Skinner vs. Oklahoma* that even though the state was determined to prevent Mr. Skinner from having children, it could not sterilize this impoverished white man as a punishment for stealing chickens and armed robbery. The Supreme Court ruled for the first time that such punishment would limit a person's rights as a human being and a citizen. The court used the concept of universal human rights to protect marriage and procreative rights, not incidentally in a case involving a white male defendant. Writing for the court, Justice William O. Douglas found that the case "touches a sensitive and important area of human rights." He declared that "marriage and procreation are fundamental to the existence and survival of the race." [20]

This 1942 court decision previsioned the concept of sexual citizenship, although the language of sexual rights had not yet been created to frame this important arena where sexual behavior, sexuality, procreation, and citizenship all intersect. Twenty-five years after the *Skinner* decision, in *Loving v. Virginia* (1967), the Supreme Court declared Virginia's antimiscegenation statute an unconstitutional violation of the Fourteenth Amendment's equal protection clause because it prohibited interracial marriage. As these and other court cases show, citizenship is a central aspect of reproductive politics and has been deeply contested throughout American history. The Supreme Court has frequently reaffirmed the fiction of racial and gender opposites to define and separate individuals, expressing its interest in controlling the bodies of both citizens and noncitizens. The ongoing impact of *Harris v. McRae*, which disproportionately affects poor women of color, shows that even if the United States can elect an African American man president, its highest court and its political system can still fail to address deeply entrenched, institutionalized human rights violations that exclude many from the benefits of equal and sexual citizenship.

The denial of sexual citizenship to poor women and other vulnerable individuals shows how lawmakers count on the lack of resources of some people to deny them access to sexual rights and sexual citizenship and to discipline individuals on account of their sexual or reproductive behavior. In October 2015, Indiana governor Mike Pence announced that his state had awarded

$3.5 million to a "crisis pregnancy center," Real Alternatives, an institution that actually functions as a deceptive antiabortion "counseling" center. In fact, in order to make this allocation, the governor had diverted funding from the budget for Temporary Assistance for Needy Families despite the fact that the federal government had allocated this money to the state of Indiana to alleviate poverty and provide financial support for low-income families, not to fund religious-based antiabortion activities.

By the beginning of 2016, eleven states provided millions of public dollars to other antiabortion, religion-based centers, thus violating the principle of separation of church and state.[21] Moreover, the Hyde Amendment, together with crisis pregnancy centers and rules governing TANF, blocks low-income women from the opportunity to plan their families and simultaneously withholds financial support for the families they have as a result of unintended pregnancies. As we've pointed out, public policies strongly suggest that poor women should simply avoid sex. The public programs that poor women depend on for health services variously refuse support for birth control, abortion, welfare, and other public services and, in the process, discipline the sexual behaviors of poor people. The alternative for poor women is to accept a long-acting reversible contraceptive (LARC). LARCs will certainly suppress pregnancy, but when public policy (and public opinion) pressure poor individuals to use only this method, this coercion constitutes a public policy commitment to a rigorous form of population control.[22] It is not difficult to imagine how pressure turns into coercion or coercion into force.[23]

Blaming poverty on the alleged bad sexual decision making of poor people has a long history. Today's shame-the-poor narratives underwrite public policies that strip public resources from people marginalized by the economic logic of neoliberalism. These narratives also reinforce the myth that anyone can pull herself up by her bootstraps in our meritocracy where work is always available, hard work is always rewarded, and inequality can always be overcome with enough personal effort. This set of beliefs, of course, embeds the idea that poor individuals have thumbed their noses at the bootstrap itinerary. And as a result, they are responsible for their own "pathetic" situations, rendering policy makers and society in general free from responsibility for the existence of poverty or the need to respond to it. So politicians cut benefits from the long-term unemployed, reduce access to food, and deny the expansion of Medicaid eligibility, claiming that, in these ways, they are fulfilling the neoliberal goal of saving the poor from their own bad decisions.

Reproductive justice pays attention to questions about whose mothering and parenting rights are affirmed and whose are harmed and diminished. Who has the right to sexual and reproductive self-determination and full sexual citizenship? Reproductive justice activists insist on the human right to engage in sexual activity without fear of violence, unwanted pregnancy, sexually transmitted infections, HIV/AIDS, or interference by the state. At the same time, reproductive justice activists place demands upon the state for support in implementing these personal decisions, because the state and the economy benefit from the reproductive capacity and the physical contributions of the citizens: persons who are employed in necessary jobs; whose incomes fuel the consumer-driven economy; who keep the population robust, contribute to Social Security, pay taxes, provide personnel for the military, and fulfill other functions of national populations. Thus, reproductive justice activists believe that demands for sex education, reproductive health services, child care, protection from pregnancy discrimination, education regarding safe sex and protection from HIV/AIDS, and a host of other supports necessary to affirm sexual human rights are each—and collectively—the right of every person. Reproductive justice activists believe that mothering is a right (as well as a responsibility) that cannot be withheld by the state or society.

Examining the concept "the right to be a mother" means we must be clear about what mothering actually means in the current economic, political, and social context. Is the right to be a mother primarily based on the biological ability to give birth? Is everyone who gives birth a woman? How do we understand ways of mothering that do not involve traditional biological processes—for example, through adoption, surrogacy, and extended families? Does everyone have the right to become a mother using any means possible? How do we understand the mothering status of women of color who are paid to take care of others' children, leaving them unable to mother their own children as well as undervalued as maternal influences? Furthermore, what distinctions can be pointed out between the right to mother and the right to parent, and are these distinctions helpful in building the movement for reproductive justice?

To unpack the concept of the human right to mother, we can explore both biological and nonbiological mothering, what writer Alexis Pauline Gumbs refers to as "radical mothering." "None of us are here unless we are mothered," she writes. "We are mothered by our movements, our families of origin and chosen family configurations and we all still struggle to mother ourselves and each other."[24]

When examined through the radical lens Gumbs describes, the status and practice of mothering encompass far more than an individual's reproductive decision making. Mothering becomes a process deeply tied to communities that suffer a myriad of intersecting oppressions, where people are constrained from making autonomous reproductive decisions. In this context, mothering becomes an act of survival, a life-affirming radical resistance to forces that deny our humanity, our interdependence, and even our existence. Radical mothers withstand oppression to create spaces for life that offer a compelling vision of the future. How we imagine and describe different or better futures is a core concern of reproductive justice, which asks, can we stop the injuries long enough to even envision the remedies?

IS MOTHERHOOD A HUMAN RIGHT?

As we have explained before, one of the key powerful ideas giving life to reproductive justice is that no right can achieve the status of a human right if it doesn't apply to all people—along with its corollary that no right is secure if it is not secure for everybody. Reproductive justice activists believe that motherhood is a human right. Articles 16 and 25 of the Universal Declaration of Human Rights state this clearly:

> Article 16: Men and women of full age, without any limitation due to race, nationality or religion, have the right to marry and to found a family.

> Article 25: (1) Everyone has the right to a standard of living adequate for the health and well-being of himself and of his family, including food, clothing, housing, and medical care and necessary social services, and the right to security in the event of unemployment, sickness, disability, widowhood, old age or other lack of livelihood in circumstances beyond his control. (2) Motherhood and childhood are entitled to special care and assistance. All children, whether born in or out of wedlock, shall enjoy the same social protection.[25]

Despite these international norms, politicians and policy makers in the United States have not viewed motherhood as a human right that must be supported as a priority for the benefit of the entire society. Even if we think only in purely economic and not humane terms, we have to acknowledge that all countries in the developed world are currently experiencing declines in working-age population, and by 2050, this segment of the population will be reduced by 5 percent.[26] Employers will have more difficulty finding both the workers and the customers that capitalism depends on for expansion. If developed countries were to increase the number of immigrants from Africa, the Middle East, and Asia allowed to settle within their borders, that decision could replenish shrinking populations. But in almost every developed country, anti-immigrant sentiment is strong. In the United States, many Republican politicians have stoked anti-immigrant sentiment so successfully that a significant part of the American public is hostile to the whole notion of immigration,[27] even though granting entry to persons from the Global South may be one of the few viable routes to population stability.[28] Of course the other viable route to population stability is to provide more generous supports for motherhood, another politically unpopular policy option in the United States.[29]

Many studies show that women seek abortions because of the continually diminishing public support for keeping a pregnancy: for example, loss of or insufficient support for maternity leave, day care, housing, employment, protection from job discrimination, and programs and protections against domestic violence.[30] Reproductive justice proponents point out the connection between supports for motherhood and improvements in general economic forecasts, justifying the claim that reproductive justice is not only the right perspective, it's the smart perspective.[31]

Monica Raye Simpson, executive director of SisterSong, argues that women of color are not simply lacking the resources they need to exercise their right to be mothers, but they are often lacking essential fundamentals. She writes, "They are concerned about feeding their children, they are concerned about making sure their child gets the medication [he or she] need[s], they are worried about their job security, they are worried about whether or not their child or partner will become the next Mike Brown [murdered in Ferguson, MO] or Eric Garner [murdered in New York City]. All of these are RJ issues."[32]

Recent data shows that motherhood poses heightened risks for many African American women because of their relatively poor health before they become pregnant. The United States is one of the few industrialized countries where maternal death rates (death during pregnancy or childbirth) are rising.[33] And African American women are four times more likely to die during childbirth than white women.[34] Most of these deaths are preventable. The Centers for Disease Control's Maternal Mortality Study Group, formed in collaboration with the American Congress of Obstetricians and Gynecologists, reviewed state-based data to identify risk factors for maternal mortality and to propose solutions to this ongoing problem.[35] The study group identified risk factors, often present before pregnancy, such as heart disease, substance abuse, obesity, and other chronic conditions, as major contributors to these deaths.[36] Clearly, there is an urgent need to reduce health disparities—that is, health statuses that are better or worse depending largely on a woman's race and class—for any and all individuals before they reach childbearing age. For example, African American women die from heart disease and related conditions within one year of pregnancy at a rate more than three times that of white women.[37]

The human right to mother necessarily involves the right to safety, security, and health care, or as the UN Universal Declaration of Human Rights puts it, motherhood requires "the right to a standard of living adequate for health and well-being" and the entitlement to "special care and assistance."

BIRTH INJUSTICES: COERCIVE MEDICINE

Reproductive justice/birth justice activists assert that women have the right to determine their own birth plans, use midwives and doulas if they choose, and have home births or use freestanding birthing centers if they prefer. The fact is that pregnant women are vulnerable to many birth injustices, harms that we can define as "obstetric violence"—for example, forced Caesarians and other unnecessary medical procedures—some of which have resulted in women being imprisoned for poor birth outcomes if they resist this treatment.[38] Indeed, many women report that they have been bullied in hospitals into accepting aggressive medical interventions they did not want or necessarily need. They are often denied midwifery services, and hospital staff members often ignore a woman's birthing plans.[39]

Ignoring women's birth preferences made national news in 2004 when a white Utah woman, Melissa Ann Rowland, was charged with murder after she refused a C-section, and one of the twins she was carrying died before birth. Ultimately, Rowland accepted a plea deal and was sentenced to eighteen months on probation. Still, this woman was a victim of coercive medicine; no nonpregnant person can be compelled to undergo any medical procedure for the benefit of another person. The obstetric violence sustained by Rowland is a human rights violation because physicians treated this parturient woman as merely a womb, denying her right of bodily integrity and effacing the decision-making authority that she would have legally possessed had she not been pregnant.

Perhaps the physicians associated with Rowland's case were using a 1984 case as a legal and medical precedent when they acted against Rowland's statement of her own interests. In the earlier case, Chicago physicians forcibly restrained a Nigerian immigrant with leather wrist and ankle ties when she refused a C-section. According to National Advocates for Pregnant Women, this woman screamed for help, but the hospital doctors obtained a judge's permission to perform the procedure. Hospitals in at least a dozen states have sought court orders to force women to have C-sections against their will.[40]

Amber Marlowe also resisted a Caesarian. Marlowe was expecting her seventh child in Pennsylvania in 2004. Because she had delivered her previous six children vaginally with no problems, she refused the doctor's order to have a C-section, explaining that the fetus showed no signs of distress, so abdominal surgery was unnecessary. Nevertheless, the hospital went to court, seeking an order to become the fetus's legal guardian so that physicians could perform the surgery. But in the meantime, Marlowe and her husband escaped from the hospital, and Marlowe safely delivered her baby girl vaginally at another facility.[41]

In many cases, physicians decide to perform Caesarians even when the need for them is unclear. Many times, they fear a malpractice suit if anything goes wrong with the vaginal delivery, and they fear the ruinous insurance rates they would be charged as a consequence of the suit. The national Caesarian rate was 4.5 percent in 1965, the first year statistics were collected. In 2014, the rate was 32.2 percent of all births.[42] The price of an uncomplicated C-section is about twice the cost of a vaginal birth, not including the hospital-stay charges. With Caesarians, women are experiencing more premature births and increased neonatal intensive care admissions, as well as infections, blood clots, and a host of other consequences of major surgery.[43]

Ending coercive medicine is a reproductive justice goal. Women deserve to give birth to their children according to their own birthing plan, without pressure or aggressive nonemergency interventions. A birthing woman must always be provided with full prior information when conditions requiring unexpected medical interventions exist, conditions that have been verified by more than one physician. Even then, women must not lose their right to refuse medical care. Reproductive justice rejects the position that a woman's disagreement with a doctor can be treated as a crime. Nor should a woman be punished for a tragic outcome to a pregnancy. There is always risk with a pregnancy, regardless of the birth method. The maternity ward should not be the first step towards prison.[44]

THE RACIAL POLITICS OF MOTHERHOOD

Reproductive justice has lofty goals requiring the reconstruction of all unjust institutions and practices that affect reproductive decision making. The needs and the voices of poor women, disabled women, women of color, immigrant women, and other vulnerable individuals must be at the center of debates about reproduction. Each of these populations can trace attacks on their reproductive capacity back to the eugenics movement's insistence that only "fit" people should reproduce and that nonwhite and nonheterosexual women's bodies are inherently pathological. Indeed, sexuality and motherhood rely on "cultural assumptions and systems of representation about race [and other characteristics] through which individuals understand their relationships within the world."[45] Further, within this white supremacist system of thought, all cultural stereotypes of women of color are sexualized. One of the core tasks of the reproductive justice framework is to challenge these dehumanizing systems, especially given the ontological uncertainty of race.[46]

Human history records a number of genocides and ethnic cleansings as states and other entities have targeted entire races and communities for harsh racial and reproductive oppression, violence, incarceration, and death. Today in the United States, white supremacy may be implicitly expressed by law enforcement policies or immigration policies that promote racial and ethnic containment. Police chiefs responding to police killings of African Americans—however disproportionate—may explain that these events simply reflect a society and a police force committed to law and order and to the protection of property. Authorities may justify separating family members—deporting Mexican parents away from their minor children in the United States, for example—as simply a matter of upholding the law.[47] When vigilantes or immigration-enforcement personnel kill people along the U.S. border with Mexico, authorities may describe the event as simply the outcome of efforts to secure the border and enforce the law.[48]

White supremacy also figures in women's persistent vulnerability to sexual violence. According to the U.S. Department of Justice, non-Native men are responsible for at least 86 percent of the reported cases of rape or sexual assault against Native American women and girls, yet few of these perpetrators are pursued or brought to court.[49] Despite the overwhelming official invocation of law and order, low-income victims of violence seldom receive justice, a state of affairs that one analyst has called "the lethality of inequality."[50] This lack of justice particularly affects the African American, Native American, Asian American, and Latino/a communities, but targets have expanded and impacts have intensified since 9/11 to include racial profiling and assaults against Muslims of any race and ethnicity.[51]

Reproductive justice invites us to examine the Black Lives Matter (BLM) movement and its work within a white supremacist culture that has most often ignored Black claims for justice. When three Black women started the Black Lives Matter movement in 2013, they insisted that America pay attention to the devaluation of Black lives by police and white vigilantes. Alicia Garza, Patrisse Cullors, and Opal Tometi responded to the unpunished murder of Trayvon Martin, a seventeen-year-old killed in 2012 by an aggressive "neighborhood watchman." After the killer was acquitted, the women met in a community-organizing school and created the hashtag #BlackLivesMatter to call attention to this outrage, to police brutality generally, and to racist violence. Defining the mission of BLM, Alicia Garza said,

> What we are fighting around are the contours of black life....We do work around policing and criminal justice, but we also take on development, affordable housing and gentrification, gender justice, trans liberation, economic justice, anti-austerity and privatization, climate justice, education, corporate accountability, and rights, dignity, and respect for gay, lesbian, and bisexual folks, because all of these issues shape the contours of black life. We're fighting back against anti-Black racism, but we're also fighting for dignity and equality for all persons.[52]

BLM and reproductive justice activists both demand the right to parent our children in safe and healthy environments free from violence by individuals or the state.[53] All children should be safe going to schools, playing in parks, or visiting friends, but when unequal citizenship intersects with racist brutality, grieving Black mothers call attention to the theft of their children's lives. Black babies too often become ancestors. In the context of racial and reproductive injustices, many Black people live in locations where random racist behavior erupts and escalates, too frequently leading to a death. White anxiety about the need to exercise social controls over African Americans has pushed police officers to commit acts such as throwing Black girls around at a pool party or in a classroom and even shooting unarmed children (unaware that their behavior was being videotaped).[54] Apparently "disobedience" on the part of unarmed Blacks can still stimulate an extrajudicial death penalty, long after the Thirteenth Amendment ended slavery in the United States. Demanding reproductive justice is a new story layered on top of an old story.

Harold Cruse, an African American studies pioneer, explained prophetically in 1968 that "White America has inherited a racial crisis that it cannot handle and is unable to create a solution for it that does not do violence to the collective white American racial ego."[55] Today, reproductive justice activists and other antiracists use the term "white fragility" to describe the inability of some white people to face harsh racial realities.[56] It is important to underscore the fact that African Americans are not reverse racists with victim complexes; they merely demand that their lives matter as much as other lives, that their children have the right to thrive, a right denied Tamir Rice, a twelve-year-old African American boy innocently playing in a park. Cleveland police killed this child who carried a toy gun in a state where it is legal to openly carry firearms.[57]

The enduring white supremacist impulse that links Black protest and Black claims for justice to criminal behavior is still vibrant today. In 2015, Maryland legislator Patrick McDonough proposed that parents of BLM protestors have their food stamps taken away as punishment for their children's activism: "I think that you could make the case that there is a failure to do proper parenting and allowing this stuff to happen, is there an opportunity for a month to take away your food stamps?"[58] McDonough, like others before him, accused Black mothers of transmitting race-based pathologies to their offspring. Black mothers have even been accused of giving birth to "superpredators" who belong in cages, locked up and excluded from educational and employment opportunities.[59] Representative Paul Ryan (R-WI) claimed in 2014, shortly before he became speaker of the U.S. House of Representatives, that young "inner city men" are "not even thinking about working or learning the value and culture of work" because they rely on government assistance.[60] This charge, along with the "youth bulge" charge that tags unemployed Black youth as likely to be radicalized troublemakers fomenting rebellion and political unrest, conveys mainstream white attitudes about the worthlessness of Black youth and their danger to society.[61] Policy makers, businessmen, and others initiated the massive expansion of the prison system as a solution for containing such youth in the 1970s and mobilizing white resentment. According to historian Naomi Murakawa, "The U.S. did not face a crime problem that was racialized. It faced a race problem that was criminalized."[62] These characterizations of Black youth and policy responses to them shape the way many Americans view the value of the children of women of color. The reproductive justice movement opposes such characterizations.

Mid-twentieth-century theories about mothers as transmitters of pathology—especially the theories of E. Franklin Frazier, the prominent Black sociologist who popularized the concept of the "Black matriarch"—blamed Black women for the condition of the African American community and family.[63] Scholars and policy makers largely overlooked racial exclusions from workplaces, unsafe neighborhoods, segregated libraries, and tragically underfunded schools when they pinned the source of "the problem" on mothers. This focus on psychology and families replaced earlier theories that claimed that race differences were the result of eugenic, biological inferiority of Blacks. By the mid-twentieth century, Frazier and others associated racial prejudice with psychological problems rooted in early childhood experiences and in negligent mothers. They ascribed racism among white men to their feelings of sexual inadequacy, frustrated aggression, and, once again, pointed at inadequate mothering, charging that white men who exhibited racism were expressing their conflicted relationships with their own mothers.[64] The media and many white Americans still blame the violence that flows from racism on individual psychology, defining hatred of others based on race as simply a personal, psychologically based problem.[65] When grand jury after grand jury decides not to bring charges against police who brutalize or kill unarmed people of color, they justify their decisions, one after the other, by claiming that these policemen were good professionals who legitimately feared for their lives.[66] These assessments and justifications do not challenge the culture of white supremacy with its rigid ideas about superiority and inferiority and its tolerance, even protection, of the consequences of these ideas.

Some white women, mostly poor ones who need various kinds of support associated with reproduction, are stigmatized and punished, too. Conservative politicians and others frequently tag such women as unfit to be mothers because they don't have enough money to give their children "the advantages" and define them as moral failures because they go ahead and have children anyway. Conservative commentator Ann Coulter and her colleagues shame poor women of all races, associating them with sexual misbehavior.[67] Some Americans who worry about the loss of white-majority population view white women who don't want children as dangerous, too, and perhaps as un-American because they "refuse" to provide white American citizens for the nation.[68]

TRANS ISSUES AND REPRODUCTIVE JUSTICE

"Transgender" is a term used to describe people whose gender identity—that is, their inner sense of being male, female, or a nonbinary gender—differs from the gender they were assigned at birth. According to some orthographic conventions, the word "trans" with an asterisk ("trans*") encompasses a whole range of identities on the gender continuum and includes people who are transgender, transsexual, genderqueer, and gender nonconforming.[69] As with many fast-evolving ways of expressing these statuses, people debate whether to use the asterisk or not.

Transgender issues are reproductive justice issues because both domains recognize that the definitions of womanhood, birthing, and mothering (among other concepts involving reproduction) do not fit neatly into the male-female binary, a construct that feels oppressive, anachronistic, and invisibilizing to some people. In addition, identity-based sexual human rights claims include the right to sexual self-definition and the right to develop individual sexual and gender identities.[70] These claims constitute a model of sexual citizenship that is not dependent on what one *does*, such as engaging in same-sex relationships, but who one *is*, or who one self-identifies as being. Transpeople make demands about self-ownership and self-determination, just as members of other identity-based movements have done in the past and do today. These demands include expectations about the right to public and social recognition and acceptance of the declared identity. They also include expectations about the right to services and conveniences that are gender appropriate. In this way claims for recognition encompass the expectation of both individual rights and collective human rights.

In a heteropatriarchal society, most humans experience sex-based socialization from birth that privileges males above females and denies the reality that many people exist on a continuum between the male-female binary. For ciswomen, transmen, and transwomen, patriarchal socialization can constitute a justification for gender-based violence, subordination, and reproductive oppression.

Transmen, transwomen, and people who self-define as trans-nonbinary encounter reproductive justice issues that the larger society generally does not acknowledge, does not understand, or rejects. Some transpeople have abortions, some use birth control, and some give birth. Some need access to family planning clinics for hormone replacement therapy. When they can access these services and experiences with dignity and safety, the human rights of transpersons are affirmed.

As society denies the identity of transpeople, it also visits the indignities of violence, homelessness, and high rates of unemployment and incarceration on transpeople. In fact, to be visibly trans is extremely dangerous in a transphobic society. Investigative reporter Zoe Greenberg reported that "in a 2000 survey of 252 gender variant residents of Washington, DC, 29 percent of respondents reported no source of income. Another 31 percent reported annual incomes under $10,000."[71] According to the Sylvia Rivera Law Project (a New York–based organization that provides free legal aid to low-income transgender, gender nonconforming, and intersex people of color), poverty and lack of job opportunities propel trans people into survival crimes such as sex work, drug sales, and theft. Given this syndrome, transpeople, especially those who are poor people of color, experience police hostility and surveillance, harassment, and incarceration. In the eyes of many law enforcement officials, simply being gender nonconforming *is* the crime. Trans folks have reported that simply walking down the street, entering a bar, or passing out leaflets can lead to arrest in some jurisdictions, an experience wryly called "walking while trans."[72] We could also call this policing practice "trans profiling" because it produces overincarceration. Police frequently profile transpersons as sex workers, particularly transpersons of color. As a number of state legislatures are busily ensuring, even using the "wrong" restroom can get a person locked up.

When trans individuals are locked up, they are likely to experience a full spectrum of anti-trans policies and practices. Many transmen and transwomen suffer rape, various forms of coercion, and denial of medical treatment in jails and prisons. When transwomen are sentenced to a male facility, they are typically at much higher risk of sexual abuse than they would be in a facility for females; this placement policy constitutes a violation of international human rights standards against torture. Such prisoners may also experience severe harassment by guards, who may accuse them of demanding special privileges when they seek safety and medical attention, including hormone treatments for gender dysphoria.[73]

Transmen able to become pregnant suffer from specific types of reproductive injustices while incarcerated. Some have had to sue because prison authorities deny them prenatal treatment, shackle them while they give birth (a practice that some prisons and jails continue to use on ciswomen giving birth, even when state law prohibits the practice), and subject them to "forced feminization" by denying them access to products "made for men," such as soaps or shaving creams. "Whether they are about health care, placement, showers, or any number of other issues, prison policies and practices for trans, intersex, and gender-nonconforming people are never about promoting anyone's safety, health, dignity, well-being, or self-determination," says Gabriel Arkles, formerly of the Sylvia Rivera Law Project. "Rather, they serve other interests, including maintenance of a patriarchal gender binary system and white supremacy. One of the ways that they do this is through limiting or destroying the reproductive potential of transgender people and other people in prison."[74] The most obvious way in which transgender and gender-non-conforming people experience reproductive oppression is by being locked up during the most fertile period of their lifetime.

Prison officials claim they place transpeople in a men's or a woman's facility based on safety considerations. In fact, these decisions are usually made only on the basis of prisoners' genitalia, not their identity; officials are frequently very eager to forestall sexual activity and the possibility of a pregnancy. Probably most important, prison officials want to retain for themselves the power to assign gender identity and prison placement, underscoring the indignity of the prisoner and the total control of the administration. Prison officials have also imposed coercive sterilization on transpeople as a strategy for marking a person's "true" gender. In addition, in some institutions, officials have refused to accept a transperson's gender identity unless that person has undergone sexual reassignment surgery (SRS).

This same reproductive injustice can also occur when low-income individuals apply for the identity papers that are necessary for receiving health care or welfare benefits, a practice that underscores the special vulnerabilities of transpersons based on their race and class. Without a government-issued identity card that matches their gender identity, individuals may be harassed, arrested, subjected to police violence, or worse. Attorney Elana Redfield, formerly on the staff of the Sylvia Rivera Law Project, explains the profound reproductive consequences of the genital-based definition of gender identity and policies of coerced SRS:

> Most policies regarding legal recognition of gender have an anatomical basis—historically, legal gender is associated with sex assigned at birth based on anatomical features (typically genitalia and reproductive organs). Thus, traditional policies of gender change require a person to conform their reproductive anatomy through surgery to the typical, expected traits of a particular sex in order to be recognized as a member of that sex. The typical idea of a woman is of a person who does not have testes; therefore they must be removed. Because a typical man does not have ovaries or a womb, these things must be removed. When people do not conform to this stereotype, such as Thomas Beatie, the transgender man who gave birth to three children, their "right" to use a term like Male is often challenged and revoked by popular opinion. Therefore, the traditional approach to gender change on government ID specifically requires genital surgery—often enumerated in detail so as to exclude non-genital surgeries.
>
> On the surface level, this is about expectations about the bodies of men and women (which of course impact all people, and particularly marginalize intersex and gender-nonconforming people). But on a deeper level ... this paradigm requires sterilization as a condition of legal recognition of gender. One must implicitly agree to compromise any existing reproductive capacity in order to obtain official designation as male or female on a government document.[75]

In summary, reproductive oppression against transpeople—especially people of color—includes denying them the access to the health care they need, denying them access to their children, segregating them from people that they might have children with, even though that may mean these individuals are exposed to extreme violence and isolation, and demanding that transpeople have surgical sterilizations or sexual reassignment surgery to meet officials definitions of gender. In short, transgender issues are reproductive justice issues.

REPRODUCTIVE JUSTICE, ADOPTION, AND FOSTER CARE

Foster care systems in the fifty states do not consistently give children under their care adequate protection, and many of the programs frequently seem to punish parents (mainly poor mothers) who do not meet various and sometimes arbitrary standards regarding parental resources and care.[76] A mother in New York, for example, with a three-year-old son took out a restraining order against the child's abusive father, who had choked her and threatened to kill her. Apparently in response to the mother's actions, the New York City child welfare authorities removed the child from her custody while she was at work, without ever proving there was a reason to separate the mother from the child.[77]

Critics of child welfare services across the country argue that mismanagement, incompetence, heavy caseloads, insufficient staff and funding, among other problems, cause long bureaucratic delays that keep children and their parents threatened and in limbo. Some children stay in harmful situations for months or even years. Yet agencies rush to place other children for adoption too quickly, forcibly terminating parental rights even of children not legally free for adoption. The vast majority of children enmeshed in foster care systems are African American, and as law professor Dorothy Roberts reports with irony, these children are "destined to be permanently separated from their irreparable parents, [and their] only salvation is to be adopted into new families."[78] The number of children in foster care grows steadily because policy makers, law enforcement officials, and service providers have abandoned the principle of family preservation, have sped up termination of parental rights, have pushed more mothers with dependent children into the workforce, and have incarcerated ever more parents with dependent children. The various public systems crack down on poor parents at the same time that policy makers have eliminated supports for these parents.[79]

Race, class, and gender biases influence decisions in the child welfare system, in the criminal justice system, and in the spaces where these two systems meet. Recently in South Carolina, Debra Harrell was arrested and incarcerated for seventeen days for letting her nine-year-old daughter play in a park while she worked at a nearby McDonald's. The authorities placed Harrell's daughter in foster care; Harrell regained custody only after a protracted court battle.

When we look at the list of crimes that poor women are charged with as they are trying to take care of their children, we can see the terrible consequences that flow from the lack of social supports for the right to mother. To be mothers, all women require a range of supports, including some degree of economic support, particularly a living wage; the ability to plan and time motherhood so as to avoid the loss of one's job; the ability to work within a stable schedule of hours so that planning and scheduling child care is possible; the ability to mother free of interpersonal violence. Policy makers, politicians, and many ordinary people claim that poor people are by definition poor decision makers. But the very lack of these supports, guarantees, and rights renders choice making all but impossible and denies dignity to poor mothers on the grounds that they do not deserve the same sexual, biological, and affective relationships and opportunities as others.

These assumptions constitute human rights violations against poor people. Most politicians apparently operate on the premise that it is politically advantageous to label certain groups of people bad decision makers and politically disadvantageous to advocate restructuring our economic and political systems to support the many diverse ways that families are comprised, including families attempting to survive on insecure, low-wage work in a neoliberal political economy.

DISABLED CHILDREN AND REPRODUCTIVE JUSTICE

Low-income children are more likely to be disabled than other children because of in-utero and childhood exposure to environmental pollutants and because their families have less access to quality health care during pregnancy and afterward. In some cases, the access problem is extreme: undocumented immigrant women may hesitate to seek prenatal care because they fear deportation; without this care, their children are at risk for a variety of harms. Thus, some children of immigrants are products of a society that denies the human right to health care. As a consequence, too many children, particularly poor children and children of color, may have disabilities in a context with few or no support systems and in a context that dehumanizes disabled people by tacitly suggesting that they should not exist because they are "burdens" on their parents and nonproductive drains on society.

Clearly, the reproductive justice perspective argues that the disabled person is *not* the burden, but the lack of social supports absolutely burdens parents who have children with special needs and burdens the children themselves. Low-income parents of color who cannot fully care for or protect their disabled children and who do not have the opportunity to claim the restorative benefits of self-care time are particularly burdened. Social policy and society in general expect parents to be uncompensated primary caregivers for their children. This work is highly gendered, as women continue to provide the majority of care. People with economic resources can, of course, hire aides, nurses, and other personal care attendants. But government agencies rarely provide such supports for low-income and working-class parents, whose families also frequently encounter a lack of Americans with Disabilities Act–compliant accommodations at school, in their apartment buildings, and in other public and private settings.

The lack of social supports violates moral imperatives and fundamental social responsibilities for assisting disabled members of society. The human rights framework illustrates the dialectic between needs and rights: Every child has a right to an education, but a blind child may need her books in Braille. This is not a special right but a special need that takes into account a disabled person's specific identity in the process of protecting and achieving human rights goals.

Antiabortionists insist that women must carry all pregnancies to term, but many of them do not support the kinds of public policies and government expenditures that would provide supports for women to make these decisions, confident that they will not unduly and solely bear the brunt of the responsibility for the child, including children with special needs. The need for comprehensive support services for disabled children and their caregivers is absolutely a reproductive justice claim.

ASSISTING MOTHERHOOD: THE RIGHT
TO PARENT AT ANY COST?

It is difficult to separate conversations about assisted reproductive technologies (ARTs) —new scientific and technological techniques and processes to boost reproductive capacity—from the history of eugenics in the United States. On the one hand, technology can liberate women by offering them more choices about getting pregnant and being mothers.[80] On the other hand, ARTs can extend the reach of patriarchy into the womb—for example, when ultrasound and amniocentesis are used to abort a female fetus. After all, we know that the widespread preference for male children has led to a world with 100 million "missing" women; that is, the number of women who should be alive in the world has been reduced by 100 million sex-selective abortions and infanticides, or more.[81] Clearly, reproductive technologies and new social norms are extending the ways that women and individuals can become mothers. Today persons can occupy a number of categories: birth mother (blood mother), various kinds and degrees of surrogate mother, othermother (a relative who takes on childcare responsibilities), and radical mother (someone who helps raise children who are not related biologically; also known as fictive kin.)[82]

As we've seen, eugenics is the pseudoscientific belief that the human race can be improved through selective breeding. Clearly, the membrane between eugenics and ART grows thinner with each new scientific breakthrough in reproductive technologies. The brave new world of "designer babies," gene-selected for certain characteristics, raises questions about which genes are desirable, which are not, and why. Deselecting for certain disabilities or racial or gender characteristics is an updated expression of eugenics.[83]

Reproductive justice activists are concerned about the slippery slope between eugenics and ART because of the poisonous history of eugenics and its periodic and contemporary reemergence. After World War II, eugenics fell into disfavor for some years in the United States because of both revulsion against the Nazi uses of eugenics and the civil rights movement's claim of human equality. But books such as Richard Herrnstein and Charles Murray's *The Bell Curve: Intelligence and Class Structure in American Life* (1994) lent a new patina of respectability to eugenics. Herrnstein and Murray claimed that African Americans are genetically predisposed to score lower on IQ tests than whites and that unqualified Blacks are the beneficiaries of affirmative action programs that merely support a culture of dependency.[84] Such pseudoscience ignores the role that substandard educational systems and preferences for white students play in constructing their assessments. In addition, they failed to account for how race structures class, and class structures educational opportunities. Prominent affirmations of *The Bell Curve*'s claims appear more than thirty years later, for example, in the words of the late Supreme Court Justice Antonin Scalia who, invoking race-based eugenics, declared approvingly in 2015 during the oral argument in the affirmative action case *Fisher v. University of Texas,*

> There are those who contend that it does not benefit African Americans to get them into the University of Texas, where they do not do well, as opposed to having them go to a less-advanced school, a slower-track school where they do well. One of the briefs pointed out that most of the black scientists in this country don't come from schools like the University of Texas. They come from lesser schools

where they do not feel that they're being pushed ahead in classes that are too fast for them.[85]

The same year that *The Bell Curve* came out, Dean Hamer and Peter Copeland published *The Science of Desire: The Gay Gene and the Biology of Behavior,* in which they claimed to have identified a "gay gene" that constitutes a biological basis for homosexuality.[86] Both books presented their findings in apparently objective, scientific terms. Both attempted to justify social problems such as racism and homophobia on the basis of genetics. This argument, of course, has implications for the variable value of the reproductive capacity of women from various groups; those with "normal genes" will have more "normal children." Critics point out that race and gender are socially constructed and that racism and homophobia are not naturally occurring phenomena but are, instead, forms of bigotry.[87]

Race-based, eugenically inflicted assaults—for example, the charge that certain people live within a "culture of poverty," or enact a culturally determined "tangle of pathology," or display culturally and biologically generated "patterns of dependency"—target African Americans and provide justifications for the futility of government programs and social supports.[88] These assaults also reinforce the idea and the reality of unequal power relationships—racial hierarchies—and emphasize individual and group "failings" instead of fundamental social and institutional injustices that must be addressed. When white "authorities" like Charles Murray claim that science, not prejudice, is the driver of injustice, then white America cannot be held accountable for the legacies of slavery and the advantages that whites derive from segregation and discrimination.

The complicated relationship between eugenics, science, and assisted reproductive technologies compels reproductive justice advocates to question the medical, ethical, and commercial issues implicated in the right to be a mother or parent. Is the right to become a parent an absolute right, regardless of the ethical implications and the medical risks to others?

Reproductive justice feminists also ask questions about surrogacy, the practice of employing a woman to provide an egg and a womb, or only a womb, to produce a baby that will be raised by others, usually the provider of the sperm and maybe the provider of the egg or another person. Does surrogacy give special weight to the idea that the only valuable child is the one who shares DNA with a parent? And since surrogacy is an expensive undertaking pursued mostly by white people, does this practice embed ideas about preserving the "white race" as well as ideas about perpetuating biological, patriarchal lineage? Surely, quality parenting can occur no matter whose DNA is in the child—through adoptions, foster parenting, collective parenting, and other nuclear-family and non-nuclear-family options. Whether through adoptions, foster care, or ART we must be vigilant in protecting the human rights of people and communities involved in these processes. When we raise these difficult issues, we are aware that there are no simple solutions. But these methods of reproduction and family building do invite us to look at the intersections of parenting and technology and consider the reproductive issues that our social mores and conventional constructions of race and gender have not yet addressed or resolved.

The mainstream media often features celebrities who have become pregnant or acquired children using reproductive technologies. Several such stories have involved complicated matters of financial support and have drawn attention to questions beyond those matters. Latina actress Sofía Vergara's ex-fiancé went to court in 2015, for example, to claim that the frozen embryos the ex-couple had created had a "right to live."[89] The man wanted to claim ownership of and oversee the gestation of the two frozen embryos. He wanted to hire a surrogate for this purpose, asking, if a woman can bring a pregnancy to term without the consent of the man who impregnated her, why can't a man bring two embryos to term even if the woman in question objects?

While the ex-fiancé does have the right to have children, of course, he does not have the right to force Vergara to be the biological mother of his children. Attempts to impregnate a woman against her will amount to rape. Forcing motherhood on an unwilling woman is equally coercive. The American Congress of Obstetricians and Gynecologists has declared that "controlling the outcomes of a pregnancy, coerc[ing] a partner to have unprotected sex, and interfer[ing] with contraceptive methods" all constitute reproductive coercion.[90]

Another celebrity case unfolded in 2014 when African American television star Sherri Shepherd fought against paying child support to her ex-husband for a baby created with his sperm and the egg of a donor. Shepherd explained that the baby was born after the couple divorced, and she was not the mother. Nevertheless, a court declared Shepherd the legal mother of the child and ordered her to pay child support to her ex-husband, a decision she contested. This case demonstrates that the legal definition of "mother" is far from fixed in our society and shows that the role of DNA in determining a woman's relation to motherhood is not clear or stable.[91]

As we noted, surrogacy as a path to pregnancy, motherhood, and parenting is a strategy generally available only to people with considerable financial resources. The exploitation of poor women hired as surrogates in the developing world, especially India, is an important subject, but not the focus of this section.[92]

Instead we look at the data on health risks associated with surrogacy in the United States. Full information is scarce, but we know that commercial surrogacy is widespread and a growing practice in the United States, with the number of babies born to gestational surrogates increasing 89 percent between 2004 and 2008.[93] Because deaths of surrogates are usually reported as pregnancy-related complications, we have little information about the experiences of female surrogates, some of whom undertake as many as six pregnancies, with the consent of their ob-gyn. Commercial surrogacy is fast becoming a popular route to pregnancy and parenthood for some infertile or same-sex couples, yet the practice and its commercial dimensions receive very little oversight, study, or regulation.[94]

Women acting as surrogates generally receive (have implanted within their uterus) a fertilized embryo to which they have no genetic relation. The embryo may have been created using the intended parents' genetic material, or the sperm and/or eggs may have been purchased in the marketplace. A medical procedure is required to implant the fertilized embryo, so clinics that provide these services are supposed to meet voluntary industry guidelines, according to the American Society for Reproductive Medicine. This group recommends that persons seeking surrogates avoid the choice of low-income women, including women who receive Medicaid or other government assistance, in order to reduce the chance that a surrogate may take on this "job" because of her financial need.[95] After all, surrogates in the United States can earn between $25,000 and $52,000 for carrying a pregnancy for nine months and giving birth, a significant sum that is not paid out until the pregnancy is confirmed, but after the surrogate has endured many medical procedures to facilitate a successful implantation and pregnancy.[96]

Critics of surrogacy accuse participants of "baby trafficking" and "commercialized slavery" and denounce the commodification of children and the commercialization of women's bodies.[97] Some critics believe that only noncompensated surrogacy should be permissible—that is, the only women the law should allow to be surrogates are individuals who carry a fetus for others for altruistic reasons, such as wanting to help a relative or bring joy to an infertile woman.[98] But others believe that banning or restricting surrogacy in this way will simply drive it underground, significantly increasing the costs and the risks.[99]

Apple and Facebook both provide a $20,000 employee benefit to cover an egg-freezing procedure, a new corporate policy that seems to address the companies' need for a stable workforce in which women are not leaving their positions (for which they received considerable, expensive training and for which they have developed considerable expertise) to rear children too soon. The new policy indeed seems to encourage some women to spend their twenties and thirties concentrating on their careers and avoiding pregnancy.[100] The benefit gives some women the confidence that their own viable eggs will be waiting for them later. In fact, the success rates for completed pregnancies under these circumstances is far from clear, with a number of experts estimating that less than 13 or 14 percent of embryos transferred from frozen eggs lead to a successful pregnancy.[101]

When young women sell their eggs, the transaction occurs within an $80 million egg-donor market that lacks federal guidelines even though these sales can make both a person's body and body parts into commodities. Without guidelines, young women are more easily exploited, especially those who need money, perhaps to pay back a student loan. Indeed, egg-donor "recruiters" advertise at elite colleges and universities around the country and concentrate their efforts on "high-end" egg donors, ignoring industry guidelines in pursuit of profits. Women "donating" these kinds of eggs have reportedly been paid up to $100,000, while other women are generally paid between $3,000 and $10,000 per round of donations. Women who donate multiple times do so in a marketplace with almost no regulations, despite the possible health risks; many are even able to obscure the fact that they have undergone the procedure previously.[102]

The fact is that egg donation is uncomfortable and possibly risky, requiring weeks of hormone injections to stimulate the ovaries for egg harvesting and then ultrasounds and surgery. Tellingly, no research exists on whether the high doses of hormones that women must take increase the risk of infertility or cancer, especially among repeat donors. And typically, there is little post-donation follow-up of the women.[103] Instead, fertility clinics invest resources in recruiting new, young, healthy, desirable donors such as women with Asian and Jewish backgrounds, actresses, models, and Ivy League students with high SAT scores.[104]

BEYOND BIOLOGY: REPRODUCTIVE JUSTICE INTERSECTIONS
Immigration

Harsh immigration laws deny immigrants and their families reproductive justice. These laws are largely the work of an anti-immigrant movement in the United States that is concerned about immigrants who allegedly take jobs away from Americans, about the complexion of the American population, and particularly about the number of nonwhite babies born in the United States.[105] By the middle of the twenty-first century, demographers predict the U.S. population will be majority people of color.[106]

We know that immigrants who arrive at the southern border of the United States have experienced a number of push-pull factors that encourage them to leave their home countries. To begin with, U.S. policies have contributed to the militarization of Latin America, including the funding and equipping of corrupt and abusive military and security forces, and have pressured governments to prevent persons fleeing these forces from leaving their countries of origin. They also include drug- and gang-related violence, persistent poverty, and other factors, all of which create various kinds of instability within countries and high levels of emigration.[107] Young, fertile women crossing the southern border of the United States are often fleeing extreme violence in their home countries and then experience rape and sexual assault on their journey to the United States. According to some who have looked closely at this situation, many women begin taking birth control pills before crossing the border because up to 80 percent are raped while in transit.[108]

Reproductive justice advocates and other proponents of human dignity argue that female migrants should have the right to be free from violence in their home country and the right to be safe on their journey to the United States. In addition, they should have full access to their human rights once they arrive in the United States. Instead, many arrive in this country denied the right to tell their stories of persecution fully, making it more likely that they will be denied asylum. Many are greeted by the anti-immigrant and antiabortion movements that have led the effort in state legislatures to deny immigrant women reproductive dignity and safety—for example, by enacting laws that exclude immigrants from access to health care. Many face detention, along with their children.[109] If they avoid detention, they may still face family separation and employers who take advantage of their undocumented status to commit wage theft (pay below the legal rates) and sexual violence.[110] In addition, many immigrant women have to defend themselves against racist allegations concerning their motives for coming to the United States.[111]

Reproductive justice intersects particularly sharply with immigrant rights in the battle over the Fourteenth Amendment to the Constitution, a guarantee ratified after the Civil War to affirm that all people born in the United States are citizens of the country. The Republican Party, especially its extremist elements, seeks to limit the Fourteenth Amendment's birth-right-citizenship provision to children born to a citizen of the United States and seeks to deny citizenship to all children born in the United States to undocumented persons, a clear violation of the Fourteenth Amendment.[112] Those who attack the human rights of immigrants often point to Mexican women, who, they charge, flock to the United States to give birth to "anchor babies," children who, as citizens, can facilitate the citizenship process for their undocumented parents of color and other family members, a process the antibirthright movement wants to extinguish. Although there is no evidence that immigrants use their U.S.-born babies for this purpose, research does exist showing that birthright citizenship helps immigrants adapt to and become a part of U.S. society.[113]

Because Republicans have not been able to void the birth-right provision of the Fourteenth Amendment, officials in some Republican-dominated states have tried to find other ways to deny citizenship rights of children born in the United States to undocumented immigrants.[114] As we noted, in McAllen, Texas, for example, officials have limited the kinds of identification that undocumented immigrants can present in order to get birth certificates for their newborns.[115]

Clearly, when citizenship is denied to babies of immigrants, these children lose their basic human right to public services such as health care, various kinds of public assistance, and education. After all, a certificate of birth is a fundamental human right, without which persons are rendered stateless, unable to function in society. To begin with, they cannot obtain legal identity papers. Such persons can end up in legal limbo, one member of a vast vulnerable population denied voting rights, representation, and citizenship benefits such as college financial aid.[116] The apartheid government of South Africa used this tactic, as have other governments determined to deny citizenship status to specific segments of their population.[117] Such policies draw directly on racist, sexist, and xenophobic impulses and taint the culture and the polity as a whole.

These same impulses have fueled the activities of "birthers" determined to delegitimize the presidency of Barack Obama. During President Obama's entire tenure, some opponents of the president repeatedly claimed that his birth certificate was forged in Hawaii or otherwise faked, that he was born in Kenya as a Muslim, and thus did not meet constitutional requirements to hold the office. Drawing on no proof whatsoever, the accusers were willing to stoke racist, anti-Muslim, and other forms of prejudice to express their opposition to the president and to immigrants generally.[118]

Policing and Parenting: Incarceration and Reproductive Justice

Reproductive justice advocates define the politics and uses of incarceration as a pressing reproductive justice issue. Advocates begin with the fact that the United States has the highest prison population rate in the world, at 716 persons per 100,000 people, adding up to more than 2.2 million incarcerated persons. The United States spends $80 billion per year on correctional facilities that lock people up and also provide health care, meals, and shelter, mostly for people excluded from the economic mainstream and from the landscape of diminished employment opportunities. Over the past forty years, $1.5 trillion has been spent on this system that punishes the poor, exploits their labor, violates their human rights, and sets up "inmates" for a life of exclusion and demonization. Andrea C. James, a former criminal defense lawyer who herself has been incarcerated, points out that even though the actual crime rate has decreased over the past twenty years, "instead of putting money into education for children, infrastructure, [and] job opportunities to invest in our future and collective prosperity as a country, we have redirected dollars to support a failed drug war and expanding prison system." [119]

The government's endless, futile, and racially targeted War on Drugs has been a war on human rights. In addition to bringing chaos and pain to countless families and communities, this war has structured the lives of vulnerable girls and women who fall "into the traps of illegal behaviors to enable a normal existence." [120] Many have been imprisoned for nonviolent survival crimes, including crimes involving controlled substances. They are sentenced to unreasonably long terms for trying to exist with too few resources; the path to prison often starts with massive unemployment and few choices outside of the underground economy. [121] Women trapped in the system risk not only incarceration but sexual and reproductive abuse in a variety of ways.

For example, some prosecutors in Nashville have, from time to time, made the acceptance of sterilization an element of plea bargaining for female defendants in drug cases, targeting women they judged as illegitimate reproducers, even though such punishments clearly violate the Supreme Court decision in *Skinner v. Oklahoma*.[122] Other investigators have identified cases in West Virginia and Virginia in which, if a woman accepted sterilization, she was granted reduced prison time. A prosecutor in Virginia recently agreed to drop some charges against a male defendant after he accepted sterilization.[123] We can't be sure how frequently these human rights abuses occur, but any such deals clearly violate basic notions of human dignity and justice.[124]

At the end of 2015, more than 200,000 women were incarcerated in the United States; this represents a growth rate of 646 percent since 1980 in federal and state prisons.[125] Over time, prisons have become key sites of injustice, where poor people are disproportionately incarcerated and incarcerated people are very likely to remain poor. Many women are incarcerated because laws originally enacted to help them now do the opposite. For example, domestic violence laws enacted to protect the victims of battering now harm the target of violence as police may arrest both the perpetrator and the battered woman, often separating the victim from her children.[126]

In 2012 Marissa Alexander, the mother of three children in Florida, was found guilty on three counts of aggravated assault for defending herself from an assault by her ex-husband, against whom she had a restraining order. She fired a warning gunshot in her attacker's direction when he attempted to beat her again. The prosecutor tried to have her sentenced to sixty years in prison; ultimately, she received twenty years for using a gun to defend herself against her batterer, arguably a profoundly unjust sentence in Florida, where the killer of teenager Trayvon Martin successfully used that state's stand-your-ground defense to escape murder charges. Alexander's sentence conveys the message that the stand-your-ground defense is not available to an

African American female victim of domestic violence but it is available to a white man (albeit one with an Afro-Peruvian grandfather) who committed murder. Alexander served three years in prison after accepting a plea deal.[127]

In some cases, women whose partners have killed their children have also gone to prison for failing to protect the children from the abusers. In Texas, Arlena Lindley's boyfriend murdered her three-year old son in 2006, after years of abuse. The boyfriend was sentenced to life in prison, but Lindley also received a forty-five-year sentence for "abuse by omission," for failing to provide a safe environment for the child.[128] An investigative reporter, Alex Campbell, found twenty-eight other cases across eleven states where mothers had been sentenced for at least ten years because they had not been able to protect their children from domestic violence perpetrated by others.[129] In these cases, the female victims were victimized all over again by the misuse of laws designed to protect victims of domestic violence.

When society punishes women for violence committed against them, we can easily lose sight of the reproductive justice issues that are embedded in many of these violent acts. Charlene, a Native American midwife, explains, "There is no justice if women are afraid all the time."[130] Personal safety is a major component of reproductive justice; the threat and reality of sexual violence directly affects women's sexual health, because in a violent environment, women are more vulnerable to unintended pregnancies, sexually transmitted infections, and physical and emotional abuse, as well as sabotage of their use of birth control or their decision to have an abortion. When reproductive and domestic violence intersect, reproductive justice activists must call attention to a wide array of issues.

Law enforcement and medical personnel have used the federal Unborn Victims of Violence Act (2004) to define fetuses as victims of crimes in cases when women have miscarried, for example, and prosecutors claim that the unborn child has been murdered.[131] Many abortion rights advocates object to the special victim status that this legislation accords fetuses, in part because they recognize the threat such legislation presents to women's rights.[132]

Pregnant women are also harmed by the War on Drugs, which has reached into the womb in ways that abortion rights advocates have foreseen. Now any pregnant woman's body may be subjected to surveillance; all pregnant women are potential suspects. Reproductive justice advocates call this dangerous intersection of reproduction and the carceral system "pregnancy policing." In this space, the dangers posed by feticide laws cause women, especially substance-abusing women, to be fearful about seeking necessary and vital medical attention, even though drug users require health care and support to get clean. Often when a woman finds out she is pregnant, she feels a strong responsibility for the fetus at the same time that she feels deep shame if she cannot control her addiction.[133] Such a person needs support and assistance, not the heavy hand of the law, a position that is supported by professional associations of physicians such as the American Academy of Pediatrics, the American College of Obstetricians and Gynecologists, and the American Medical Association.

The Unborn Victims of Violence Act and other such legislation define drug users as illegitimate mothers. These laws that punish vulnerable women ignore the context in which many fertile women live, a context structurally distorted by racism, systemic poverty, and inadequate health care.

One recent study lays out the long-term strategy that has tied the War on Drugs to racial targeting.[134] An analysis of over four hundred cases in which a woman's pregnancy was the basis for her arrest and incarceration found that African American women comprised over half of the cases.[135] Pregnant Black women are more likely to be tested by health care providers, reported to authorities (often without their knowledge until they are arrested), and targeted for the removal of their children by child welfare authorities.

Rennie Gibbs was caught in the net of pregnancy policing when she was sixteen. At thirty-six weeks of pregnancy, Gibbs was admitted to a hospital in Mississippi. Doctors induced labor, but the infant was stillborn because the umbilical cord was wrapped around its neck. Despite this non-drug-related cause of infant death, Gibbs was charged with homicide, and a Lowndes County grand jury indicted her for "depraved heart murder" because traces of a "cocaine byproduct" were allegedly found in her blood although no traces of any drugs were found in the infant's blood. After years of fighting the prosecution, the charges against Gibbs were dropped, but the prosecutor reserved the right to reinstate them. This is one of a surge of cases that are the result of prosecutions of low-income women of color under "fetal harm laws." As Lynn Paltrow, executive director of National Advocates for Pregnant Women and cocounsel for Gibbs put it, "The biggest threats to life—born and unborn—do not come from mommies—but rather [from] poverty, barriers to health care, persistent racism, and environmental hazards." Paltrow added, "Prosecutions like these increase risks to babies by frightening women away from care and using tax dollars to expand the criminal justice system rather than to fund nurse-family partnerships that actually protect the health of the children."[136]

In Wisconsin and several other states, authorities can arrest women at any stage of their pregnancies if they use or admit to past use of alcohol or drugs during pregnancy. In 2015, a white woman, Tamara Loertscher, was one of three thousand women in Wisconsin under surveillance, being actively investigated, or recently arrested for allegedly using drugs while pregnant, according to National Advocates for Pregnant Women.[137] Some jurisdictions are bringing criminal charges against women even after they give birth to a healthy baby. In 2014, the Alabama Supreme Court, ruling that a woman can be charged with chemical endangerment of a fetus if she uses a controlled substance while pregnant, upheld the conviction of Sarah Hicks, an African American woman who gave birth to a healthy baby who nevertheless tested positive for cocaine. Health professionals had requested medical care and treatment for Hicks while she was pregnant. Instead of receiving help, however, she was imprisoned. Since the chemical endangerment law was passed in 2006, more than one hundred women who became pregnant and tested positive for a controlled substance have been arrested. Some have experienced pregnancy losses, but the majority— like Sarah Hicks—have continued their pregnancy to term and have given birth to a healthy child. The legal actions against these women have depended upon the definition of the word "child" in Alabama law, which refers not only to a baby but also to a fertilized egg and draws on antiabortion definitions of "personhood." Pointedly, there is no exception from prosecution for pregnant women who use legal substances prescribed by physicians. Further, pregnant women who use alcohol (a legal but far more fetal-damaging substance, which can cause fetal alcohol syndrome) are not prosecuted. Their behavior is treated as a public health issue, and authorities simply warn alcohol-using pregnant women of the dangers involved. Eighteen states consider drug use while pregnant to be de facto child abuse. In these states, women who stand at the intersection of a failed social policy on drugs and pregnancy are vulnerable to arrest, punishment, and official degradation generally.[138]

Reproductive justice advocates oppose this punitive treatment of pregnant women because it reflects a policy that turns a public health problem into a matter for the criminal justice system. Critics note that under this policy, authorities imagine neither the community nor the medical establishment as sources of assistance or support for women who need both. The policy seems only concerned with trapping individuals within the criminal justice system. Indeed, the regime that criminalizes pregnant women supports few drug treatment centers that are brave enough to admit a pregnant addicted woman.[139] Jennifer Johnson, an African American Florida woman, the first person convicted after having given birth to a baby who tested positive for cocaine, had sought assistance at a drug-treatment clinic and had been turned away.[140] Her 1989 conviction was overturned in 1992 by the Florida Supreme Court, partly out of the concern that the threat of imprisonment or loss of their children may drive women away from seeking vital prenatal care. The fact is that most women convicted under these laws are poor and Black or Latina. In Florida, women of color are ten times more likely to be reported for substance abuse than white women, although rates of drug use are actually higher for whites.[141]

In another disturbing development, Purvi Patel, an Asian American woman living in Indiana, was sentenced to twenty years in prison in 2015 for feticide and neglect of a dependent. She was accused first, of taking abortion pills and causing the death of her fetus (a self-induced abortion) and second, of killing the fetus after it was born alive (feticide). In the absence of specific evidence to support either charge, Patel was basically convicted of failing to give birth to a surviving child. Lynn Paltrow, Patel's cocounselor, called the conviction "a shocking new application of Indiana's feticide law, which was intended to criminalize 'knowing or intentional termination of *another's* pregnancy.' Turning this law into one that can be used to punish a woman who herself has an abortion is an extraordinary expansion of the scope and intention of the state's law."[142] Patel's conviction was overturned in July 2016, but she still faces charges that she knew the infant was born alive, based on a controversial and historically discredited "lung float test" that prosecutors used to argue that the infant was not stillborn.[143] Another Indiana woman, Bei Bei Shuai, a Chinese immigrant, was also prosecuted and imprisoned in 2010 under Indiana's feticide law after she unsuccessfully attempted suicide, and the fetus she was carrying died. The murder and attempted feticide charges were dropped in August 2013, when she accepted a plea agreement by pleading guilty to criminal recklessness.[144]

A Black woman in Georgia, Kenlissia Jones, obtained a commercial form of misoprostol (a drug used for medical abortions) from an Internet source in order to terminate her own pregnancy.[145] Abortion is legal in Georgia, but Jones wanted a more private way to terminate her pregnancy. When she ended up having to go to the hospital, she was arrested for "malice murder," a crime that can carry life in prison or the death penalty. The reproductive justice community was outraged, particularly since Georgia abortion laws do not call for the prosecution of women for self-induced abortions. Eventually the charges against her were dropped; however, authorities have told her that she is still at risk for rearrest for possession of a dangerous drug.

These cases are examples of the ways that states have established separate and unequal laws for pregnant people, a clear violation of both reproductive justice principles and of the guarantee of equal protection under the law. In all of these cases, the laws and legislators who crafted them may seem to address the health and well-being of fetuses and babies and women. In fact, legislators seem most committed to establishing the legal personhood of fetuses. They are typically quite a bit less committed to the well-being of children once they are born and even less interested in the well-being of poor pregnant women of color.[146]

A reproductive justice analysis also explores the intersection of sexual violence and incarceration in the lives of young girls of reproductive age. For example, we know that before they were incarcerated, this population of girls has experienced sexual abuse at a rate 4.4 times the rate of boys. A total of 31 percent of incarcerated girls have previously experienced sexual abuse; 41 percent have experienced physical abuse; 39 percent emotional abuse; and 84 percent family violence. Not surprisingly, many girls seek to escape the environments in which they have encountered trauma and abuse by running away from home, fighting at home, engaging in substance abuse, choosing older partners to "protect" them, and experiencing failure at school. Boys account for more than two-thirds of juvenile arrests, but girls account for 29 percent, for crimes such as prostitution (76 percent), curfew violations (29 percent), liquor law violations (40 percent), and disorderly conduct (35 percent). Also notable is that Black girls are 20 percent more likely to be detained than white girls, but Native American and Alaskan Native girls are 50 percent more likely to be detained than white girls. More than 40 percent of incarcerated girls identify as LGBTQ.[147]

Incarceration of girls and women during the most fertile time of their reproductive lives means that many end up subjected to reproductive abuses such as shackling during childbirth, denial of abortion and birth control services, visitation abuses, food scarcity leading to low-birth-weight babies, and lack of privacy.[148] Birth justice activists have protested forced C-sections, unnecessary medical interventions, and shackling. A number of states have enacted laws banning the use of shackles on incarcerated women during labor, delivery, and recovery, yet in these states and elsewhere, this practice that the American Medical Association calls "barbaric" continues.[149] In thirty-eight states, the law permits authorities to shackle a woman during labor and birth.[150] These birth injustices constitute gender-based violence, or birth abuse, particularly because they are enacted upon on women without public voices, women who are seen as state property, or noncitizens lacking human rights.

What are the long-term, intergenerational effects of these experiences? First, the most drastic result of racialized incarceration policies in the United States is that one in fourteen African American children has at least one parent behind bars. Experts note that, typically, these children suffer from low self-esteem, poor mental and physical health, and other problems, some of which are classified as epigenetic—that is, the manifestation of alterations in gene expression that can persist and be transmitted across generations and can contribute to an expanding progression of problem behaviors, including increased levels of family disintegration, violence, substance abuse, obesity, stress, and mental health issues.[151] These outcomes of overincarceration affect populations possessing the fewest resources to combat such developments.[152]

Women who mother from prison are typically beset by fears, despondency, guilt, and shame.[153] Many of these women, two-thirds of whom were the primary caretaker of at least one child before incarceration, define themselves as "bad mothers," persons who violated the basic norms of caring for their children. Still, despite feeling ashamed and isolated from their children, many women work hard to stay connected to them by making "every [phone] conversation ... a clipped verbal dance of concern, love, anger, discipline, and inquisition."[154] If they are fortunate—if they are able to maintain good family contact—they fill their personal lockers with pictures of missed family weddings, graduations, births, and funerals.[155]

Many incarcerated mothers are leery of signing powers of attorney or documents giving temporary guardianship of their children to others because they worry that these documents may be used to terminate their parental rights. On the outside, children struggle to survive without their mother. Some are cared for by grandparents or other relatives; others end up in foster care.[156]

Issues associated with visiting are particularly difficult for incarcerated women who are not permitted visits from their children, or whose children have no one to bring them to see their mother, or no money to travel with an adult companion for visits at an institution hundreds of miles from their home, or who are too scared or ashamed to visit.[157] When fathers are incarcerated, mothers often bring the children to visit; when mothers are the ones behind bars, there may be no one to carry out this difficult task.[158] Many women whose children do visit are joyful but also profoundly frustrated by the institutional constraints placed on visits, such as not being able to hold their baby or only being able to kiss their child only once at arrival and once at departure, under the threat that any violation of these and dozens of other regulations will lead to immediate termination of the visit and of all visiting privileges in the future.[159] Some mothers anticipate the moment when their children turn sixteen and can visit on their own without a supervising adult. Others mourn children who died during their draconian sentences, sometimes ten years, for minor drug offenses.[160]

Many women cannot find their children after they are released, especially when laws allow termination of parental rights if the parent has been out of the child's life for two years or, under the federal Adoption and Safe Families Act of 1997, if a child has been in foster care for fifteen of the past twenty-two months.[161] Since many women leave prison with no place to live and without employment, they lack the resources to fight for their rights to reunite with their children.[162] Moreover, a woman with a criminal record is banned from accessing welfare, public housing, student loans, and other social services, all of which would help her set up a new life with her children.[163]

For women who are or have been incarcerated, Mother's Day is a particularly profound event because that holiday gives them an opportunity to claim their right to mother their own children and to protest the devastating removal of their children by child welfare authorities, or to protest abusive sterilization policies and other practices that prevented them from being a mother in the first place. The right and capacity of many women—especially incarcerated women—to be mothers is so often denied, questioned, and threatened that they are shocked when many white women and privileged women in general denigrate Mother's Day as a meaningless, commercialized holiday. For women whose motherhood is thwarted, threatened, and denied, this is a day of special anguish and heartfelt claims.[164]

Housing, Gentrification, and Reproductive Justice

Reproductive decision making is affected by policies that shape neighborhood gentrification, housing, and land use. When a person decides whether to become a parent, she is likely to consider factors such as the availability of affordable housing. Can I give my child her own bedroom and a safe play space? The woman considering whether or not to have a child knows that housing has implications beyond crucial matters regarding where to sleep, eat, and conduct family life. Housing location determines the quality of schools, the availability of transportation, access to affordable, convenient day care, proximity to employment, and the presence or absence of environmental risks.[165]

Certainly, municipalities and corporations—expressing racist contempt—have put a disproportionate number of toxic dumps in or near low-income communities.[166] These dumps, along with aging sewer systems, the absence of political will to upgrade infrastructure, and the presence of other environmental degradations, have deprived many poor communities of even potable water while exposing children to highly toxic lead poisoning and other harmful effects.[167] Some low-income communities are "food deserts," because large grocery chains, typically a community's source of fresh fruits and vegetables and other healthy foods, define these neighborhoods as insufficiently profitable and stay away, at least until developers have gentrified the former working-class neighborhood.[168]

Neighborhood gentrification is the process of transforming an area inhabited by poor or working-class people into a neighborhood for wealthier people, usually by renovating decrepit older buildings, making them into high-priced, highly profitable housing. In this process, lower-income individuals are pushed out, no longer able to afford the new rents nor able to purchase the snazzy, expensive refurbished dwellings.[169] Before gentrification, basic municipal services may be frayed and disappearing: public schools may be shutting down and fire stations and hospitals closing, all of which cripples the viability of the community. After gentrification, these institutions return, their funding restored, the community revitalized, the neighborhood providing a sufficient tax and voter base to demand and pay for basic services.[170]

Federal housing policies, linked to banking and real estate practices, have over decades, pursued urban renewal, planned disinvestment, gentrification, subprime loans, redlining, and foreclosures, all of which have, separately and together, ensured both racially segregated housing and intergenerational poverty. Generation after generation of low-income individuals, very often people of color, have been forced by official programs and policies, along with the real estate industry's development strategies, to move away from their own communities, where they can no longer afford to live. In the process, low-income people of color have lost out on the opportunity to achieve economic security—or wealth accumulation—through home ownership, the most common way that Americans have passed wealth to the next generation. These policies and practices have enriched the banks and benefitted developers but have deepened discrimination against families of color and have placed harsh stresses on the reproductive decision making of millions of women because of the lack of wealth and other resources.[171]

In neighborhoods where low-income people must rear their families, public transportation is completely inadequate, even though residents must have access, without cars, to jobs, doctor's appointments, schools, and stores, to begin with. The lack of buses and other kinds of public transportation tends to geographically contain poor people, isolating them from higher-income neighborhoods and job opportunities. For example, public funding has been slashed or discontinued for bus service in Clayton County, Georgia,[172] and Arlington County, Virginia,[173] low-income communities, while public funding schemes have excluded extensions of subway systems into nearby wealthier communities in Cobb County, Georgia,[174] and the Georgetown section of Washington, DC,[175] making them largely inaccessible to people who do not own cars. Public transportation policies lock racially segregated housing and schools into place and undermine the safety and life opportunities for children of color.[176] These matters are at the heart of the reproductive decision-making process for millions of people in the United States and of paramount concern to reproductive justice analysts.

Education and Reproductive Justice

When people decide whether and when to have a child, they naturally consider what kind of a future the child will have. At the center of this question is concern about what kind of education their child can get. Will school be challenging and nurturing and prepare the child for a successful, independent life? Will the child be safe in school and also safe for traveling back and forth from home to school? All parents worry about the future and safety of their children. But parents of color also have to worry if their children will make it home from school or from a friend's house without being killed. African American parents, especially, have to have "the talk" with their children, not about sex, but about how to "behave if they get pulled over or if a cop stops them on the street" and how to "get out of that conversation alive."[177]

Some parents of color know that their neighborhood schools, underfunded and unsafe, cannot adequately educate their children. They have used false addresses to enroll their children in predominantly white schools with far more educational resources. In Connecticut, Ohio, and elsewhere, mothers have been punished—even sent to prison—for trying to obtain a decent education for their children.[178] Clearly, education is a reproductive justice issue.

The most profoundly underfunded schools in America, almost all in communities of color, constitute the so-called school-to-prison pipeline, a process that violates reproductive justice and the human right to raise children in safe and healthy environments. The pipeline consists of a series of policies and practices that push children out of schools and into the juvenile and criminal justice system. A disproportionate number of children of color—especially African American and Latino children—are arrested for what in-school police define as school-based misbehavior, such as burping in class.[179] As schools turn over responsibility for routine school discipline to municipal law enforcement, young children are caught in punitive nets, given police records for behaviors that would have formerly been matters for school counselors to deal with. In Louisiana, for example, an eighth-grade student was arrested for battery after allegedly throwing Skittles candy at another child on a school bus. When the student complained that the police officer twisted his arm, he was also charged with resisting arrest and held at a juvenile detention center for six days. U.S. Department of Education data shows that in most states Black, Latino, and disabled students get referred to police and courts disproportionately. In addition, other studies show that when a critical mass of Black students attends a school, the administration typically adds so-called resource (police) officers to the staff.[180] The volume of these school-based referrals suggests that zero-tolerance policies and school policing are exacerbating the school-to-prison pipeline by criminalizing behavior better dealt with outside courts.[181]

Extending the impact of these unjust policies further, some analysts like Michelle Alexander and Marian Wright Edelman of the Children's Defense Fund call the process a "cradle-to-prison" pipeline, citing the effects of poverty, unequal access to health and mental health care, low-quality schools, and a malfunctioning child welfare system, all of which constitute the context for the miseducation of Black children.[182] This continuum describes the complex web of economic, social, and political factors that push children into the criminal justice system. Schools can serve as pre-prison programs that prioritize incarceration over education.

Underfunded schools cannot keep their students safe from the structural forces of oppression nor do these schools have the resources—curricular materials, age-appropriate books, and other materials—to teach their students about the structural systems that produce inequality and violence in the United States. With a grade 6–12 curriculum that lacks these perspectives, young people are denied the information they need to function within a school, a society, and a criminal justice system that has been substantially shaped by racism, sexism, and homophobia.[183]

Public education is under broad attack today and the consequences are frightening and depressing for millions of Americans in the process of deciding whether or not to become parents, even in an era when birth control and abortion services are also under attack and difficult or nearly impossible to access in many parts of the country. Today, the language of "school choice" sanitizes and justifies the resegregation of schools in the United States even while suggesting that all parents have productive choices to make between good options.[184] Diminished funding for public schools, the rise of privately sponsored, publicly subsidized charter schools, attacks on teacher protections and professionalism, state school board control of textbook content (including material that denies slavery and evolution), and the overreliance on testing are some of the political strategies that hurt neighborhood schools, student learning, public education, and society in general.[185] These developments have harmful impacts on the reproductive decision making and the parenting of low-income people, especially people of color. These developments especially harm young people of color, widely defined as children with deficits, particularly if they have learning difficulties, limited English proficiency, or physical disabilities. Attacks on public education also deepen the privileges of wealthier children, families, and communities where genuine school choice may be exercised. In these communities, parents can be reasonably confident that their children can receive a high-quality education relevant to the labor market, providing the basis for lives of relative economic independence.[186]

Environmental Issues and Reproductive Justice

Reproductive justice calls for a world in which all women and parents achieve the human right to have children (or have the right to decide not to), raise families, and work and play in safe environments that do not threaten anyone's reproductive health or the health of their communities. Clearly these life events and conditions require a societal commitment to environmental justice as well as to reproductive justice, as these programs intersect in so many ways. As Native American midwife, Katsi Cook, observes, "Women are the first environment.... From the bodies of women flow the relationship of the generations both to society and the natural world."[187]

First of all, reproductive justice activists insist that mainstream environmental and reproductive rights movements incorporate a racial analysis because without a consideration of the racialized geography of environmental degradation and the lack of resources in communities of color to resist and combat the impacts of environmental toxicities on reproductive health, both movements are limiting their goals and missing their mark. As with access to quality education, access to quality environments must not be the privilege and protector only of wealthier and white Americans.[188]

In recent years, many women in the United States report that they plan to refrain from having children because they believe this is the only environmentally sound position they can take in an "overpopulated," overconsuming society.[189] They cite the fact that Americans constitute 5 percent of the world's population but consume 24 percent of the world's energy. According to the Sierra Club, a child born in the United States will create thirteen times more ecological damage over the course of his or her lifetime than a child born in Brazil. The average American will use as many resources as thirty-five people in India and consume fifty-three times more goods and services than someone living in China.[190] Nonetheless, reproductive justice activists suggest that each individual has the human right to determine if and when to become a parent and that no one has the responsibility to remain childless based on concern for the "environmental good." The number of people on the Earth is far less problematic than the irresponsible consumption patterns of people, corporations, and the military-industrial complex—a question of quality, not quantity.

Reproductive justice/environmental justice advocates argue that environmental degradation is not chiefly caused by over-population.[191] They do affirm, however, that these reports of American behavior appropriately associate the state of the environment—and climate change—with U.S. patterns of consumption and environmental degradation, including both military and corporate impacts. The United States, like other countries, needs to replenish its population to keep the economy robust, to replace aging workers, to bolster the tax base that pays for old age supports such as Social Security and Medicare, and to keep the country vibrant, generally. Moreover, when old-line environmentalists invoke "overpopulation," they are generally characterizing the putative reproductive behavior of poor women and women of color, who, they claim, have too many children they can't afford to raise and that society cannot afford to support.[192] In reality, all women in the United States, including poor women, have about two children or fewer, on average. Again, as with education, we surely don't want to live in a country where only wealthier persons have access to a profoundly basic human right: the right to reproduce.

To create population policies that target the bodies of the poorest and most vulnerable women obscures the health and material needs of these women while blaming them for environmental degradation. Such policies also obscure the broader, industrial causes of resource depletion and other environmental problems. Over the past several decades, the environmental justice movement—and activists drawing attention to the intersection of reproductive justice and environmental justice—have pointed out that landfills, incinerators, and power plants are almost always built where poor people of color live, causing especially high rates of cancers, infertility, miscarriage, and birth anomalies in communities that already lack adequate health care facilities. Those who draw attention to these matters provide many examples. They cite industrial waste and contamination in the Gulf states, causing long-term residents, mostly African American and Latino/a, to test positive for chemicals linked to infertility, miscarriage, low birthrate, low sperm count, and developmental and respiratory disorders for children exposed in utero. Mohawk and other Indigenous peoples have organized to demand remediation of toxic waste sites such as the PCB-filled open lagoons leaking into the St. Lawrence River, a crucial waterway for Mohawks. The toxins are contaminating the Mohawks' food chain, including the milk of lactating mothers. And Latino/a activists are demanding attention to the fact that 66 percent of their population lives in areas of the United States where air quality does not meet EPA standards, causing disproportionately negative impacts on pregnant Latina women and children.[193]

As we've stressed throughout, the decision to parent a child is a deeply personal one that needs to be made according to one's own needs, abilities, and preferences. The context in which such decisions are made can, of course, be affected both by the censorious politics of "overpopulation" and by external environmental conditions. Effectively advocating for environmental and climate justice means objecting to the persistent claim that those with the least power are causing the most harm and highlighting the real causes and effects of climate change and environmental degradation. Reproductive justice activists work towards building a just and sustainable world—a world where clean, renewable energy has freed us from the shackles of fossil fuel addiction. We desire a world where communities are made whole and have the resources to be prepared and resilient in the face of environmental disasters.

Reproductive justice activists focus on building societies in which the reproductive advantages and disadvantages of individuals and communities are not structured by race and class and other characteristics, are not enforced by law and policy, and do not ensure the perpetuation of inequality and injustice in America. Reproductive justice is the place to begin building this world.

Epilogue

Reproductive Justice on the Ground

Our description of reproductive justice is clearly a portmanteau that holds transformative ideas, encompassing visions, and powerful mandates. And equally clearly, the process of fully realizing and implementing this new paradigm will be long and complicated. But still we can offer snapshots of what reproductive justice looks like on the ground. This epilogue is a sampler of six ways that reproductive justice occupies the heart of an organization that began with individuals, became a community, and is thriving as a vital center of collective action.

Each of these six organizations was founded by and is led by women of color, with a constituency largely of individuals of color. This does not signify that reproductive justice is a concept and a movement exclusively for persons of color. On the contrary, reproductive justice expresses the requirements that all persons have when they strive to achieve sexual and reproductive health, safety, and dignity for themselves and their communities. Pressed by historical oppressions and animated by extraordinary creativity and determination, women of color have been the pioneers, defining and organizing for reproductive justice. They have demonstrated the ultimate uselessness and lack of relevance of the narrow rhetoric of "choice" and have begun to show the inevitable power of this new cluster of ideas that constitute reproductive justice. These pioneers and the collective activity they have fashioned over recent decades represent a model and a roadmap for us all.

Each of the six pieces that follow describes how reproductive justice provides both a restorative tonic and a capacious framework. Each organization has created itself using core principles of reproductive justice that link one organization to the other and to many others. Each organization, because of its own focus and goals, interprets, emphasizes, and expands reproductive justice principles uniquely, as well.

At the heart of each of the pieces is a strong commitment to *intersectional* analysis and the belief that building alliances— being an ally, working collectively—across human rights issues constitutes the perfect expression of intersectionality in action. Each piece speaks in one way or another about the *lived experiences* of persons struggling to construct a life and to build a world governed by reproductive justice. Becoming a participant in that effort requires a commitment to self-determination and self-help and requires having the right to be a parent as much as it requires the right not to be a parent. Each of the pieces also shows the adaptability and applicability of reproductive justice, as it variously connects with individuals working to achieve, for example, birth justice and sexual justice. Finally, each of these voices, in various ways, expresses a profound belief in paying the closest attention to the condition of the community and its history because, ultimately, the individual can achieve only the degree of health, safety, and dignity that the various resources available within the community make possible.

NEW VOICES FOR REPRODUCTIVE JUSTICE
*—LaTasha D. Mayes, founder and executive
director of New Voices*

When I hear or say the words "tapping into the infinite potential of Black women and girls," I envision in my mind the beautiful faces and collective genius that have the power to change Pittsburgh and the world. I never imagined that I would be here, in Pittsburgh, at thirty-four, leading New Voices for Reproductive Justice, a multistate human rights organization dedicated to the health and humanity of Black women and girls in Pennsylvania and Ohio. Life has a funny way of delivering on the promises of things you say you would never do.

I am one of many who came to Pittsburgh for school, work, or love. My path was a 95-percent scholarship to the College of Business Administration at the University of Pittsburgh. When financial accounting, intro to marketing, and business economics were not enough for my soul, you could find me in Black Consciousness with the late Rob Penny and raising hell in the Women's Studies department (now called Gender, Sexuality and Women's Studies). Beyond the classroom, I committed myself to activist campus leadership that would include real life-and-death scenarios of racism, sexism, and homophobia on campus like in the film *Higher Learning.* The precise moment I was politicized about race and gender, I was in my dorm room and I heard about how Black women in Congress attempted to block the certification of George W. Bush as president after the 2000 election, to no avail.

My first act of resistance for reproductive freedom occurred when I was spokesperson for the Plan B campaign to create access to emergency contraception at Student Health Services, a venue that was closed at night and on the weekends. How convenient! I did not know all the language to articulate intersectional oppression then, nor did I even have the confidence in myself to speak and affirm my own experiences as my expertise. I did not know I was worthy enough to prioritize myself as a Black woman fighting for social justice. But we won ... our campaign demands were met.

After this victory, I could not help but feel that this win *included me but was not about me* or any of the other Black women or women of color students. The feminism I encountered on campus was fierce but far from representing the critical understanding of how all parts of my identity impacted my ability to ever know reproductive freedom. I was turned off by the one-dimensional ideas of third-wave feminists who praised my womanhood but ignored my Blackness. With an academic, career, and life path turned toward civic engagement and an inevitable Corporate America takeover looming, I said to myself and to others, "I will never do reproductive *anything* ever again."

I graduated with honors in 2003, left a legacy of badassness on campus, and entered into adulthood. You could not tell me that I was not going to San Francisco to complete my Coro Fellowship in Public Affairs. I received my acceptance letter and it mocked me as I read it: "Looks like you're staying in Pittsburgh." I was actually fine with that. I just knew if I was going to stay in Pittsburgh that I had to change Pittsburgh.

I began looking for professional students of color in the spaces that I had been part of creating on campus, like Sisters Beyond the Surface, Black Women's Week, and Minorities in Pittsburgh Conference. My quest included many conversations with my best friends in which we concluded that progressive political spaces did not exist for young women of color, especially when it came to spaces devoted to reproductive rights. We decided that we needed to develop new voices of leadership in Pittsburgh. Just around this time in 2003, the Feminist Majority began national planning for the March for Choice, a massive demonstration for reproductive rights scheduled for April 25, 2004, in Washington, DC. My feminist mentor asked me to be part of the Western Pennsylvania planning committee. I could see right away that the same white- women-centric feminist dynamics were playing out in the same way they had when I was in college, and I said no thanks. That is, until I met Malika Redmond and Alma Speed Fox.

Before Gmail, the hot thing was Hotmail. One day in this time frame, I received an e-mail from a young Black woman, Malika Redmond, who was from Pittsburgh but lived in Atlanta. She was coming home to visit, and she was looking for young Black women and women of color who might be interested in organizing for the March for Women's Lives—the replacement name for the March for Choice, a substantive title-change initiated successfully by women of color. I still wasn't convinced that I should be part of this effort, but then I met Alma Speed Fox— the mother of the civil rights and women's rights movements in Pittsburgh.

I met Alma Speed Fox when I made a simple request to use a community park for a project, and our interaction quickly developed into a lasting friendship that became instrumental in the birth of the reproductive justice movement in Pittsburgh. Ms. Fox essentially told me I had no choice but to organize Black women and women of color. I had inherited that legacy and a vision to transform a rust-belt city like Pittsburgh. With Malika providing support through the National Center for Human Rights Education and the initiative New Voices for Reproductive Justice, and Ms. Fox guiding me, in just forty days, we organized a busload of Black women and women of color to attend the March for Women's Lives. As the crowds grew, I knew I had found the movement for me. I was home.

On the ride back, after the march, the women asked, "What are we going to do when we get back to Pittsburgh?" I had not thought that far. I guess I had thought that this was it: we'd go to the march, and we'd go home. But twelve years later, New Voices is a multistate organization in Pennsylvania and Ohio that has served and engaged over 50,000 Black women and girls, women of color, and queer and trans* people of color and has participated in building a powerful and influential movement for reproductive justice.

COLORADO ORGANIZATION FOR LATINA OPPORTUNITY AND REPRODUCTIVE RIGHTS (COLOR)

—Cristina Aguilar, executive director of COLOR

AMENDMENT 67: EMBRACING OUR CULTURE AND MOBILIZING OUR COMMUNITY TO ACHIEVE REPRODUCTIVE JUSTICE

The Colorado Organization for Latina Opportunity and Reproductive Rights (COLOR) is building a movement of Latinas, their families, and allies. We focus on leadership development, organizing, and advocacy to create opportunities and achieve reproductive justice. We envision Latinas and their families having the knowledge, freedom, and power to access a full range of opportunities that promote the health of their bodies, minds, and spirit.

COLOR wants to ensure the reproductive and sexual health of our community. We advocate for reproductive rights. But the heart of our work is a commitment to reproductive justice. We believe reproductive justice exists when all individuals have the power, access and resources to make healthy decisions about their bodies, sexuality, relationships, and families for themselves and their community.

We are committed to ensuring that women of color are able to access abortion care when they need it, but our commitments go further than that. We are committed to the right of all persons to have a child, the right not to have a child, the right to parent the children we have with dignity, the right to control our birthing options, the right to choose our sexual partners, and the right to control our own gender. Our 2014 fight against Amendment 67 in the Colorado state legislature brought many of these areas of passion and principle together.

Amendment 67 marked the legislature's third attempt in six years to pass a measure that would expand the definition of the words "person" and "child" in Colorado's criminal code to include "unborn human beings." This redefinition could have enormous potential to restrict access to abortion, fertility services, and many common forms of contraception. Activists who opposed "personhood language" also feared that antiabortion forces would use the expanded definition to criminalize pregnant women's behavior or some pregnancy outcomes, a development we have seen more and more often in recent years—for example, when laws are written so that a woman who has a miscarriage is at risk of arrest or interrogation. This recurrent legislative effort in Colorado was an extreme example of the attacks on women's ability to make their own decisions about whether they have a child and about how to build their families; these attacks fall hardest on low-income women and women of color.

Gina Millan, a community and parent organizer at COLOR does not typically share her story, but she spoke out on this policy. When Gina was in college, she had to leave school because of family problems. She found herself pregnant and without any family support or a partner, so she decided to have to have an abortion. Living in Mexico at the time, where abortion was illegal, she had to resort to a clandestine clinic where she felt she was putting her health at risk. Also the clinic doctor treated her disrespectfully.

Gina went on to get married and have a daughter. During her subsequent pregnancy, doctors told Gina that this time the pregnancy was high risk. After that, she worked hard to take all necessary precautions, but she found herself bleeding late one evening. When she went to the emergency room, the doctor told Gina and her husband that the placenta had detached and that she had lost the pregnancy. She later said that in spite of the physical hurt, the greatest pain was "apologizing to my daughter, who was six years old at the time, and telling her that she was not going to have a brother or a sister."

Many women are extremely sad when they experience pregnancy loss, especially when these experiences are made harder by barriers to abortion and additional health care services in other countries and right here in this country. Together with COLOR, Gina fought hard to defeat Amendment 67, knowing that she had walked in the shoes of women who would be hurt by a lack of safe abortion care, women who could be prevented from accessing reproductive health care to plan their families, and women who could face a miscarriage and then have to endure interrogation or investigation if the personhood policy were pushed through.

COLOR approached this ballot initiative as a reproductive justice issue. We also approached it with the determination to apply our COLOR flavor of intersectional organizing. We saw this as an opportunity to halt a harmful policy and as a chance to empower our community through knowledge, education, and information. We led a robust grassroots effort focused on Latina voters in eight counties throughout the state. We brought together activists of different ages and looked at how to create a campaign that would build a stronger community and not simply do things the way they had always been done. We demanded that we be at the table as equal partners. We insisted that whether or not we had the same money or staffing capacity as other organizations, we had a lot to give to the campaign and to the conversation.

When the question of language translation came up, we pushed back on the idea that COLOR would translate a few core materials for our people. Instead, we insisted that *all* campaign materials and messages had to be translated. Otherwise, the implication was that Spanish speakers deserved a lesser campaign experience without the same access to information as English speakers. We also made it clear that it was not our job to make this comprehensive translation project happen. We explained that translation and interpretation are professional services with standards. Campaigns and coalitions must prioritize and invest in these services from the outset rather than naively burden native speakers or groups representing these communities with this "task." Instead of minimizing or marginalizing the importance of translation, we argued that translation is critical to ensuring that campaigns make linguistic fairness available to all key communities, no matter their language.

We have the power to open our own gates or breach the gates when necessary. We did not wait to be invited to talk to pollsters who were crafting the questions and testing the messages that would have an impact on the direction of the campaign. We held our own meetings with power brokers to emphasize and leverage the expertise of our community. We put ourselves in the position to advocate for and advise on Latina focus groups in English and Spanish. This helped us to forge ties that will benefit our community for future battles and victories and to build stronger alliances.

We conducted our campaigns without losing a sense of who we are. One of the best *cafecito* events that COLOR hosted during the campaign season brought together friends and families along with funk music and an outdoor fire. We generated a buzz that we know how to throw a party and host a fiercely effective, intersectional canvass. Grounded in cultura, we employed our cafecito model of having *comida, pan dulce,* and *música* as an entrée to our canvass kickoffs. We also made the event welcoming, because too often, political spaces can be intimidating—both during the campaign and beyond.

COLOR hosts events in our own homes. We have food and music that represents our culture. We invite a diverse set of partners. We organize and rally together, but we also dance together. We value an intergenerational approach and are committed to an intergenerational leadership pipeline. We have a program that trains and supports young Latinas to engage in the political process and are developing a program that supports young parents. We also hold up the stories of our founders and share our history as ways of respecting those who have built the foundation we stand on now.

Our approach has resulted in nods from national organizations for "revolutionizing the way Latinas organize in Colorado." But we know that we are just leveraging our collective strength, empowering our community to be part of the change we are creating, and breathing culture into our work.

We are intentional about the way that we do our work. We believe that community is at the center of achieving complete physical, mental, spiritual, political, economic, and social well-being of women and girls. We know that we cannot achieve reproductive justice without Latinas of all ages and experiences by our side. We also know that we must build a movement that includes the talents and the lived experiences of our community.

In the end, Amendment 67 was defeated with a strong turnout from the Latino community voting against this harmful measure. We were a key part of the victory and modeled how to do work in a way that doesn't just tack Latinas on. We engaged with our community as a valued partner and leader on critical issues. We are not and will not be an afterthought. We will tell our stories and mobilize our voices and our votes to make a difference.

SISTERLOVE

—Dázon Dixon Diallo, founder and director of SisterLove, Inc. and a pioneer in the women's HIV/AIDS and reproductive justice arenas

BRINGING THE S INTO THE RJ FRAMEWORK

SisterLove is on a mission with two parts. We are working to eradicate both the impact of HIV and the existence of sexual and reproductive oppression in the lives of all women and their communities in the US and around the world.

SisterLove, Inc., is a twenty-five-year-old reproductive justice organization with a focus on sexual health and well-being through prevention and through care for women dealing with HIV, STIs, unintended pregnancy, and violence. SisterLove is an active collaborator and partner with a number of networks, coalitions, and movement-building organizations. We are committed to ensuring that the human rights framework of liberty, justice, and dignity is at the center of social change efforts to protect and advance the sexual and reproductive health and rights of women and their families. We draw strength from the resilience and determination of the women we serve. And we need a lot strength because we work at many dangerous intersections where the lives of so many women and girls are shaped. We work to transform the policy frame that defends women's *choices* into a policy frame that asserts women's *agency* to make decisions that are best for themselves and their families. Notably, we broaden the reproductive justice movement to include *sexual justice* as an integral part of the framework.

SISTERLOVE'S PREP CAMPAIGN: A SEXUAL REPRODUCTIVE JUSTICE EFFORT

In 2012, the Food and Drug Administration (FDA) approved Truvada for use as pre-exposure prophylaxis, or PrEP. The preventative treatment (a daily pill), when used consistently by HIV negative individuals, provides a discreet method for decreasing a person's risk—by 92 percent and more—of contracting HIV through sexual contact. Shortly after the FDA's approval, Sister-Love's founder and president, Dázon Dixon Diallo, brought together a group of advocates to establish the US Women and PrEP Working Group. This group quickly became the leading—and remains the only—group in the United States that focuses predominantly on women's lack of access to PrEP and on the absence of research dealing with women and PrEP. In comparison, a significant number of organizations focus on providing men who have sex with men access to PrEP. These conditions reflect the general disregard of the unique needs of women in the face of the HIV epidemic. And ignoring women's needs reflects the widespread failure to connect reproductive justice issues and HIV. The sexual and reproductive justice framework is at the foundation of the working group's perspective, an expression of SisterLove's mission to articulate the HIV epidemic as a sexual and reproductive justice issue.

Diallo's engagement with the HIV/AIDS movement began with her work in the feminist health movement, where *self-help*—the power to determine one's own reproductive health and well-being –has been a core feature of feminist-centered, high-quality sexual and reproductive health information and services, including abortion and family planning. Similarly, women in the HIV movement have made self-help—in this case, placing the power to prevent HIV in women's own hands— a rallying cry for people working in the sexual and reproductive justice movement as well as for advocates of antiviolence and HIV for nearly three decades. SisterLove, as an HIV/sexual/ reproductive-justice service provider and advocacy organization, is leading the campaign for implementation of PrEP in the United States to include a focus on women's sexual and reproductive health needs because PrEP has enormous potential to empower women who are at risk for and living with HIV.

Advocates for PrEP draw on women's right to sexuality and to sexual justice. For one thing, this preventative treatment provides, to some extent, a degree of sexual liberation. Individuals who take the daily pill are taking the opportunity to stop thinking only about disease avoidance and start thinking about their own sexual well-being. But in a culture that continues to condemn or ignore a woman's right to sexual pleasure, we can hardly be surprised that medical authorities and researchers don't focus on PrEP for women who are at risk of exposure to

HIV. Instead, medical authorities and others have been quick to promote the use of antiretroviral (ARV) therapy to prevent mother-child transmission of HIV when this use of ARVs was discovered in 1994. The lack of a similar nationwide response to the development and proven effectiveness of PrEP suggests a widespread lack of interest and urgency when the subject is protecting women from exposure to HIV through sexual contact.[1]

To understand the meaning of this phenomenon, we can consider the disproportionate impact of HIV on women of color. In the state of Georgia, for example, black heterosexual women constitute 75% of all women living with HIV. We can also consider the history of biomedical and reproductive oppression that Black women have suffered throughout American history, ranging from forced pregnancy and childrearing during slavery to forced sterilization afterward. Keeping these matters in mind helps us understand that using the HIV lens to advocate for PrEP for women is to advocate for sexual justice and reproductive justice as intrinsically intersectional human rights; we are promoting sexual health and pleasure as a right. The working group uses this framework in concert with SisterLove's mission. The framework gives strength to its message that the HIV epidemic is a matter of sexual and reproductive justice.

LINKING HIV SERVICES TO SEXUAL AND REPRODUCTIVE HEALTH SERVICES

The US Women and PrEP Working Group conducts its policy, advocacy, and outreach through the sexual and reproductive justice framework, underscoring the linkages between HIV and sexual and reproductive health services and stressing the intersectional focus of the group's research and advocacy approaches. The group tackles the social determinants of health that frustrate treatment and prevention efforts and disempower those who are living with and at risk of HIV.[2] The group's advocacy efforts include raising awareness about the lack of insurance options for many people living with HIV and the disparities in coverage of PrEP. Moreover, advocates recognize that while PrEP can be a vehicle for empowerment, its existence may also potentially embolden the clients of sex workers to demand or expect condomless sex.

The working group presses for researchers studying PrEP efficacy to stop treating transgender women and men who have sex with men as a single population and instead to look at each group as distinct in identity and experience. The working group calls for service providers to be trained in providing care that is gender affirming and trauma informed and for research efforts into the impact of PrEP on pregnant women and on infants whose mothers have taken PrEP during the period of breastfeeding. Finally, the working group calls for all women to have access to community education about PrEP's efficacy if used autonomously, without a condom, as an act that can promote the empowerment and bodily self-determination of women in situations in which a partner may be unwilling to wear a condom.[3]

The 2015 national HIV/AIDS strategy update neglected to mention family planning or reproductive health services as arenas for providing HIV prevention care.[4] Yet, in many instances, a family planning clinic is the main or only point of access to health care that a woman may receive in a year; this is typically the case for women in communities at increased risk of exposure to HIV.[5] Providing HIV care and access to PrEP in family planning clinics is a way to provide a space where women can expect to receive guidance about their risk of exposure to HIV and to have a physician provide a prescription to PrEP when they are at risk. These linkages are particularly necessary for women of color in the southern states, a population disproportionately at risk of exposure to HIV. This connection, so important to the advocacy of the working group, particularly highlights the role of HIV and sexual justice within the reproductive justice framework.

NATIVE YOUTH SEXUAL HEALTH NETWORK

—Krysta Williams, advocacy and outreach
coordinator, and Erin Konsmo, media arts justice
and projects coordinator, Native Youth
Sexual Health Network

We like to think about reproductive justice in the context of reclaiming voice and naming values that Indigenous communities have long held and that we have long been attacked for. We can begin with the idea of our basic self-determination over our lands and bodies and the relationships we have to land, language, culture, and each other. These concepts are profoundly distinct from Western capitalist notions of private ownership that have to do with nation-specific ways of life, kinship models, and governance structures.

We Indigenous peoples have been organizing for our rights since long before the various waves of feminisms and the pro-choice movement and long before the naming of reproductive justice by and for women of color. Nevertheless, Indigenous women, families, youth, and communities in general are still left out of these narratives of herstory. This is the case despite the fact that we have suffered through many forms of reproductive oppression and genocide in the past and in the present. Indeed, we have much to teach and to share within a context of consensual solidarity that centers our own understanding of who we are as peoples.

In many ways, though, reproductive justice has breathed new life into youth organizing. Particularly for us at the Native Youth Sexual Health Network, reproductive justice has provided another way to honor ancestral teachings, restore our ways of life, and build stronger movements for the future. Reproductive justice has provided a kind of translation in English to describe our realities and resist the push from the non-profit-industrial complex to maintain a single-issue focus. The very concept of reproductive justice has allowed us to take a stand and resist the hierarchal imperialism of state-manufactured health care. It has allowed us to center our self-determination so that we decide for ourselves what is best for our bodies, communities, and human rights in ways that acknowledge where this all went wrong in the first place.

It is no secret that Indigenous forms of reproductive justice were made illegal on purpose for many years, including ceremonies, gatherings, and cultural practices, as well as the criminalization of midwifery and a forced conformity to hetero, patriarchal settler governance. It is also true that our communities have always been organizing and resisting the ongoing colonialism that is still inherent to our relationship with the state and the violence it inflicts daily. For example, Indigenous women were, and continue to be, at the forefront of the movement for informed consent as a strategy for resisting historical and ongoing forced sterilization. In addition, many ceremonial practitioners and healers have continued to provide care despite threats to their lives.

Reproductive justice makes room for self-determination for all persons who invoke this language to decide for themselves what it looks like and means for them. However, this framework also means our movements have to know each other's histories, resist erasure of each other from those histories, and, of course, actually acknowledge, honor, and learn from these teachings. For our communities, reproductive justice can also include all of what we know to be true ancestrally and all of what we learn from the legacies of organizers before us.

For us, centering Indigenous self-determination is a real way to respond to the constant erasure and displacement that Indigenous peoples face from so-called progressive movements, from structures of oppression, and from settlers as well as from the internalized racism that is constantly being reinforced and fed to us. In practice, this means being able to reshape and give life to young people's organizing efforts whether or not they have "activist cred" or a degree or a nonprofit job.

It makes sense for us to organize beyond and around the U.S.-Canada imperial border because so many of our communities are transected by this border and face violence at the hands of both countries. Also the very existence of this border is a reproductive justice issue. Border imperialism perpetuates and upholds violence against Indigenous bodies by the historical and present-day violent reinforcement of the doctrine of discovery and assertion of colonial ownership of Indigenous lands and territories.

Our relationship to reproductive justice is also reminding each other about the inherent and necessary connection to land, not to the state. In order to uphold this connection, we have utilized multiple frameworks including queer Indigenous feminisms that teach us about how critical it is to organize for the land and our bodies simultaneously. Homophobia and transphobia were and still are about the removal of Indigenous bodies from the land. Queer Indigenous feminisms are about movements that follow the leadership of Two Spirit, LGBTTQQIA Indigenous people.[6]

When we overlook interventions against our bodies and fail to respond and resist—or respond as if our bodies and the land are not interrelated—we respond to only a portion of the injustice. If we are not seeking justice for our bodies, then who are we seeking to protect the land for?

Responses to our bodies must move beyond recognition of states to a future where the state does not actually exist. Efforts to pursue harm reduction—that is, relief from state policies that abuse our bodies—are important to our survival. But our organizing goals must move beyond policy reform and other efforts to enhance or protect our status under the state. Our goals must imagine and embody new futures, always. Youth in our network generate much of this imagining, around kitchen tables, walking for the land and water, birthing babies, helping other queer/Two Spirit youth survive, creating narratives for our bodies through art that pushes back on stereotypes, healing intergenerational trauma, finding pleasure, and more. Even as we endure colonial violence and crisis, we hold onto each other's bodies and try to imagine and enact different futures.

SISTERSONG WOMEN OF COLOR REPRODUCTIVE JUSTICE COLLECTIVE
—Monica Simpson, executive director of SisterSong

ON THE INTERSECTION OF REPRODUCTIVE JUSTICE AND BLACK LIVES MATTER

On July 13th, 2013, the nation anxiously awaited the verdict in the case against George Zimmerman, the self-appointed neighborhood security guard who shot and killed Trayvon Martin, an unarmed young man on his way home with a bag of Skittles he just purchased at a 7-Eleven store. The smiling face of the young chestnut-brown teenage boy gone too soon was burned into our minds, and many of us chanted the mantra "I am Trayvon Martin" as a way to stand in solidarity. Many of us were convinced that Zimmerman was guilty, but as Black Americans, we know all too well that the U.S. legal system has historically and repeatedly expressed its commitment to white supremacy, exonerating white people while demonizing, criminalizing, incarcerating, and killing Black people. In this case, the outcome was consistent with history: allowing George Zimmerman to walk away a free man while Trayvon Martin's family was left to grieve their son resting six feet in the ground.

Black people wanted justice. We chanted "Black Lives Matter" in the streets and on social media, and a new movement for Black liberation was born. Led by Black women, young people, queer people, transpeople, elders, and allies, Black Lives Matter was no longer simply a pointed hashtag; it was our powerful rallying call. And we were ready.

Out of the shadows of the Trayvon Martin case, a group of Black women, also in Florida, emerged with their own call to action. Naming themselves "Free Marissa Now," they constituted an alliance of activists and organizers working to free Marissa Alexander, a black mother who had fired a warning shot in an effort to defend her family from her abusive partner. The shot harmed no one, and Alexander, who, nine days earlier, had given birth, justified her action as a proper response to a man who had threatened her life. Alexander described her warning shot as consistent with Florida's stand-your-ground law. Nevertheless, Alexander was convicted, sentenced to a twenty-year term, and imprisoned, unlike Zimmerman who successfully used this same defense in explaining his murder of Trayvon Martin, an unarmed person.

In 2010, just a few years before both the death of Trayvon Martin and Marissa Alexander's conviction and imprisonment, SisterSong formed the Trust Black Women Partnership to defeat the racist antichoice billboard campaign that had begun in Georgia with the intention of shaming Black women for their reproductive decisions, equating Black women's abortions with genocide, and promoting antiabortion legislation. Over time, Trust Black Women had waged a successful campaign, and the billboards had become rare. But both the attacks on the lives of Black women and our claim to self-determination had grown; Marissa Alexander's case showed us that not all of the attacks were centered on abortion.

After building relationships with the leaders of Free Marissa Now and working with local activists in Jacksonville, Florida, SisterSong made a decision, one that some people thought was radical: to partner with Free Marissa Now in order to demand justice for Alexander and to frame the injustice perpetrated against her as reproductive oppression. SisterSong took the position that Alexander's wrongful incarceration embodied issues that the reproductive justice movement needed to be on the front lines for, much as the movement needed to be on the front lines for any attack on our human right to have a child or prevent pregnancy.

Although the reproductive health, rights, and justice movements were fighting off antichoice legislation across the nation, SisterSong veered from the path to organize with grassroots activists in Florida, a very politically charged state in the South, at a very politically charged moment. We believed that the Alexander case opened an opportunity for SisterSong to lean more forcefully into our framework rooted in human rights and intersectionality. This was an opportunity to move from theory to practice and to trust the expertise and leadership of those who are directly impacted by the issues we are committed to addressing.

We also believed—then and now—that it is important to work across movements in order to build alliances. It was clear to us that if we wanted to boost support for reproductive health and rights issues, we needed to show up as allies for other movements, especially in cases where intersectional analysis shows that we are natural allies. Alexander's case stimulated us to draw parallels between the reproductive justice movement and the movement working on criminal justice reform and domestic violence. Together with the Free Marissa Now campaign, SisterSong cohosted the Standing Our Ground Against Reproductive Oppression, Gender Violence, and Mass Incarceration Summit in Jacksonville, Florida, in July 2014. The event culminated in a march to the Duval County Courthouse with a rally there to demand the release of Marissa Alexander. The two-day summit included panel discussions about the intersecting issues of criminal justice reform, domestic violence, child welfare, and reproductive justice, thus bringing the reproductive justice movement solidly into alignment with Black Lives Matter. This grassroots organizing effort helped create a national focus on Marissa Alexander's case, and ultimately she was released.

The Black Lives Matter movement continued to grow and so did the antiabortionists' attacks on the Black community. Attackers gained momentum by co-opting the language and strategies and riding off of the success of the Black Lives Matter movement. They saw this movement moment as an opportunity to once again use abortion to drive a wedge into the Black community for their own political purposes.[7]

From Mike Brown in Ferguson, Missouri, to Sandra Bland in Texas, Black people were dying just for being Black. Mothers were losing their sons. Black women were dying before having an opportunity to decide whether or not they wanted to parent. Black women were contemplating motherhood. They thought about whether they made enough money to support a child and about the quality of their school district. They also worried about dying in childbirth or having to identify their young son in a morgue after police shot him on a playground, like Tamir Rice in Cleveland.

Black reproductive justice leaders had to respond. SisterSong relaunched Trust Black Women and expanded the partnership, becoming the first reproductive justice organization to publicly connect Black Lives Matter with reproductive justice. We know that our reproductive decisions are inextricably linked to our lived experience as Black people, a status that is burdened with all forms of oppression. We know that we need to make this clear in order to dismantle and defeat the pro-lifers' attempts to divide us. Trust Black Women initiated a solidarity statement with Black Lives Matter to articulate these connections and our commitment to working together against all attacks on the lives of Black people. The Trust Black Women Statement of Solidarity with Black Lives Matter says:

> The United States has a long history of overpolicing and overcriminalizing Black bodies that started with the forced removal of Africans from our homeland. Ever since we were brought here against our will, this country has been a hostile birthing environment for Black women and a dangerous place to raise Black children. Our lives are at stake. To realize a future where Black Lives Matter, we must Trust Black Women. To Trust Black Women is to affirm that Black Lives do Matter.

As the national reproductive justice collective whose foundation is supported by people of all ethnicities and identities, SisterSong understands the importance of collective action and being in political solidarity. Like Black Lives Matter, the reproductive justice movement was created by Black women over twenty years ago; therefore, we are committed to the fight for black liberation. We proclaim boldly that Black Lives Matter and that we should always Trust Black Women.

INTERNATIONAL CENTER FOR TRADITIONAL CHILDBIRTH

—Shafia M. Monroe, founder, president, and CEO of the International Center for Traditional Childbirth

Babies dying and mothers crying are at the heart of the mission of the International Center for Traditional Childbirth (ICTC), as a birth justice organization. ICTC exists to increase the number of midwives, doulas, and healers of color in order to empower families and to reduce infant and maternal mortality.

ICTC, based in Portland, Oregon, aims to halt the epidemic of Black babies born prematurely and too small, events that are the result of many structural factors in the United States, including health inequities, racism-induced stress, and the lack of access to midwives and doulas of color. Indeed, Black women and infants continue to have the worst birth outcomes of any racial-ethnic cohort in the United States. Black women have the highest rate of preterm birth and low-birth-weight babies. Black women lose their babies at a rate that is almost 2.3 times greater than white women. In addition, the Black maternal mortality rate is three times higher than the rate for white women.

In response to these conditions of birth, life, and death, ICTC, as a birth justice organization, intersects vibrantly with the reproductive justice framework. "Birth justice" refers to the right to give birth with whom, where, when, and how a person chooses. Today the law and public policies penalize many women who claim that the right to control their own pregnancies, births, and postpartum experiences are simply claiming their human rights. These are women determined to exercise the right to feed their babies from their own breasts, to birth at home, to have access to VBAC (vaginal births after Caesarean delivery) services, and to have the option of birthing under the guidance of a midwife from their own community. ICTC organizes to reduce the high infant and maternal mortality rate in the African American community by training Black midwives and ICTC Full Circle Doulas, as leaders to champion the birth justice movement.

Why do Black women and other women of color so frequently lack access to midwives of color from their own communities? After all, the history of Black midwives and other midwives of color in the United States is a vibrant history of expert practitioners attending births in their own communities deep into the twentieth century, until the American Medical Association persuaded state legislatures to criminalize traditional childbirth practices completely. In the first decades of the twentieth century, up to 50 percent of births in the United States were supervised by midwives; today only about 1 percent of births are. Historical sociologist Keisha Goode explains that the racist dimension of this campaign is still alive today: Black midwives attending the births of Black women's babies constitute a very small fraction of that 1 percent. Moreover, predominantly white midwifery programs and professional organizations have had a history of racial exclusiveness.[8] To combat these obstacles and to promote maternal and infant health in communities of color, ICTC honors our past and embraces our future, engages youth in civic activities, seeks to improve birth outcomes and to address systemic barriers that have prevented Black midwives and doulas and midwives of color from full participation in the profession. Since 1991 ICTC has trained over four hundred doulas of color, one-third of whom have gone on to become midwives.

ICTC accomplishes a great deal with limited resources. Most recently, ICTC led the initiative to have doulas—certified professionals who provide personal, nonmedical support to women and families throughout a woman's pregnancy, childbirth, and postpartum experience—recognized by the state of Oregon so that these birth attendants could receive Medicaid reimbursement and, through their work, decrease health inequities in Oregon's birth outcomes. Beginning in 2011, ICTC worked in partnership with the Oregon Coalition to Improve Birth Outcomes and state legislators to enact a bill that mandated research and created a committee of stakeholders that produced a comprehensive report showing that doulas improved birth outcomes for women who face a disproportionately greater risk of poor birth outcomes, disproportionately women of color. When women had doula support, costs associated with maternal and infant care declined as well.

In 2013, ICTC announced a stunning victory: certified doula services were approved for reimbursement by Medicaid, a development that makes doulas accessible to many women who could otherwise not afford their services. This development drew in part on the Cochrane database, the gold standard for analysis of human health care and health policy research, which has described doula services as options that "all women should be ... encouraged to have," especially when "the provider is not an employee of the [hospital], when epidural analgesia is not routinely used, and when support begins early in labor."

Another ICTC victory occurred in early 2016, when ICTC was finally invited to join the steering committee of US MERA (United States Midwifery Education, Regulation, and Association), a collaborative working group of organizations representing the midwifery industry. US MERA describes its goals as "ensuring a highly qualified midwifery workforce that will increase access to midwifery care and improve the health of women, infants, and families in our country." But despite this mission and repeated efforts of ICTC, US MERA had not, until 2016, been willing to admit ICTC, the only autonomous organization that represents the interests of midwives of color, to its steering committee.

The absence of midwives of color from the US MERA decision-making table reflected an absence of cultural humility on the part of that organization and contributed to the systemic racism that creates and perpetuates barriers for midwives of color to enter the field and serve their communities. As a consequence of these kinds of exclusions, communities of color have faced a shortage of midwives of color who can provide culturally appropriate services in ways that improve birth outcomes. On February 23, 2016, after many months of hard work between ICTC and US MERA, ICTC received and accepted an invitation to be a US MERA member, bolstering ICTC's work to increase the number of midwives and doulas of color, diversifying the midwife and doula workforce, and improving infant and maternal health in the African American community.

Today, under the leadership of founder, president, and CEO Shafia M. Monroe, ICTC continues its targeted and wide-ranging work, supporting federal and state legislative initiatives to promote better health for women and their babies, including bills promoting comprehensive and effective maternity services, breastfeeding promotion, and protections for premature infants. ICTC has also worked for the passage of H.R. 1054 to establish federal recognition of Certified Professional Midwives and Medicaid reimbursement for doula services for low-income women. ICTC works with the American College of Nurse Midwives and allied midwifery organizations, the U.S. Birthing Project, Black Women's Health Imperative, SisterSong, and ICTC state representatives. ICTC also supports traditional birth practices in Ghana, Colombia, Haiti, South Africa, Indonesia, and elsewhere, and holds doula trainings and the Black Midwife and Healers Conference in the United States every year, keeping birth justice in the forefront to save Black babies and end genocide.

•   •   •

In the United States, some mainstream reproductive rights organizations such as Planned Parenthood and feminist organizations such as the National Organization for Women have declared their allegiance to key concepts of reproductive justice. As we noted, the New York City Department of Health and Mental Hygiene's Sexual and Reproductive Health Unit of its Bureau of Maternal, Infant and Reproductive Health has committed itself to using the reproductive justice framework in constructing its programs and services. In September 2014, the South African minister of social development, Bathabile Dlamini, defined reproductive justice as a global framework and noted that "Feminists and particularly black feminists across the world are beginning to refer to reproductive justice as a concept that best explains the realities of poor and marginalised women in many parts of the world." Surely, each organization, each governmental entity, and each official inflects the meaning of "reproductive justice" somewhat differently, reflecting differences in culture, history, health imperatives, politics, and other crucial variables.

And just as surely, as we have acknowledged, the process of bringing the principles of reproductive justice to life—fully realizing and implementing them—will be a long and complicated process. But these organizations and scores of others around the world are proving that reproductive justice is a framework that speaks to millions of people because its human-rights core and its creative spaciousness support ways for individuals to think about, plan for, and realize full personhood in harmony with their reproductive capacity.

ACKNOWLEDGMENTS

LORETTA

My profound thanks to the SisterSong family past and present, the Five Colleges Women's Studies Research Center, Rickie Solinger, Dázon Dixon Diallo, Juanita Williams, Toni Bond Leonard, Alice Skenadore, Marlene Gerber Fried, Lynn Roberts, bell hooks, Joyce Follet, Sherrill Redmon, Nkenge Toure, Faye Williams, Alice Cohan, Jean Caini, Gloria Steinem, Karen Pittleman, and my son, Howard Michael Ross, and the entire Burton-Ward-Ross family to which I am proud to offer this product of your unending encouragement of me.

RICKIE

My daughter, Nell Geiser, has been my most important teacher for many years; she continued to guide me this time. Many thanks to Khiara Bridges for joining me with gusto, grace, and brilliance and to Naomi Schneider for embracing the Reproductive Justice book series. Zakiya Luna told me in no uncertain terms that Loretta Ross and I had to write the first book in the series, and we obeyed her, full-heartedly. I am grateful beyond words to Loretta for agreeing to work with me and for joining me in forging both a book and a bond. Jim Geiser, as always, listened to new paragraphs and pages and was eager to support me in all ways. Zachary, Molly, Dean, and Ruby—their household of love, fairness, and beauty—are, together, a model for a gentler and more just future.

NOTES

INTRODUCTION

1. Cheryl Chastine, "Cisgender Women Aren't the Only People Who Seek Abortions, and Activists' Language Should Reflect That," *RH Reality Check,* March 18, 2015.

1. A REPRODUCTIVE JUSTICE HISTORY

1. William Faulkner, *Requiem for a Nun* (New York: Random House, 1951).

2. The term "management" is drawn from Barbara Gurr, *Reproductive Justice: The Politics of Health Care for Native American Women* (New Brunswick, NJ: Rutgers University Press, 2015).

3. Ibid., 26.

4. Harriet A. Washington, *Medical Apartheid: The Dark History of Medical Experimentation on Black Americans from Colonial Times to the Present* (New York: Doubleday, 2007).

5. See Khiara M. Bridges, *Reproducing Race: An Ethnography of Pregnancy as a Site of Racialization* (Berkeley: University of California Press, 2011).

6. Kathleen M. Brown, *Good Wives, Nasty Wenches, and Anxious Patriarchs: Gender, Race, and Power in Colonial Virginia* (Chapel Hill: University of North Carolina Press, 1996), 207.

7. Quoted in Carol Berkin and Leslie Horowitz, *Women's Voices, Women's Lives: Documents in Early American History* (Boston: Northeastern University Press, 1998), 13.

8. Kristen Fischer, *Suspect Relations: Sex, Race, and Resistance in Colonial North Carolina* (Ithaca, NY: Cornell University Press, 2002), 124; Brown, *Good Wives, Nasty Wenches,* 198.

9. Dorothy Roberts, *Killing the Black Body: Race, Reproduction, and the Meaning of Liberty* (New York: Pantheon, 1997), 29–30; Brown, *Good Wives, Nasty Wenches,* 210; Brenda Stevenson, "Distress and Discord in Virginia Slave Families, 1830–1860," in *In Joy and Sorrow: Women, Family, and Marriage in the Victorian South,* ed. Carol Bleser (New York: Oxford University Press, 1992), 53; Marie Jenkins Schwartz, *Born in Bondage: Growing Up Enslaved in the Antebellum South* (Cambridge, MA: Harvard University Press, 2000) 18; Jennifer M. Spear "Colonial Intimacies: Legislating Sex in French Louisiana," *William and Mary Quarterly* 60 (2003): 95; Wilma A. Dunaway, *The African-American Family in Slavery and Emancipation* (New York: Cambridge University Press, 2003), 54.

10. See generally Edward E. Baptist, *The Half Has Never Been Told: Slavery and the Making of American Capitalism* (New York: Basic Books, 2014); Dunaway, *The African-American Family,* 81.

11. Dunaway, *The African-American Family,* 129–40.

12. Richard Follett, "Heat, Sex, and Sugar: Pregnancy and Childbearing in the Slave Quarters," *Journal of Family History* 28 (2003): 510–39.

13. Ibid.

14. Dunaway, *The African-American Family,* 136–38.

15. Katherine Paugh, "The Politics of Childbearing in the British Caribbean and the Atlantic World during the Age of Abolition, 1776–1838," *Past and Present* 221(2013): 119–60.

16. Peggy Cooper-Davis, *Neglected Stories: The Constitution and Family Values* (New York: Hill and Wang, 1993), 373; Darlene Clark Hine and Kathleen Thompson, *A Shining Thread of Hope: The History of Black Women in America* (New York: Broadway Books, 1998), 98–99; Deborah

Gray White, *Ar'n't I a Woman? Female Slaves in the Plantation South* (New York: Oxford University Press, 1985), 84–89; Janet Farrell Brodie, *Contraception and Abortion in Nineteenth-Century America* (Ithaca, NY: Cornell University Press, 1994), 52–53; Stephanie Shaw, "Mothering under Slavery in the Antebellum South," in *Mothering and Motherhood: Readings in American History,* ed. Janet Golden and Rima Apple (Columbus, OH: Ohio University Press, 1997), 309.

17. Baptist, *The Half Has Never Been Told,* chapter 2; Theda Perdue, *Slavery and the Evolution of Cherokee Society,* (Knoxville: University of Tennessee Press, 1979), 99–100.

18. Theda Perdue, *Cherokee Women: Gender and Cultural Change, 1700–1835* (Lincoln: University of Nebraska Press, 1998); Theda Perdue and Michael D. Greene, *The Cherokee Removal: A Brief History with Documents* (New York: St. Martin's, 1995); John Ehle, *Trail of Tears: The Rise and Fall of the Cherokee Nation* (Garden City, NY: Doubleday, 1988); Albert L. Hurtado, *Indian Survival on the California Frontier* (New Haven: Yale University Press, 1988); David E. Stannard, *American Holocaust: The Conquest of the New World* (New York: Oxford University Press, 1992); Rebecca Tsosie, "Changing Women: The Crosscurrents of American Indian Feminine Identity," in *Unequal Sisters: A Multicultural Reader in U.S. Women's History,* 3rd ed., ed. Vicki Ruiz and Ellen Carol DuBois (New York: Routledge, 2000), 565–86.

19. Linda K. Kerber, *Women of the Republic: Intellect and Ideology in Revolutionary America* (Chapel Hill: University of North Carolina Press, 1980); Mary Beth Norton, *Liberty's Daughters: The Revolutionary Experience of American Women, 1750–1800* (Ithaca, NY: Cornell University Press, 1980); Ruth H. Block, "American Feminine Ideals in Transition: The Rise of the Moral Mother, 1785–1815," *Feminist Studies* 4 (1978): 101–26; Nancy Cott, "Passionless: An Interpretation of Victorian Sexual Ideology, 1790–1850," *Signs* 4 (1978): 219–36.

20. Cornelia Hughes Dayton, "Taking the Trade: Abortion and Gender Relations in an Eighteenth-Century New England Village" *William and Mary Quarterly* 48 (1991): 19–49; John M. Riddle, *Eve's Herbs: A History of Contraception and Abortion in the West* (Cambridge, MA: Harvard University Press, 1997); Londa Schiebinger, *Plants and Empire: Colonial Bioprospecting in the Atlantic World* (Cambridge, MA: Harvard

University Press, 2004); Susan E. Klepp, *Revolutionary Conceptions: Women's Fertility and Family Limitation in America, 1760–1820* (Chapel Hill: University of North Carolina Press, 2009).

21. David A. Blackmon, *Slavery by Another Name: The Re-enslavement of Black Americans from the Civil War to World War II* (New York: Doubleday, 2008).

22. Eric Foner, *Reconstruction: America's Unfinished Revolution, 1863–1877* (New York: Harper & Row, 1988), 564–612.

23. Joanne Goodwin *Gender and the Politics of Welfare Reform: Mothers' Pensions in Chicago, 1911–1929* (Chicago: University of Chicago Press, 1997); Gwendolyn Mink and Rickie Solinger, eds., "Part I: 1900–1940," in *Welfare: A Documentary History of U.S. Policy and Politics* (New York: New York University Press, 2003); Michele Mitchell, *Righteous Propagation: African Americans and the Politics of Racial Destiny after Reconstruction* (Chapel Hill: University of North Carolina Press, 2004).

24. Rickie Solinger, "Extreme Danger: Women Abortionists and Their Clients before *Roe v. Wade,*" in *Not June Cleaver: Women and Gender in Postwar America, 1945–1960*, ed. Joanne Meyerowitz (Philadelphia: Temple University Press, 1994), 335–57; Isabel Wilkerson, *The Warmth of Other Suns: The Epic Story of America's Great Migration* (New York: Vintage, 2011).

25. David Wallace Adams, *Education for Extinction: American Indians and the Boarding School Experience, 1875–1928* (Lawrence: University Press of Kansas, 1995); Julie Davis, "American Indian Boarding School Experiences: Recent Studies from Native Perspectives," *Organization of American Historians Magazine of History* 15 (Winter, 2001): 20–22; Gurr, *Reproductive Justice.*

26. Adams, *Education for Extinction,* 210, 211.

27. Gwendolyn Mink, *The Wages of Motherhood: Inequality in The Welfare State, 1917–1942* (Ithaca, NY: Cornell University Press, 1995); Erika Lee, *At America's Gates: Chinese Immigration during the Exclusion* (Chapel Hill: University of North Carolina Press, 2003).

28. Andrea Tone, *Devices and Desires: A History of Contraceptives in America* (New York: Hill and Wang, 2001), 86.

29. Peggy Pascoe, *What Comes Naturally: Miscegenation Law and the Making of Race in America* (New York: Oxford University Press, 2009); see especially 118, "Racial Coverage of Miscegenation Laws, 1939."

30. Alexandra Minna Stern, *Eugenic Nation: Faults and Frontiers of Better Breeding in Modern America* (Berkeley: University of California Press, 2005); Paul Popenoe and Roswell Johnson, *Applied Eugenics* (New York: Macmillan, 1926); Ian Haney Lopez, *White by Law: The Legal Construction of Race* (New York: New York University Press, 1998); Wendy Kline, *Building a Better Race: Gender, Sexuality, and Eugenics from the Turn of the Century to the Baby Boom* (Berkeley: University of California Press, 2001).

As Stern points out, eugenicists in the past did not limit their scope to hereditary biological processes. They addressed a wide range of subjects, including immigration and demographics, economics, environmentalism, state surveillance, land use policies, scientific racism, the mental health and criminal justice systems, foreign policy, and militarism. Proponents frankly recognized that controlling land, resources, and labor are keys to controlling the world. Stern, *Eugenic Nation*, 3.

For the purposes of this analysis of reproductive control, however, we focus on a few strands of the eugenics movement.

31. Roger Daniels, *Guarding the Golden Door: American Immigration Policy and Immigrants since 1882* (New York: Hill and Wang, 2004).

32. Johanna Schoen, "Fighting for Child Health: Race, Birth Control, and the State in the Jim Crow South," *Social Politics* 4 (1997): 90–113; Tone, *Devices and Desires*, 152, 160; Jessie M. Rodrique, "The Black Community and the Birth Control Movement," chapter 29 in *We Specialize in the Wholly Impossible: A Reader in Black Women's History,* ed. Darlene Clark Hine, Wilma King, and Linda Reed (Brooklyn, NY: Carlson, 1995), 507; Jane Kwong Lee, "A Richer Life for All," in *Unbound Voices: A Documentary History of Chinese Women in San Francisco,* ed. Judy Yung, (Berkeley: University of California Press, 1999), 252–53; Maxine Davis, *Women's Medical Problems* (New York: Pocket Books, 1953), 90; Sandy Polishuk, *Sticking to the Union: An Oral History of the Life and Times of Julia Ruuttila* (New York: Palgrave, 2003), 66.

33. Ellen Chesler, *Woman of Valor: Margaret Sanger and the Birth Control Movement in America* (New York: Simon and Shuster, 1992), 320–41; Laura Briggs, *Reproducing Empire: Race, Sex, Science and U.S. Imperialism in Puerto Rico* (Berkeley: University of California Press, 2002), 83; Kline, *Building a Better Race.*

34. Constance M. Chen, *"The Sex Side of Life: Mary Ware Dennett's Pioneering Battle for Birth Control and Sex Education* (New York: New Press, 1996), 301; Chesler, *Woman of Valor,* 331; Carol McCann, *Birth Control Politics in the United States, 1916–1945* (Ithaca, NY: Cornell University Press, 1994), 75; Linda Gordon, *The Moral Property of Women: A History of Birth Control Politics in America* (Champaign: University of Illinois Press, 2002) , 226; Tone, *Devices and Desires,* 113.

35. Chesler, *Woman of Valor,* 300; Leslie J. Reagan, *When Abortion Was a Crime: Women, Medicine, and Law in the United States, 1867–1973* (Berkeley: University of California Press, 1997), 137–59.

36. Buck v. Bell, 274 U.S. 200 (1927).

37. Daniel J. Kevles, *In the Name of Eugenics: Genetics and the Uses of Human Heredity* (Cambridge, MA: Harvard University Press, 1995), 116.

38. After the collapse of the mortgage industry in 2008, Republicans routinely blamed poor homeowners for industry-wide failures, claiming that poor people borrowed more money than they could pay back. Analysts have refuted this narrative, assigning responsibility to the mortgage financialization industry itself. See Gretchen Morgenson and Joshua Rosner, *Reckless Endangerment: How Outsized Ambition, Greed, and Corruption Led to Economic Armageddon* (New York: Henry Holt, 2011) and Michael Lewis, *The Big Short* (New York: Norton, 2010), for example.

39. Chesler, *Woman of Valor,* 294–95.

40. Kevles, *In the Name of Eugenics,* chapter 8.

41. Molly Ladd-Taylor, *Mother-Work: Women, Child Welfare and the State 1890–1930* (Champaign: University of Illinois Press, 1994); Joanne Goodwin, *Gender and the Politics of Welfare Reform* (Chicago: University of Chicago Press, 1997).

42. Mink and Solinger, "Part I: 1900–1940."

43. Ira Katznelson, *Fear Itself: The New Deal and the Origins of Our Time* (New York: Liveright, 2013), 259–60; Winifred Bell, *ADC* (New York: Columbia University Press, 1965).

44. Tone, *Devices and Desires,* 135; Alice Kessler-Harris, *Out to Work: A History of Wage-Earning Women in the United States* (New York: Oxford University Press, 1982); Marynia Farnham and Ferdinand Lundberg,

Modern Woman: The Lost Sex (New York: Harper and Brothers, 1947); Lizabeth Cohen, *A Consumers' Republic: The Politics of Mass Consumption in Postwar America* (New York: Knopf, 2003).

45. See generally Daniel Moynihan, *The Negro Family: The Case for National Action* (Washington, DC: Office of Policy Planning and Research, U.S. Department of Labor, March 1965); Roberts, *Killing the Black Body;* Rickie Solinger, *Wake Up Little Susie: Single Pregnancy and Race before Roe v. Wade* (New York: Routledge, 2000); Martin Gilens, *Why Americans Hate Welfare: Race, Media, and the Politics of Antipoverty Policy* (Chicago: University of Chicago Press, 2000).

46. See, for example, Elena Gutiérrez, *Fertile Matters: The Politics of Mexican-Origin Women's Reproduction* (Austin: University of Texas Press, 2008).

47. See generally Daniel Callahan, ed., *The American Population Debate* (New York: Doubleday, 1971); see, for example, David E. Lilienthal, "300,000,000 Americans Would Be Wrong," *New York Times Magazine,* January 9, 1966; also see John B. Calhoun, "Population Density and Social Pathology," in *The Urban Condition: People and Policy in the Metropolis,* ed. Leonard J. Duhl (New York: Basic Books, 1963), 33–43; "Crime: Rising Tide, Its Upsurge Stirs a Quest for Causes and Cures," *Newsweek,* August 16, 1965, 21.

48. Director, Department of Public Welfare, Mecklenburg County, North Carolina, Population Crisis, Hearings, 89th Congress, 1st sess., part 3B, 1773; Committee on Population, *The Growth of U.S. Population: Analysis of the Problems and Recommendations for Research, Training and Service,* National Academy of Sciences-National Research Council, Washington, DC, publication 1279, 1965; Lois Wille, "The Tug of War on Birth Control: What It's About," *Chicago Daily News,* September 13–18, 1966, parts 1, 2, 3, 4.

49. Gary London, Health Division, Office of Economic Opportunity, Population Crisis, Hearings, 90th Congress, 1st sess., Part 1, 98.

50. "Union Sets Up Birth Control Clinic," *Washington Post/Times Herald,* January 15, 1965, A-9.

51. Donald T. Critchlow, *Intended Consequences: Birth Control, Abortion, and the Federal Government in Modern America* (New York: Oxford University Press, 1999), 49.

52. Jennifer Nelson, *Women of Color and the Reproductive Rights Movement* (New York: New York University Press, 2003); Jennifer Nelson, *More Than Medicine: A History of the Feminist Women's Health Movement* (New York: New York University Press, 2015); Felicia Kornbluh, *The Battle for Welfare Rights: Politics and Poverty in Modern America* (Philadelphia: University of Pennsylvania Press, 2007); Rickie Solinger, *Beggars and Choosers: How the Politics of Choice Shapes Adoption, Abortion, and Welfare* (New York: Hill and Wang, 2002).

53. See generally Solinger, *Wake Up Little Susie.*

54. Ibid.; Ann Fessler, *The Girls Who Went Away: The Hidden History of Women Who Surrendered Children for Adoption in the Decades before* Roe v. Wade (New York: Penguin, 2006).

55. Carole Joffe, *Doctors of Conscience: The Struggle to Provide Abortion before and after* Roe v. Wade (Boston: Beacon Press, 1995); Rickie Solinger, *The Abortionist: A Woman against the Law* (New York: Free Press, 1994).

56. Iris Lopez, *Matters of Choice: Puerto Rican Women's Struggle for Reproductive Freedom* (New Brunswick, NJ: Rutgers University Press, 2008).

57. Jean Hardisty, *Mobilizing Resentment: Conservative Resurgence from the John Birch Society to the Promise Keepers* (Boston: Beacon Press, 1999).

58. Zakiya Luna and Kristin Luker, "Reproductive Justice," *Annual Review of Law and Social Science* 9 (2013): 327–52.

59. Martin Bauml Duberman, *Stonewall* (New York: Penguin Books, 1994); David Carter, *Stonewall: The Riots That Sparked the Gay Revolution* (St. Martin's, 2004).

60. See Gutiérrez, *Fertile Matters.*

61. Gurr, *Reproductive Justice,* 125.

62. Roberts, *Killing the Black Body,* 91.

63. Nelson, *Women of Color and the Reproductive Rights Movement,* 140–45.

64. Gutiérrez, *Fertile Matters;* Nelson, *Women of Color and the Reproductive Rights Movement,* chapter 2.

65. Roberts, *Killing the Black Body,* 90.

66. These practices and policies were recommended by the American College of Obstetricians and Gynecologists and widely adopted. Gordon, *The Moral Property of Women,* 343–44.

67. Roberts, *Killing the Black Body*, chapters 2 and 3.

68. *Congressional Record–House*, vol. 123, pt. 16, June 17, 1997, 19698–19715.

69. Rachel Roth, *Making Women Pay: The Hidden Costs of Fetal Rights* (Ithaca, NY: Cornell University Press, 2000).

70. Nelson, *Women of Color and the Reproductive Rights Movement*; Nelson, *More Than Medicine*.

71. Jael Silliman, Marlene Gerber Fried Loretta Ross, and Elena R. Gutiérrez, *Undivided Rights: Women of Color Organize for Reproductive Justice* (Cambridge, MA: South End Press, 2004).

2. REPRODUCTIVE JUSTICE IN THE TWENTY-FIRST CENTURY

1. SisterSong Women of Color Reproductive Justice Collective, http://sistersong.net. SisterSong formerly was the Women of Color Reproductive *Health* Collective. We changed our name in 2011.

2. Zora Neal Hurston, www.goodreads.com/quotes/409934-if-you-are-silent-about-your-pain-they-ll-kill-you.

3. Audre Lorde, *Sister Outsider: Essays and Speeches* (Trumansburg, NY: Crossing Press, 1984), 37.

4. Gloria Anzaldúa, *Borderlands/La Frontera: The New Mestiza* (San Francisco: Aunt Lute Books, 1987), 81.

5. These were the twelve founding mothers of the concept of reproductive justice and their affiliations at the time:

Toni M. Bond, Chicago Abortion Fund

Reverend Alma Crawford, Religious Coalition for Reproductive Choice

Evelyn S. Field, National Council of Negro Women

Terri James, American Civil Liberties Union of Illinois

Bisola Maringay, National Black Women's Health Project, Chicago Chapter

Cassandra McConnell, Planned Parenthood of Greater Cleveland

Cynthia Newbille, National Black Women's Health Project (now Black Women's Health Imperative)

Loretta J. Ross, Center for Democratic Renewal

Elizabeth Terry, National Abortion Rights Action League of
 Pennsylvania
"Able" Mabel Thomas, Pro-Choice Resource Center, Inc.
Winnette P. Willis, Chicago Abortion Fund
Kim Youngblood, National Black Women's Health Project

6. Black Women on Health Care Reform held a press conference the next day to underscore the purpose of the ad. The press conference featured African American Congresswomen Eleanor Holmes Norton, Maxine Waters, Carrie Meek, Cynthia McKinney, and Eva Clayton.

7. The women in the 2003 SisterSong plenary and workshop on reproductive justice included the following:

Byllye Avery, National Black Women's Health Project Founder
Adriane Fugh Berman, National Women's Health Network
Jatrice Gaithers, Planned Parenthood of Metropolitan Washington
Rosalina Palacios, National Latina Health Organization
Dorothy Roberts, Northwestern University School of Law
Malika Saada Saar, Rebecca Project for Human Rights founder
Eveline Shen, Asian Pacific Islanders for Reproductive Health
Jael Silliman, Ford Foundation (affiliation listed for identification only)
Barbara Smith, Combahee River Collective cofounder

8. The name March for Women's Human Rights was originally suggested at the SisterSong conference, but was likely little understood by some of the mainstream groups, so a name used for previous marches was recycled.

9. These included environmental justice issues, the war against Iraq, and the international debt crisis of the Global South.

10. Zakiya Luna, "Marching toward Reproductive Justice: Coalitional (Re) Framing of the March for Women's Lives," *Sociological Inquiry* 80, no. 4 (November 2010): 554–78.

11. Jael Silliman, Marlene Gerber Fried, Loretta Ross, and Elena Gutiérrez, *Undivided Rights: Women of Color Organize for Reproductive Justice* (Boston: South End Press, 2004).

12. An example of a "quick win" was the campaign for the Family Medical Leave Act, started by feminists in 1984 and finally turned into

law in 1993, signed by President Clinton, provided unpaid leave for up to three months for families, an important new benefit for workers. However, many activists, especially women of color, protested that unpaid leave helped only those who could afford to be without an income for three months. The supporters of the bill pushed back, saying that Congress would approve only unpaid leave at that time, and future opportunities would develop to expand to paid leave for low-wage workers. Twenty-two years later, low-income people are still waiting.

13. Forward Together (formerly Asian Communities for Reproductive Justice), *A New Vision for Reproductive Justice, 2005,* http://strongfamiliesmovement.org/assets/docs/ACRJ-A-New-Vision.pdf.

14. Ibid.

15. Rebecca Davis, "Minister Bathabile Dlamini: Reproductive Justice's Newly Vocal Champion," *Daily Maverick,* June 11, 2014, http://www.dailymaverick.co.za/article/2014–06–11-minister-bathabile-dlamini-reproductive-justices-newly-vocal-champion/.

16. Bernice Johnson Reagon, "Coalition Politics: Turning the Century," in *Home Girls: A Black Feminist Anthology,* ed. Barbara Smith (New York: Kitchen Table Press, 1983), 365.

17. Kimberlé Crenshaw, "Intersectionality and Identity Politics: Learning from Violence against Women of Color" in *Feminist Theory: A Reader,* 2nd ed., ed. Wendy Kolmar and Frances Bartkowski (New York: McGraw-Hill, 2005), 50.

18. Frances Beal, "Double Jeopardy: To Be Black and Female," in *The Black Woman,* ed. Toni Cade Bambara (1970; New York: Washington Square Press, 2005), 109; Kalamu Ya Salaam and Toni Cade Bambara, "Searching for the Mother Tongue: An Interview with Toni Cade Bambara," chap. 5, in *Savoring the Salt: The Legacy of Toni Cade Bambara,* ed. Linda Janet Holmes and Cheryl A. Wall (Philadelphia: Temple University Press, 2008), 58–69.

19. The Combahee River Collective's name commemorated a river in South Carolina where 750 slaves were freed on June 2, 1863, in a raid planned and led by ex-slave Harriet Tubman, the only military campaign in American history planned and led by a woman. Combahee River Collective, "Black Feminist Statement," in *All the Women Are*

White, All the Blacks Are Men, But Some of Us Are Brave: Black Women's Studies, ed. Gloria T. Hull, Patricia Bell Scott, and Barbara Smith (Westbury, NY: Feminist Press, 1982).

20. Gloria Anzaldúa and Cherríe Moraga, *This Bridge Called My Back,* 2nd ed. (New York: Kitchen Table Press, 1983), 263. Also available in *Savoring the Salt: The Legacy of Toni Cade Bambara,* ed. Linda Janet Holmes and Cheryl A. Wall (Philadelphia: Temple University Press, 2007); Thabiti Lewis, *Conversations with Toni Cade Bambara* (Jackson: University of Mississippi Press, 2012).

21. Bernice Johnson Reagon wrote, "The 'our' must include everybody you have to include in order for you to survive." "Coalition Politics: Turning the Century," in *Homegirls: A Black Feminist Anthology,* ed. Barbara Smith (New York: Kitchen Table Press, 1983), 365.

22. Reagon, "Coalition Politics," 359.

23. Moya Bailey, "They Aren't Talking About Me," Crunk Feminist Collective, March 14, 2010, http://www.crunkfeministcollective .com/2010/03/14/they-arent-talking-about-me/; Keir Bristol, "On Moya Bailey, Misogynoir, and Why Both Are Important," Visibility Project, May 27, 2014, www.thevisibilityproject.com/2014/05/27/on-moya-bailey-misogynoir-and-why-both-are-important/.

24. Settler colonialism was and is an ongoing wealth-accumulation process of emigrants permanently occupying territories and forming new communities, displacing original or indigenous inhabitants through elimination, subjugation, containment, and genocide. It is contrasted with processes that extract labor or natural resources, while leaving the original inhabitants in place. Settler colonialism requires the legitimization of settler sovereignty over people and land, so that access to resources, development, scientific advancements, and education are restricted. Political, economic, and cultural hegemony result, which benefits the colonists rather than the previous people living in the land. Settler colonial relationships are both gendered and sexualized, according to Neferti Tadiar: "The economies and political relations of nations are libidinally configured, that is, they are grasped and effected in terms of sexuality," so that the issues of colonial, race, and gender oppression cannot be separated. Quoted in Andrea Smith, "Sexual Violence as a Tool of Genocide," chap. 1, in *Conquest: Sexual*

Violence and American Indian Genocide (Cambridge, MA: South End Press, 2005), 8.

25. Audre Lorde, "Age, Race, Class and Sex: Women Redefining Difference," in *Feminist Theory: A Reader,* 2nd ed., ed. Wendy Kolmar and Frances Bartkowski (New York: McGraw-Hill, 2005), 50.

26. Lilly Ledbetter was hired by Goodyear in 1979 and retired in 1998. She learned that she and other women managers had been paid considerably less than their male counterparts. The lawsuit eventually reached the Supreme Court, which ruled that because she did not file the suit 180 days from her first paycheck, she had no right to sue, even though she did not know at the time what comparable men were earning. Ledbetter v. Goodyear Tire and Rubber Co., 550 U.S. 618 (2007). Obviously, the company did not advertise that it was paying women less, so despite the disparate outcomes she could prove, the bar was higher because she had to prove the company intentionally paid women less and do so within a limited time frame. Justice Ruth Bader Ginsburg dissented, and Congress eventually passed the Lilly Ledbetter Fair Pay Act of 2009 addressing the 180-day issue, while leaving intact the question of intent vs. outcome.

27. *Congressional Record–House,* vol. 123, pt. 16, June 17, 1977, 19698–19715.

28. Burwell v. Hobby Lobby Stores, 134 S. Ct. 2751 (2014).

29. It is likely that a ninth category may be digital rights because societies are quickly moving towards separating people between those who do and do not have digital access to technology. For example, much of banking, health care, education, communication, taxation, and regulation have become digitally accessible, and in some cases, required. Those who are on the outside of the digital divide of technology may be unable to receive an education, transact banking needs, or obtain immediate health care assistance. In a short while, cash transactions may indicate a certain level of poverty rather than wealth.

30. Office of the High Commissioner for Human Rights, "Universal Declaration of Human Rights" (UDHR), United Nations, adopted by the UN General Assembly, December 10, 1948, http://www.ohchr.org/EN/UDHR/Documents/UDHR_Translations/eng.pdf.

31. Dázon Dixon Diallo, "HIV/AIDS and the Women's Health Movement," *HIV Risk Reduction* 8, no. 1, HIV Early Intervention Services (EIS), Georgia Department of Human Resources, Office of Addictive Disease, n.d., http://hiveis.com/documents/WomensHealthMovement_ Dazon.pdf.

32. The primary international treaty that covers women is the Convention on the Elimination of All Forms of Discrimination Against Women (CEDAW), which was signed by President Jimmy Carter in 1979 but has yet to be ratified by the Senate. It takes a two-thirds majority of the Senate to ratify a treaty (the House of Representatives is not required). Once ratified, an international treaty has the same legal power as a law passed by Congress, and states are compelled to comply.

33. William Korey, "The Key to Human Rights Implementation," in *International Conciliation* (New York: Carnegie Endowment for International Peace, 1968), 49.

34. The International Commission for Air Navigation (ICAN) was an international governing body that was formed by the Convention Relating to the Regulation of Aerial Navigation in 1922 under the direction of the League of Nations, the forerunner to the United Nations. Currently, the United Nations oversees the International Civil Aviation Organization to manage the administration and governance of the Convention on International Civil Aviation to safely and efficiently coordinate more than 100,000 daily flights around the world. See the ICAO website, http://www.icao.int/about-icao/Pages /default.aspx . Similar international cooperative arrangements exist for postal and communications services.

35. Dorothy Roberts, *Shattered Bonds: The Color of Child Welfare* (New York: Basic Civitas Books, 2002), 248. See also "Convention on the Prevention and Punishment of the Crime of Genocide," article 2, (d) and (e), http://www.hrweb.org/legal/genocide.html.

36. Misty Rojo, "Gov. Jerry Brown Signs SB 1135, Prison Anti-Sterilization Bill," *San Francisco Bay View,* September 26, 2014, http:// sfbayview.com/2014/09/gov-jerry-brown-signs-sb-1135-prison-anti-sterilization-bill/; Alexandra Stern, *Eugenic Nation: Faults and Frontiers of Better*

Breeding in Modern America (Berkeley: University of California Press, 2005); Dorothy Roberts, *Killing the Black Body: Race, Reproduction, and the Meaning of Liberty* (New York: Pantheon, 1997).

37. Smith, "Sexual Violence as a Tool of Genocide," 35–46.

38. Roberts, *Shattered Bonds*, 248.

39. Forward Together (formerly Asian Communities for Reproductive Justice), *A New Vision for Reproductive Justice, 2005*, www.reproductivejustice.org.

40. Jessica Yee Danforth, Native Youth Sexual Health Network, Statement delivered by Action Canada for Population and Development (ACPD) and International Indian Treaty Council, 25th Session of the Human Rights Council, Item 3: Interactive Dialogue with the Independent Expert on the Issue of Human Rights Obligations Relating to the Enjoyment of a Safe, Clean, Healthy And Sustainable Environment, http://www.nativeyouthsexualhealth.com/march112014.pdf.

41. Silliman et al., *Undivided Rights*, 131–33.

42. Gabrielle Glaser, "A Son Given Up for Adoption Is Found after Half a Century, and Then Lost Again," *New York Times,* July 10, 2015.

43. Rickie Solinger and Mie Nakachi, *Reproductive States: Global Perspectives on the Invention and Implementation of Population Policy* (New York: Oxford University Press, 2016).

44. Jennifer Nelson, *Women of Color and the Reproductive Rights Movement* (New York: New York University Press, 2003), chap. 5.

45. This argument is right only if one allows that poverty somehow defines competence. However, human rights activists deny this non sequitur because poverty is more likely a predictor of more poverty, but not mental capacity or competence. Poor people have poor children; wealthy people have wealthy children. It is not a result of intelligence, or proof that we live in a meritocracy, but of unequal opportunity. See Barbara Ehrenreich, *Nickel and Dimed: On (NOT) Getting By in America* (New York: Henry Holt, 2001).

46. Buck v. Bell, 274 U.S. 200 (1927).

47. Harriet A. Washington, *Medical Apartheid: The Dark History of Medical Experimentation on Black Americans from Colonial Times to the Present* (New York: Harlem Moon, Broadway Books, 2006), 203–4.

48. Elena Gutiérrez, *Fertile Matters: The Politics of Mexican-Origin Women's Reproduction* (Austin: University of Texas Press, 2008).

49. Sonya Borrero, Nikki Zite, Joseph E. Potter, and James Trussell, "Medicaid Policy on Sterilization—Anachronistic or Still Relevant?" *New England Journal of Medicine* 307 (January 9, 2014): 102–4.

50. David Harvey, *A Brief History of Neoliberalism* (Oxford and New York: Oxford University Press, 2005), 165. This discussion of neoliberalism relies on Harvey's *Brief History*. Also see Susan Strange, *The Retreat of the State: The Diffusion of Power in the World Economy* (Cambridge, UK: Cambridge University Press, 1996); Henry Giroux, *Against the Terror of Neo-Liberalism: Politics Beyond the Age of Greed* (Boulder, CO: Paradigm, 2008).

51. See, for example, Thomas J. Sugrue, *The Origins of the Urban Crisis: Race and Inequality in Postwar Detroit* (Princeton, NJ: Princeton University Press, 1996).

52. For a vivid description of this phenomenon, see Rick Pearlstein, *Nixonland: The Rise of a President and the Fracturing of America* (New York: Scribner's, 2008).

53. Ruth Rosen, *The World Split Open: How the Modern Women's Movement Changed America* (New York: Viking Penguin, 2000).

54. William Saletan, *Bearing Right: How Conservatives Won the Abortion War* (Berkeley: University of California Press, 2003).

55. See Jean Hardisty, *Mobilizing for Resentment: Conservative Resurgence from the John Birch Society to the Promise Keepers* (Boston: Beacon Press, 1999); Leonard Zeskind, *Blood and Politics: The History of the White Nationalist Movement from the Margins to the Mainstream* (New York: Farrar Straus Giroux, 2009).

56. Michelle Alexander, *The New Jim Crow: Mass Incarceration in the Age of Colorblindness* (New York: New Press, 2010), 194.

57. Tara Herivel and Paul Wright, eds., *Prison Nation: The Warehousing of America's Poor* (New York: Routledge, 2003); Alexander, *The New Jim Crow*.

58. This discussion relies in part on Tamar Kraft-Stolar, "Reproductive Injustice: The State of Reproductive Health Care for Women

in New York State Prisons," A Report of the Women in Prison Project (New York: Correctional Association of New York, 2015), http://www.correctionalassociation.org/wp-content/uploads/2015/03/Reproductive-Injustice-FULL-REPORT-FINAL-2–11–15.pdf; Rebecca Project on Human Rights and The National Women's Law Center, "Mothers Behind Bars: A State by State Report Card and Analysis of Federal Policies on Conditions of Confinement for Pregnant and Parenting Women and the Effects on Their Children," (Washington, DC: Authors, 2010), http://www.rebeccaprojectjustice.org/images/stories/files/mothersbehindbarsreport-2010.pdf.

59. Julia Sudbury, ed., *Global Lockdown: Race, Gender, and the Prison-Industrial Complex* (New York: Routledge, 2005); Beth E. Richie, *Arrested Justice: Black Women, Violence, and America's Prison Nation* (New York: New York University Press, 2012); Rickie Solinger, Paula C. Johnson, Martha L. Raimon, Tina Reynolds, and Ruby C. Tapia, eds., *Interrupted Life: Experiences of Incarcerated Women in the United States* (Berkeley: University of California Press, 2010).

60. William H. Frey, "New Projections Point to a Majority Minority Nation in 2044," *The Avenue* (blog), Brookings Institute, December 12, 2014, https://www.brookings.edu/blog/the-avenue/2014/12/12/new-projections-point-to-a-majority-minority-nation-in-2044/.

61. Aviva Galpert, "Demographic Winter: Right-Wing Prophecies of White Supremacy's Decline and What They Mean for Reproductive Justice," Political Research Associates, July 3, 2014, http://www.politicalresearch.org/2014/07/03/demographic-winter-right-wing-prophecies-of-white-supremacys-decline/#.

62. bell hooks, *Feminist Theory from Margin to Center* (Boston: South End Press, 1984), 52.

63. Domenico Montenaro, "Obama Performance with White Voters on Par with Other Democrats," *NBC News,* November 9, 2012, http://firstread.nbcnews.com/_news/2012/11/19/15282553-obama-performance-with-white-voters-on-par-with-other-democrats.

64. Stephen D. Foster, Jr., "Top 10 Quotes That Prove That Neurosurgeon Ben Carson Doesn't Have the Brain to be President," Addicting Info, November 15, 2014, http://www.addictinginfo.org/2014/11/15/top-10-

quotes-that-prove-neurosurgeon-ben-carson-doesnt-have-the-brain-to-be-president/.

65. Loretta Ross, Heidi Williamson, Laura Jimenez, and Serena Garcia, "Race, Gender and Abortion: How Reproductive Justice Activists Won in Georgia," Policy Report, SisterSong Women of Color Reproductive Justice Collective, October 2010, http://www.trustblackwomen.org/SisterSong_Policy_Report.pdf (abridged version). See also Carole Joffe and Jennifer Reich, *Reproduction and Society Interdisciplinary Readings* (New York: Routledge, 2015), 76.

66. Catherine Dunn, "Shopping While Black: America's Retailers Know They Have a Racial Profiling Problem: Now What?" *International Business Times*, December 15, 2015, http://www.ibtimes.com/shopping-while-black-americas-retailers-know-they-have-racial-profiling-problem-now-2222778. See also Nadra Nittle, "Online Shopping While Black," November 15, 2015, http://www.racked.com/2015/11/25/9769638/cyber-monday-shopping-while-black; George E. Schreer, Saundra Smith, and Kirsten Thomas, "Shopping While Black: Examining Racial Discrimination in a Retail Setting," *Journal of Applied Social Psychology* 39, no. 6 (2009): 1432–44.

67. Katie McKay Bryson, Lynda Pickbourn and Betsy Hartmann, *Population in Perspective: A Curriculum Resource*, 2nd ed., (Amherst, MA: Hampshire College, 2013), 25. See also Galpert, "Demographic Winter."

68. Jenny A. Higgins, "Celebration Meets Caution: LARC's Boon, Potential Busts, and the Benefits of a Reproductive Justice Approach," Association of Reproductive Health Professionals, *Contraception Journal*, April 2014, http://www.arhp.org/Publications-and-Resources/Contraception-Journal/April-2014.

69. Ian Haney López, *Dog Whistle Politics: How Coded Racial Appeals Have Reinvented Racism and Wrecked the Middle Class* (New York: Oxford University Press, 2014).

70. See, for example, Alexander, *The New Jim Crow;* Beverly I. Moran and Stephanie M. Wildman, "Race and Wealth Disparity: The Role of Law and the Legal System," *Fordham Urban Law Journal* 4 (2007): 1219–38; Khiara M. Bridges, *Reproducing Race: An Ethnography of Pregnancy as a Site of Racialization* (Berkeley: University of California

Press, 2011). The U.S. Census Bureau reported that in 2014, the rate of homeownership was 72.3 percent for non-Hispanic whites; for the category "All Other Races," the rate was 55.3 percent. Among "Blacks Alone," the rate was 42.1 percent and for Hispanics, 44.5 percent. Robert R. Kallis and Melissa Kressin, "Residential Vacancies and Homeownership in the Fourth Quarter 2014" (press release), U.S. Census Bureau News, CB15–08 (Washington, DC: U.S. Department of Commerce, January 29, 2015), http://www.census.gov/housing/hvs/files/qtr414/currenthvspress.pdf.

71. Anzaldúa, *Borderlands/La Frontera*, 63.

72. Barbara Smith, ed., Preface, *Homegirls: A Black Feminist Anthology* (New York: Kitchen Table Press, 1983), xxxiii.

73. Paula M.L. Moya, "Postmodernism, 'Realism,' and the Politics of Identity: Cherríe Moraga and Chicana Feminism," in *Feminist Genealogies, Colonial Legacies, Democratic Futures*, ed. M. Jacqui Alexander and Chandra Talpade Mohanty (New York: Routledge, 1997), 125–26.

74. Lynn Paltrow, "Pregnancy, Childbirth and Parenting," National Advocates for Pregnant Women, http://www.advocatesforpregnant women.org/issues/pregnancy_childbirth_and_parenting, n.d., accessed October 16, 2016.

75. Law Students for Reproductive Justice is now If/When/How: Lawyering for Reproductive Justice, www.ifwhenhow.org.

76. Notably, the Feminist Majority Foundation and the local chapter of the American Civil Liberties Union strongly supported linking the two ballot initiatives, yet this was not the decision of the primary national organizations leading the antipersonhood campaign.

77. Audre Lorde, "The Master's Tools Will Never Dismantle the Master's House," *Sister Outsider: Essays and Speeches* (Trumansburg, NY: Crossing Press, 1984), 112.

3. MANAGING FERTILITY

1. Jessie M. Rodrique, "The Black Community and the Birth Control Movement," in *Passion and Power: Sexuality and History*, ed. Kathy Peiss and Christina Simmons (Philadelphia: Temple University Press, 1989), 138–54.

2. Andrea Smith, "Beyond Pro-Choice versus Pro-Life: Women of Color and Reproductive Justice," *National Women's Studies Association Journal* 19 (Spring 2005): 131–33.

3. Robin West, "From Choice to Reproductive Justice: De-Constitutionalizing Abortion Rights," *Yale Law Journal* 118 (2009): 1409.

4. Sarah London, "Reproductive Justice: Developing a Lawyering Model," *Berkeley Journal of African American Law and Policy* 71 (2011): 88; Reproductive Health and Technologies Project, *Two Sides of the Same Coin: Integrating Economic and Reproductive Justice* (Washington, DC: RHTP, August 2015), 9, http://rhtp.org/wp-content/uploads/2016/08/Two-Sides-of-the-Same-Coin-Integrating-Economic-and-Reproductive-Justice.pdf.

5. Loretta Ross, "Understanding Reproductive Justice," November 2006, updated March 2011, http://www.trustblackwomen.org/our-work/what-is-reproductive-justice.

6. Miriam Zoila Pérez, "A Tale of Two Movements," *Colorlines,* January 22, 2015.

7. London, "Reproductive Justice," 77.

8. Barbara Gurr, *Reproductive Justice: The Politics of Health Care for Native American Women* (New Brunswick, NJ: Rutgers University Press, 2015), 34.

9. Cynthia Soohoo, "Hyde-Care for All: The Expansion of Abortion-Funding Restrictions under Health Care Reform," *CUNY Law Review* 15 (2012): 399.

10. Gurr, *Reproductive Justice,* 26; Burwell v. Hobby Lobby Stores, Inc., 134 S. Ct. 2751 (2014).

11. West, "From Choice to Reproductive Justice," 1413–14.

12. Ibid., 1413–17.

13. Potter Stewart, Harris v. McRae, 448 U.S. 297 (1980), 316–17.

14. West, "From Choice to Reproductive Justice," 1414; *Harris v. McRae,* 316.

15. Soohoo, "Hyde-Care for All," 407–8, 442; Jessica Arons and Madina Agénor, *Separate and Unequal: The Hyde Amendment and Women of Color* (Washington, DC: Center for American Progress, December 2010), 7, https://www.americanprogress.org/issues/women/report/2010/12/06/8808/separate-and-unequal/; *Harris v. McRae,* 314.

16. Guttmacher Institute, "State Policies in Brief as of May 1, 2015, Restricting Insurance Coverage of Abortion," 2015, http://www.guttmacher.org.

17. Copelon quoted in Soohoo, "Hyde-Care for All," 396, 441.

18. See, for example, Rhonda Williams, *The Politics of Public Housing: Black Women's Struggles against Urban Poverty* (New York: Oxford University Press, 2005); Nicholas Dagen Bloom, *Public Housing That Worked: New York in the 20th Century* (Philadelphia: University of Pennsylvania Press, 2008); Lisa Levenstein, *A Movement without Marches: African American Women and the Politics of Poverty in Postwar Philadelphia* (Chapel Hill: University of North Carolina Press, 2009).

19. Loretta Ross, "Anti-Abortion PreNDA Legislation," *Collective Voices: Black Abortion* 6 (2011): 15; Laura L. Lovett, "Fight the Legacies," *Collective Voices: Black Abortion* 6 (2011), 35; Soohoo, "Hyde-Care for All," 397; Rhonda Copelon, "Losing the Negative Right of Privacy," *New York University Review of Law and Social Change* 18 (1990–91): 22.

20. Joane Nagel, quoted in Gurr, *Reproductive Justice*, 27; Lisa C. Ikemoto, "Abortion, Contraception, and the ACA: The Realignment of Women's Health," *Howard University School of Law Journal* 55 (2012): 733, 742.

21. Kathryn J. Edin and H. Luke Shaefer, *$2 a Day: Living on Almost Nothing in America* (Boston: Houghton Mifflin Harcourt, 2015); *Nuestra Voz, Nuestra Salud, Nuestro Texas: The Fight for Reproductive Heath in the Rio Grande Valley* (New York: National Latina Institute for Reproductive Health and Center for Reproductive Rights, November 2013), http://www.nuestrotexas.org/pdf/NT-spread.pdf.

22. Manny Fernandez, "Hurdles as Immigrants Seek Texas Birth Certificates for Children," *International New York Times*, September 17, 2015, http://www.nytimes.com/2015/09/18/us/illegal-immigrant-birth-certificates.html.

23. Loretta Ross, Heidi Williamson, Laura Jimenez, Serena Garcia, and SisterSong National Office, *Race, Gender and Abortion: How Reproductive Justice Activists Won in Georgia*, SisterSong Policy Report, October 2010, http://www.trustblackwomen.org/SisterSong_Policy_Report.pdf.

24. Gurr, *Reproductive Justice,* 26; Ross, "Anti-Abortion PreNDA Legislation," 14; Sujatha Jesudason and Susannah Baruch, *Race and Sex in Abortion Debates: The Legislation and the Billboards* (Oakland, CA: Generations Ahead, December 21, 2011), http://www.generations-ahead .org/files-for-download/success-stories/RaceAndSexSelection.pdf.

25. University of Chicago Law School, National Asian Pacific American Women's Forum, and Advancing New Standards in Reproductive Health, *Replacing Myths with Facts: Sex-Selective Abortion Laws in the United States,* June 2014, https://napawf.org/wp-content/uploads /2014/06/Replacing-Myths-with-Facts-final.pdf.

26. Ross et al., *Race, Gender and Abortion.*

27. London, "Reproductive Justice," 78. Among the Supreme Court decisions that added restrictions on abortion access are Webster v. Reproductive Health Services 492 U.S. 490 (1989) and Rust v. Sullivan 500 U.S. 173 (1990). Indicative of the court's unwillingness to consider the actual conditions of women's lives and the actual impacts of its decisions, the court asserted in *Rust* that its refusal to facilitate a woman's access to her abortion right could not be considered a "penalty," and claimed in *Webster* that restrictions to abortion access left poor women "no worse off." A number of states did look at funding restrictions in the 1970s and 1980s from a woman's perspective. These states analyzed their actual impact on women and found that "denial of coverage for medically necessary abortions was inconsistent with the purposes of Medicaid and state commitments to provide for the health of the poor." California and Minnesota went so far as to take the position that states had an obligation to "provide more, not less, protection for the rights of poor women." Soohoo, "Hyde-Care for All," 415; Reproductive Health and Technologies Project, *Two Sides of the Same Coin.*

28. Andrea Smith, *Native Americans and the Christian Right: The Gendered Politics of Unlikely Alliance* (Durham, NC: Duke, 2008), 238.

29. Michelle Alexander, *The New Jim Crow: Mass Incarceration in the Age of Colorblindness* (New York: New Press, 2010).

30. Soohoo, "Hyde-Care for All," 292–93.

31. Adrienne Nickerson, Ruth Manski, and Amanda Dennis, "A Qualitative Investigation of Low-Income Abortion Clients' Attitudes toward Public Funding for Abortion," *Women and Health* 54 (2014): 672–

86; Guttmacher Institute, "State Policies in Brief"; Soohoo, "Hyde-Care for All," 420.

32. Soohoo, "Hyde-Care for All," 416–18; Ikemoto, "Abortion, Contraception, and the ACA," 761.

33. This is Barbara Gurr's term; see Gurr, *Reproductive Justice,* 30.

34. Ibid., 29; see Rickie Solinger and Mie Nakachi, eds., *Reproductive States: Global Perspectives on the Invention and Implementation of Population Policy* (New York: Oxford University Press, 2016).

35. Jennifer Nelson, *More Than Medicine: A History of the Feminist Women's Health Movement* (New York: NYU Press, 2015), 209.

36. Jill E. Adams and Jessica Arons, "A Travesty of Justice: Revisiting *Harris v. McRae,*" *William and Mary Journal of Women and the Law* 21 (2014): 5–57.

37. "Nuestro Texas: A Reproductive Justice Agenda of Latinas," (New York: National Latina Institute for Reproductive Health and Center for Reproductive Rights, January 2015), 38, http://www.nuestrotexas.org/wp-content/uploads/2015/01/CRR_ReproJusticeFor Latinas_v9_single_pg.pdf; Reproductive Health and Technologies Project, *Two Sides of the Same Coin,* 10.

38. Addendum, "Responses to the Questionnaire on Risks and Challenges Faced by Women Human Rights Defenders and Those Working on Women's Rights and Gender issues," to *Report Submitted by the Special Rapporteur on the Situation of Human Rights Defenders, Margaret Sekaggya,* United Nations General Assembly, Human Rights Council, 16th sess., agenda item 3, December 20, 2010, 52.

39. Ikemoto, "Abortion, Contraception, and the ACA," 767.

40. Reproductive Health and Technologies Project, *Two Sides of the Same Coin,* 20.

41. Guttmacher Institute, "Contraceptive Use in the United States," fact sheet, July 2015; *Nuestra Voz, Nuestra Salud, Nuestro Texas,* 41.

42. Sharon Lerner, "The Real War on Families: Why the U.S. Needs Paid Leave Now," *In These Times,* August 8, 2015; Reproductive Health and Technologies Project, *Two Sides of the Same Coin,* 4.

43. U.S. Department of Labor, "DOL Fact Sheet: Paid Family and Medical Leave," updated June 2015, http://www.dol.gov/wb/PaidLeave /PaidLeave.htm.

44. National Women's Law Center, "Pharmacy Refusals 101," Birth Control Resources, August 4, 2015, http://www.nwlc.org/resource /pharmacy-refusals-101.

45. Reginald A. Byron and Vincent J. Roscigno, "Relational Power, Legitimation, and Pregnancy Discrimination," *Gender and* Society 28 (2014): 435–62; First Amendment Defense Act, H.R. 2802, 114th Cong. (2015–2016), https://www.congress.gov/bill/114th-congress/house-bill /2802.

46. In recent years, the disability rights movement has advocated effectively for the reproductive rights of individuals with disabilities, and in the process, it has created perspectives and language that aim to fuel the reproductive rights claims of these persons, create intersectional alliances, and reshape mainstream thinking about reproductive politics, policies, and services. See, for example, Dorothy Roberts and Sujatha Jesudason, "The Case of Race, Gender, Disability, and Genetic Technologies," *Du Bois Review: Social Science Research on Race* 10 (Fall 2013): 313–28.

47. *Nuestra Voz, Nuestra Salud, Nuestro Texas,* 9–10, 50–51.

48. Reproductive Health and Technologies Project, *Two Sides of the Same Coin,* 13–16; Arons and Agénor, *Separate and Unequal,* 13, 15–16; Ross, "Understanding Reproductive Justice."

49. *Nuestra Voz, Nuestra Salud, Nuestro Texas,* 16–18; Arons and Agénor, *Separate and Unequal,* 23; *Nuestra Voz, Nuestra Salud, Nuestro Texas,* 39.

50. *Nuestra Voz, Nuestra Salud, Nuestro Texas,* 23–24; 36, 42; National Family Planning and Reproductive Health Association, "Title X, Budget and Appropriations"; Reproductive Health and Technologies Project, *Two Sides of the Same Coin,* 10. "In Texas, from 2000–2010, the unmet need for publicly subsidized contraception increased by 30% to 1,690,150, with one-half of the women in need being Latina." *Nuestra Voz, Nuestra Salud, Nuestro Texas,* 15.

51. *Nuestra Voz, Nuestra Salud, Nuestro Texas,* 31, 39, 44; Reproductive Health and Technologies Project, *Two Sides of the Same Coin,* 6.

52. Arons and Agénor, *Separate and Unequal,* 25.

53. Reproductive Health and Technologies Project, *Two Sides of the Same Coin,* 16–17.

54. Ibid.

55. M. A. Biggs, J. Neuhaus, D. G Foster, "Mental Health Diagnoses Three Years after Receiving or Being Denied an Abortion in the United States," *American Journal of Public Health,* 105, no. 12 (December 2015): 2557–63; Reproductive Health and Technologies Project, *Two Sides of the Same Coin,* 20; *Nuestra Voz, Nuestra Salud, Nuestro Texas,* 23, 33; Arons and Agénor, *Separate and Unequal,* 18.

56. For a fuller discussion of this phenomenon see Gurr, *Reproductive Justice,* chapter 1.

57. The Guttmacher Institute defines an "unintended pregnancy" as one that "was either mistimed or unwanted (51% of pregnancies). If a woman did not want to become pregnant at the time the pregnancy occurred, but did want to become pregnant at some point in the future, the pregnancy is considered *mistimed* (31% of pregnancies). If a woman did not want to become pregnant then or at any time in the future, the pregnancy is considered *unwanted* (20% of pregnancies)." "Unintended Pregnancy in the United States," fact sheet, July 2015.

58. Gilda Sedgh, Susheela Singh, and Rubina Hussain, "Intended and Unintended Pregnancies Worldwide in 2012 and Recent Trends," *Studies in Family Planning* 43 (2014): 301–14.

59. Byllye Avery, "Lifting as We Climb: Women of Color, Wealth, and America's Future," *Collective Voices: Black Abortion Issue* 6 (2011): 5; Allison Stevens, "Single Mothers' Poverty Spikes after Welfare Overhaul," *Women's eNews,* July 3, 2008; Addendum, "Responses to the Questionnaire," 53.

60. Isabel Sawhill, "Beyond Marriage," *New York Times,* September 14, 2014, http://www.nytimes.com/2014/09/14/opinion/sunday/beyond-marriage.html; Reproductive Health and Technologies Project, *Two Sides of the Same Coin,* 23.

61. Ikemoto, "Abortion, Contraception, and the ACA," 746.

62. Guttmacher Institute, "Unintended Pregnancy in the United States," fact sheet, February 2015; Claudia Goldin and Lawrence F. Katz, "The Power of the Pill: Oral Contraceptives and Women's Career and Marriage Decisions," *Journal of Political Economics* 110 (2002): 766; Adam Sonfield, Kinsey Hasstedt, and Rachel Benson Gold,

Moving Forward: Family Planning in the Era of Health Reform (New York: Guttmacher Institute, March 2014), 5, https://www.guttmacher.org/report/moving-forward-family-planning-era-health-reform.

63. Reproductive Health and Technologies Project, *Two Sides of the Same Coin*, 3–5.

64. Laurie Sobel, Alina Salganicoff, Nisha Kurani, Jennifer Wiens, Kimsung Hawks, and Linda Shields, *Coverage of Contraceptive Services: A Review of Health Insurance Plans in Five States* (Menlo Park, CA: Kaiser Family Foundation, April 2015), http://files.kff.org/attachment/report-coverage-of-contraceptive-services-a-review-of-health-insurance-plans-in-five-states; Sonfield, Hasstedt, and Gold, *Moving Forward*, 4.

65. Susan A. Cohen, "No Conspiracy Theories Needed," *Collective Voices: Black Abortion Issue* 6 (2011): 32.

66. Reproductive Health and Technologies Project, *Two Sides of the Same Coin*, 1–2, 11–13.

67. Melissa Moore, "Reproductive Health and Intimate Partner Violence," *Family Planning Perspectives*, 31 (November–December 1999): 302–6, 312.

68. "Reports to Police of Abuse during Pregnancy Signal Risk of Adverse Outcomes," *Perspectives on Sexual and Reproductive Health*, 36 (January–February 2004): 38–39.

69. Charity Woods, "Reproductive Violence and Black Women," *Collective Voices: Black Abortion Issue* 6 (2011): 30; Martha Kempner, "Native American Women Still Don't Have Access to OTC Emergency Contraception," RH Reality Check, March 24, 2015, https://rewire.news/article/2015/03/24/native-american-women-still-dont-access-otc-emergency-contraception/.

70. See, for example, Loretta Ross, "Trust Black Women Partnership," *Collective Voices: Black Abortion Issue* 6 (2011): 19.

71. Reproductive Health and Technologies Project, *Two Sides of the Same Coin*, 3; Sharon Lerner, "The Real War on Families: Why the U.S. Needs Paid Leave Now," *In These Times*, August 18, 2015.

72. Sawhill, "Beyond Marriage"; Jenny A. Higgins, "Celebration Meets Caution: LARC's Boons, Potential Busts, and the Benefits of a Reproductive Justice Approach," *Contraception* 89 (2014), 237–38.

73. See, for example, Kathryn Edin and Maria Kefalas, *Promises I Can Keep: Why Poor Women Put Motherhood before Marriage* (Berkeley, CA: University of California Press, 2011); Higgins, "Celebration Meets Caution," 238–39; Jo Jones, William Mosher, and Kimberley Daniels, "Current Contraceptive Use in the United States, 2006–2010 and Changes in Patterns of Use since 1995," National Council for Health Statistics, Division of Vital Statistics, *National Health Statistics Reports* 60 (October 18, 2012), http://www.cdc.gov/nchs/data/nhsr/nhsr060.pdf.

74. Dani McLain, "Long-Acting Contraception Makes Teen Pregnancy Rates Plummet. So Why Are Some Women Still Skeptical?" *Nation,* November 16, 2015.

75. Higgins, "Celebration Meets Caution," 239–40.

76. Ibid., 240.

77. Soohoo, "Hyde-Care for All," 399–400.

78. Center for Reproductive Rights, Human Rights Watch, and Latin American and Caribbean Committee for the Defense of Women's Rights, *Defenders of Sexual Rights and Reproductive Rights: A Briefing Paper to the Special Rapporteur on Human Rights Defenders,* March 18, 2008, 4–5, http://reproductiverights.org/sites/crr.civicactions.net/files/documents/CRR_HRW_CLADEM_BriefingPaper_SRHRD.pdf.

79. Heidi Williamson, "Affirming Sexual Rights: Passion and Punishment," *Collective Voices: Black Abortion Issue* 6 (2011): 16.

80. Ross, "Understanding Reproductive Justice." Ross drew on the ACRJ essay "A New Vision for Reproductive Justice" for this observation. Forward Together (formerly Asian Communities for Reproductive Justice), *A New Vision for Reproductive Justice, 2005,* http://strongfamiliesmovement.org/assets/docs/ACRJ-A-New-Vision.pdf.

81. Cait Gillies, "Reproductive Justice is Economic Justice," National Center for Law and Economic Justice (unpublished manuscript, May 1, 2014); Reproductive Health and Technologies Project, *Two Sides of the Same Coin,* 3.

82. Byllye Avery, "Defending Abortion Rights as Black Women," *Collective Voices: Black Abortion* (2011): 6

83. Reproductive Health and Technologies Project, *Two Sides of the Same Coin,* 3; Joan C. Williams and Shauna L. Shames, "Mothers Dreams:

Abortion and the High Price of Motherhood," *University of Pennsylvania Journal of Constitutional Law* 6 (2004): 818; Olivia Morgan and Karen Skelton, eds., *Shriver Report: A Woman's Nation Pushes Back from the Brink,* A Study by Maria Shriver and the Center for American Progress (New York: Palgrave Macmillan, 2014); John Schmitt and Janelle Jones, *Bad Jobs on the Rise* (Washington, DC: Center for Economic and Policy Research, September 2012), http://cepr.net/documents/publications /bad-jobs-2012–09.pdf; Lonnie Golden, *Irregular Work Scheduling and Its Consequences,* Briefing Paper no. 394, Economic Policy Institute, April 9, 2015, http://www.epi.org/publication/irregular-work-scheduling-and-its-consequences/.

84. Lerner, "The Real War on Families."

85. West, "From Choice to Reproductive Justice," 1431–32; Cornelia T. Pillard, "Our Other Reproductive Choices: Equality in Sex Education, Contraceptive Access, and Work-Family Policy, *Emory Law Journal* 56 (2007): 941–91.

86. Ikemoto, "Abortion, Contraception, and the ACA," 736–37; *Nuestra Voz, Nuestra Salud, Nuestro Texas,* 31; Reproductive Health and Technologies Project, *Two Sides of the Same Coin,* 22; Addendum, "Responses to the Questionnaire," 52; Soohoo, "Hyde-Care for All," 435; Sonfield, Hasstedt, and Gold, *Moving Forward.*

87. Trust Black Women, "Statement of Solidarity with African American Women," http://www.trustblackwomen.org/take-action/join/44.

88. Cherisse Scott, "New Billboards Bring Message to Empower and Inspire Black Community," RH Reality Check, October 7, 2015, https://rewire.news/article/2015/10/07/new-billboards-bring-messages-empower-inspire-black-community/; Ikemoto, "Abortion, Contraception, and the ACA," 738; Ross et al., *Race, Gender, and Abortion,* 16; Center for Reproductive Rights, "Texas Latinas Rising," March 26, 2015, http://www.reproductiverights.org/feature/texas-latinas-rising; Black Women for Wellness in collaboration with the California Women's Law Center, *Sisters in Control,* March 2007, http://www.bwwla.org /publications/Sisters-in-Control.pdf.

89. Trust Black Women, "Statement of Solidarity."

90. Black Women for Wellness, *Sisters in Control;* Miriam Zoila Pérez, "Worried about Women of Color? Thanks, But No Thanks, Anti-

Choicers. We've Got It Covered," RH Reality Check, February 24, 2010, https://rewire.news/article/2010/02/24/worried-about-women-color-thanks-thanks-antichoicers-weve-covered/.

91. Pérez, "Worried about Women of Color?"; London, "Reproductive Justice," 71–102.

92. Quoted in Nelson, *More Than Medicine*, 206.

4. REPRODUCTIVE JUSTICE AND THE RIGHT TO PARENT

1. Zakiya Luna and Kristin Luker, "Reproductive Justice," in *Reproduction and Society*, ed. Carol Joffe and Jennifer Reich (New York: Routledge, 2015), 245.

2. Centers for Disease Control, "Births: Final Data for 2013," *National Vital Statistics Report* 64, no. 1 (January 15, 2015): 6; Isabel Sawhill, "Family Complexity: Is It a Problem, and If So, What Do We Do?" *Annals of the American Society of Political and Social Science*, 654 (2014): 241; Sarah L. Hayford, Karen Benjamin Guzzo, and Pamela J. Smock, "The Decoupling of Marriage and Parenthood? Trends in the Timing of Marital First Births, 1945–2002," *Journal of Marriage and Family*, 76, no. 3 (2014): 520.

3. Gwendolyn Mink, "Afterword: Postmaternalist Welfare Politics" in *The Wages of Motherhood: Inequality in the Welfare State, 1917–1942* (Ithaca, NY: Cornell University Press, 1995), 176.

4. Rickie Solinger, "Poisonous Choice," in *Bad Mothers: The Politics of Blame in Twentieth-Century America*," ed. Molly Ladd-Taylor and Lauri Umansky (New York: New York University Press, 1998), 383.

5. Kate W. Strully, David H. Rehkopf, and Ziming Xuan, "Effects of Prenatal Poverty on Infant Health: State Earned Income Tax Credits and Birth Weight," *American Sociology Review* 75, no. 4 (August 11, 2010): 559.

6. Camara Phyllis Jones, Clara Yvonne Jones, Geraldine S. Perry, Gillian Barclay, and Camille Arnel Jones, "Addressing the Social Determinants of Children's Health: A Cliff Analogy," supplement, *Journal of Health Care for the Poor and Underserved* 20, no. 4 (November 2009): 2.

7. Andrea Smith, "American Studies without America: Native Feminisms and the Nation-State," *American Quarterly* 60, no. 2 (June 2008): 312.

8. Greg J. Duncan, Kathleen M. Ziol-Guest, and Ariel Kalil, "Early Childhood Poverty and Adult Attainment, Behavior, and Health," *Child Development* 81, no. 1 (January-February 2010): 306.

9. Gretchen Livingston and D'Vera Cohn, "U.S. Birth Rate Falls to a Record Low; Decline Is Greatest among Immigrants," *Social and Demographic Trends,* Pew Research Center, November 29, 2015, 1, http://www.pewsocialtrends.org/2012/11/29/u-s-birth-rate-falls-to-a-record-low-decline-is-greatest-among-immigrants/.

10. Isabel Molina Guzmán, "Gendering Latinidad through the Elián News Discourse about Cuban Women," *Latino Studies* 3, no. 2 (2005): 188; Le'Brian Patrick, "Vagrant Frontiers: Black Gay Masculinity and a Quest for Community—The Issues That Shape My Viewpoint," in *Hyper Sexual, Hyper Masculine?: Gender, Race and Sexuality in the Identities of Contemporary Black Men,* ed. Brittany C. Slatton and Kamesha Spates, (Surrey, UK, and Burlington, VT: Ashgate, 2014), 60.

11. Dorothy Roberts, *Killing the Black Body: Race, Reproduction and the Meaning of Liberty,* (New York: Pantheon Books, 1997), 209, 245; see generally, Gwendolyn Mink, *Whose Welfare?* (Ithaca, NY: Cornell University Press, 1999); Kaaryn S. Gustafson, *Cheating Welfare: Public Assistance and the Criminalization of Poverty* (New York: New York University Press, 2011), 61; Felicia Ann Kornbluh, *The Battle for Welfare Rights: Politics and Poverty in Modern America* (Philadelphia: University of Pennsylvania Press, 2007).

12. Ian Haney López, *Dog Whistle Politics: How Coded Racial Appeals Have Reinvented Racism and Wrecked the Middle Class* (New York: Oxford University Press, 2014), 3.

13. It is important to note that the mortality rates for African Americans, although decreasing, still significantly exceed those of this group of midlife white people. See Josh Freeman, "Rising White Midlife Mortality: What are the Real Causes and Solutions?" *Medicine and Social Justice,* November 14, 2015, http://medicinesocialjustice.blogspot.com/2015/11/rising-white-midlife-mortality-what-are.html.

14. Jason M. Fletcher, "New Evidence of the Effects of Education on Health in the US: Compulsory Schooling Laws Revisited," *Social*

Science and Medicine 127 (2015): 106; Wei Zhang, Hamilton McCubbin, Laurie McCubbin, Qi Chen, Shirley Foley, Ida Strom, and Lisa Kehl, "Education and Self-Rated Health: An Individual and Neighborhood Level Analysis of Asian-Americans, Hawaiians, and Caucasians in Hawaii," *Social Science and Medicine* 70 (2010): 568.

15. Monica Potts, "What's Killing Poor White Women?" *American Prospect* 24, no. 4 (July-August 2013).

16. Kathryn Kost and Stanley Henshaw, *U.S. Teenage Pregnancies, Births and Abortions, 2010: National and State Trends by Age, Race, and Ethnicity*, Guttmacher Institute, May 2014, https://www.guttmacher.org/sites /default/files/report_pdf/ustptrends10.pdf. See also Amanda Peterson Beadle, "Teen Pregnancies Highest in States with Abstinence-Only Policies," *ThinkProgress*, April 20, 2012, http://thinkprogress.org/health /2012/04/10/461402/teen-pregnancy-sex-education.

17. Diane Richardson, "Constructing Sexual Citizenship: Theorizing Sexual Rights," *Critical Social Policy* 20, no. 1 (February 2000): 105.

18. United Nations Fourth World Conference on Women: Action for Equality, Development, and Peace, "C. Women and Health," *Platform for Action*, Beijing, China, September 1995, http://www.un.org /womenwatch/daw/beijing/platform/health.htm.

19. Michel Desjardins, "The Sexualized Body of the Child: Parents and the Politics of 'Voluntary' Sterilization of People Labeled Intellectually Disabled," in *Sex and Disability*, ed. Robert McRuer and Anna Mollow (Durham, NC: Duke University Press, 2011), 69–71; Roberta Cepko, "Involuntary Sterilization of Mentally Disabled Women," *Berkeley Women's Law Journal* 8 (1993): 126.

20. *"Skinner vs. Oklahoma:* Significance, Oklahoma Prisoner Sterilization," http://law.jrank.org/pages/13137/Skinner-v-Oklahoma.html; Victoria F. Nourse, *In Reckless Hands:* Skinner v. Oklahoma *and the Near Triumph of American Eugenics* (New York: Norton, 2008).

21. Harry Targ, "The Idea of the Deep State and 'Real Alternatives,'" *Diary of a Heartland Radical* (blog), November 8, 2015, http:// heartlandradical.blogspot.com/2015/11/the-idea-of-deep-state-and-real.html.

22. George F. Brown and Ellen H. Moskowitz, "Moral and Policy Issues in Long-Acting Contraception," *Annual Review of Public Health* 18 (1997): 393–94.

23. There are a variety of conceptive options. Some are provider dependent, like LARCs, requiring medical staff to administer and remove. Others options enable women to use them independent of a provider. If a contraceptive can be used or removed only with a provider's consent, this offers the possibility of pressure and/or coercion that is directly inflected by the social context in which the woman is embedded and her personal power to influence the provider's decisions. On the other hand, women-controlled options such as condoms, cervical caps, diaphragms, and contraceptive sponges are not provider dependent and should be offered as well with a sturdy informed-consent regimen. Questions of effectiveness and risks should be decided by the person using the method. Underlying assumptions about whether women are "good contraceptors" or able to effectively use birth control may be tinged by class, racial, or age biases. See Rachel Benson Gold, "Guarding against Coercion While Ensuring Access: A Delicate Balance," *Alan Guttmacher Institute Policy Review* 17, no. 3 (Summer 2014).

24. Alexis Pauline Gumbs, Mai'a Williams, and China Martens, eds., *Revolutionary Mothering: Love on the Frontlines* (Oakland: PM Press, 2015).

25. United Nations, *Universal Declaration of Human Rights*, 1948, www.un.org/ed/documents/udhr/.

26. Greg Ip, "How Demographics Rule the Global Economy," *Wall Street Journal*, November 22, 2015, http://www.wsj.com/articles/how-demographics-rule-the-global-economy-1448203724; Martin C. Libicki, Howard J. Shatz, and Julie E. Taylor, Summary, *Global Demographic Change and Its Implications for Military Power* (Santa Monica: RAND, 2011), xxiii, http://www.rand.org/content/dam/rand/pubs/monographs/2011/RAND_MG1091.pdf.

27. Fifty-eight percent of Republicans polled in a recent Pew research study view allowing a path to citizenship for people here illegally as "a reward for doing something wrong." Additionally, 59 percent of Republicans polled said the Republican Party had not done a good job representing their views on immigration, and the numbers are higher among Republicans who do not support legal pathways to

immigration for those here illegally. Pew Research Center, "Broad Public Support for Legal Status for Undocumented Immigrants, Other Attitudes about Immigration More Mixed," June 4, 2015, http://www.people-press.org/2015/06/04/broad-public-support-for-legal-status-for-undocumented-immigrants/.

28. Andrei Rogers and James Rayner, "Immigration and the Regional Demographics of the Elderly Population in the United States," *Journal of Gerontology: Social Sciences* 56, no. 1 (2001): S53.

29. Keith Cunningham-Parmeter, "(Un)Equal Protection, Why Gender Equality Depends on Discrimination," *Northwestern University Law Review* 109, no. 1 (2005): 5.

30. M. Antonia Biggs, Heather Gould, and Diane Greene Foster, "Understanding Why Women Seek Abortions in the US," *BMC Women's Health* 13, no. 29 (July 5, 2013): 1; Rachel K. Jones, Lori F. Frowirth, and Ann M. Moore, "'I Would Want to Give My Child, Like, Everything in the World': How Issues of Motherhood Influence Women Who Have Abortions," *Journal of Family Issues* 29, no. 1 (2008): 82; Joan C. Williams and Shauna L. Shames, "Mothers' Dreams: Abortion and the High Price of Motherhood," *University of Pennsylvania Journal of Constitutional Law* 6, no. 4 (2004): 822–23; Robin West, Justin Murray, and Meredith Esser, eds., *In Search of Common Ground on Abortion: From Culture War to Reproductive Justice,* Gender in Law, Culture, and Society (Surrey, UK, and Burlington, VT: Ashgate, 2014), 144.

31. Council of Economic Advisors, *The Economics of Paid and Unpaid Leave,* Executive Office of the President of the United States, July 2014, https://www.whitehouse.gov/sites/default/files/docs/leave_report_final.pdf, 8, 22; Jonathan Kohn, "An Obama Economist Explains How to Help Working Moms," *New Republic,* September 22, 2014, https://newrepublic.com/article/119519/betsey-stevenson-interview-economic-impact-work-family-policies.

32. Simpson quoted in Miriam Zoila Pérez, "A Tale of Two Movements," *Colorlines,* January 22, 2015, http://www.colorlines.com/articles/tale-two-movements.

33. Victoria Kavanaugh, "Maternal Mortality Review—Each Death Matters," *Women's Health Activist* (National Women's Health Network) 40, no. 2 (March-April 2015): 6.

34. Francine Coeytaux, Debra Bingham, and Nan Strauss, "Maternal Mortality in the United States: A Human Rights Failure," in *Reproduction and Society*, ed. Carol Joffe and Jennifer Reich (New York: Routledge, 2015), 154.

35. American College of Obstetricians and Gynecologists, *Maternal Mortality Review*, accessed January 21, 2016, http://www.acog.org /About-ACOG/ACOG-Departments/Public-Health-and-Social-Issues /Maternal-Mortality-Review.

36. Kavanaugh, "Maternal Mortality Review, 6.

37. Myra J. Tucker, Cynthia J. Berg, and William M. Callaghan, "The Black-White Disparity in Pregnancy-Related Mortality from Five Conditions: Differences in Prevalence and Case-Fatality Rates," *American Journal of Public Health* 97, no. 2 (February 2007): 24–51.

38. Pamela Harris, "Compelled Medical Treatment of Pregnant Women: The Balancing of Maternal and Fetal Rights, Note," *Cleveland State Law Review* 49 (2001): 151.

39. Khiara M. Bridges, *Reproducing Race: An Ethnography of Pregnancy as a Site of Racialization* (Berkeley: University of California Press, 2011), 88.

40. The Nigerian woman's name was withheld for privacy reasons by those reporting on the case. Lisa Collier Cool, "Could You Be Forced to Have a C-Section?" National Advocates for Pregnant Women, May 2005, http://www.advocatesforpregnantwomen.org /articles/forced_c-section.htm; Elizabeth Eggleston Drigotas, "Comment, Forced Caesarian Sections: Do The Ends Justify the Means?" *North Carolina Law Review* 70 (1991–92): 297; Veronica E. B. Holder, Janet Gallagher, and Michael T. Parsons, "Court-Ordered Obstetrical Interventions," *New England Journal of Medicine* 316, no. 19 (May 7, 1987): 1192.

41. Collier Cool, "Could You Be Forced to Have a C-Section?"; Lloyd Vries, "Debate Revived on Mother's Rights," *CBS News*, May 19, 2004, http://www.cbsnews.com/news/debate-revived-on-mothers-rights/.

42. Childbirth Connection, "Cesarean Section Trends 1989–2014," fact sheet, August 2016, http://www.nationalpartnership.org/research-library/maternal-health/cesarean-section-trends-1989–2014.pdf.

43. Lisa Girion, "More C-Sections, More Problems," *Los Angeles Times*, May 17, 2009, http://articles.latimes.com/2009/may/17

/business/fi-cover-birth17; Anibal Faúndes and José Guiherme Cecatti, "Which Policy for Caesarian Sections in Brazil? An Analysis of Trends and Consequences," *Health Policy and Planning* 8, no. 1 (1993): 37; National Collaborating Centre for Women's and Children's Health, "Care of the Woman after CS," in *Caesarian Sections* (London: Royal College of Obstetrics and Gynaecologists Press, 2004), 77.

44. Michelle Oberman, "Commentary: The Control of Pregnancy and the Criminalization of Femaleness," *Berkeley Women's Law Journal* 7 (1992): 1; Elizabeth L. Thompson, "The Criminalization of Maternal Conduct during Pregnancy: A Decision-Making Model for Lawmakers," *Indiana Law Journal* 64 (1988–89): 359.

45. Siobhan B. Somerville, *Queering the Color Line,* (Durham, NC: Duke University Press, 2000), 17.

46. Dorothy Roberts, "The Invention of Race," in *Fatal Invention: How Science, Politics, and Big Business Re-create Race in the Twenty-First Century* (New York: New Press, 2011), 3.

47. Spencer Ackerman and Daniel Hernandez, "Homeland Security Secretary Defends Deportation of Central Americans," *Guardian,* January4,2016,http://www.theguardian.com/us-news/2016/jan/04/us-authorities-begin-deportations-of-central-american-asylum-seekers.

48. Ryan Lenz, "Investigating Deaths of Undocumented Immigrants on the Border," Intelligence Report, Southern Poverty Law Center, August 26, 2016, https://www.splcenter.org/fighting-hate/intelligence-report/2012/investigating-deaths-undocumented-immigrants-border.

49. Amnesty International, *Maze of Injustice: The Failure to Protect Indigenous Women from Sexual Violence in the USA* (New York: Amnesty International Publications, 2007), 4.

50. Adam Gaffney, "Baltimore's Secret History of Death: Racism, Corporate Greed and the Most Infamous Mass-Poisoning in American History," *Salon,* May 6, 2015, http://www.salon.com/2015/05/06/a_secret_history_of_death_in_baltimore_how_segregation_corporate_greed_ravaged_its_black_population/.

51. Samuel Walker, Cassia C. Spohn, and Miriam DeLone, *The Color of Justice: Race, Ethnicity, and Crime in America,* 5th ed. (Belmont, CA: Cengage, 2012), 2.

52. Ethan Corey, "Connecting the Dots between the 'Identity Politics' of Black Lives Matter and Class Politics," *In These Times,* October 27,2015,http://inthesetimes.com/working/entry/18545/Blacklivesmatter-fightfor15-paneldiscussion.

53. Kenrya Rankin, "Black Lives Matter Partner with Reproductive Justice Groups to Fight for Black Women," *Colorlines,* February 9, 2016,https://www.colorlines.com/articles/black-lives-matter-partners-reproductive-justice-groups-fight-black-women.

54. Henry A. Giroux, "Terrorizing Students: The Criminalization of Children in the U.S. Police State," *Truthout,* November 11, 2015, http://www.truth-out.org/opinion/item/33604-terrorizing-students-the-criminalization-of-children-in-the-us-police-state.

55. Cruse quoted in Roberts, *Killing the Black Body,* 245.

56. The term "white fragility" was developed by Robin DiAngelo. See "White Fragility," *International Journal of Critical Pedagogy* 3, no. 3 (2011), http://libjournal.uncg.edu/ijcp/article/view/249.

57. Timothy Williams and Mitch Smith, "Cleveland Officer Will Not Face Charges in Tamir Rice Shooting Death," *New York Times,* December 28, 2015, http://www.nytimes.com/2015/12/29/us/tamir-rice-police-shootiing-cleveland.html.

58. Joanna Rothkoff, "Maryland Legislator's Evil Proposal: Take Food Stamps Away from Parents of Protestors," *Salon,* April 30, 2015, http://www.salon.com/2015/04/30/maryland_legislators_evil_proposal_take_food_stamps_away_from_parents_of_protestors/.

59. Valentine Stevenson, "Ben Carson: 'Children Raised by Single Mothers End Up Poor and Become Criminals," *DC Pols,* October 8, 2015,http://dcpols.com/ben-carson-children-raised-by-single-parents-end-up-poor-and-become-criminals/; Patrick F. Fagan, "The Real Root Cause of Violent Crime: The Breakdown of Marriage, Family, and Community," Heritage Foundation, March 17, 1995, http://www.heritage.org/research/reports/1995/03/bg1026nbsp-the-real-root-causes-of-violent-crime.

60. Igor Volsky, "Ryan Defends Comments on Lazy 'Inner City' Men," *ThinkProgress,* March 13, 2014, http://thinkprogress.org/economy/2014/03/13/3399441/ryan-research-lazy-inner-cities/.

61. Anne Hendrixson, "The 'Youth Bulge': Defining the Next Generation of Young Men as a Threat to the Future," *Different Takes,* Hampshire College Population and Development Program, no. 19 (Winter 2003), 2.

62. Naomi Murakawa, *The First Civil Right: How Liberals Built Prison America* (New York: Oxford University Press, 2014), 3.

63. Anthony M. Platt, "Between Scorn and Longing, Frazier's *Black Bourgeoisie*," in *E. Franklin Frazier and Black Bourgeoisie,* ed. James E. Teele (Columbia: University of Missouri Press, 2002), 71.

64. Ruth Feldstein, *Motherhood in Black and White: Race and Sex in American Liberalism 1938–1985* (New York: Cornell University Press, 2000), 157.

65. Evelyn Y. Young, "The Four Personae of Racism: (Mis)Understanding Individual vs. Systemic Racism," *Urban Education* 46, no. 6 (2011): 1449.

66. Harry Bruinius, "Eric Garner Case 101: Why Grand Juries Rarely Indict Police Officers," *Christian Science Monitor,* December 9, 2014, 17.

67. Sadhbh Walshe, "The Right's Poverty Plan: Shame Poor Kids and the Vaginas That Birthed Them," *Guardian,* March 12, 2014, http://www.theguardian.com/commentisfree/2014/mar/12/conservative-poverty-plan-birth-control-food-stamps; Hannah Groch-Begley, "How Conservative Media's Slut Shaming Helped Inspire a Scientific Study," *Media Matters for America,* March 11, 2014, http://mediamatters.org/blog/2014/03/11/how-conservative-medias-slut-shaming-helped-ins/198432; Susie Madrak, "Conservative Heroine Ann Coulter: Tell Poor People Keep Your Knees Together before You're Married," *Crooks and Liars,* March 10, 2014, http://crooksandliars.com/2014/03/conservative-heroine-ann-coulter-tell-poor.

68. Maureen A. Craig and Jennifer A. Richeson, "On the Precipice of a 'Majority-Minority' America: Perceived Status Threat from the Racial Demographic Shift Affects White Americans' Political Ideology," *Psychological Science* 25, no. 6 (2014): 1189.

69. The Cicada Collective in Texas is a queer and trans people-of-color-centered organization that aims to provide access to reproductive resources to the gender-nonconforming community.

70. Richardson, "Constructing Sexual Citizenship," 118.

71. Zoe Greenberg, "Sentenced to Abuse: Trans* People in Prison Suffer Rape, Coercion, Denial of Medical Treatment," RH Reality Check, May 12, 2015, https://rewire.news/article/2015/05/12/sentenced-abuse-trans-people-prison-suffer-rape-coercion-denial-medical-treatment/.

72. Chase Strangio, "Arrested for Walking While Trans: An Interview with Monica Jones," American Civil Liberties Union, April 2, 2014,https://www.aclu.org/blog/arrested-walking-while-trans-interview-monica-jones.

73. "Gender dysphoria" is term that describes a medical condition in which one's gender identity differs from the gender assigned at birth, causing clinically significant distress. If untreated, gender dysphoria can lead to suicide, self-mutilation, self-castration, and other forms of self-harm.

74. Gabriel Arkles, "Prisons as a Tool for Reproductive Oppression: Cross-Movement Strategies for Gender Justice," Sylvia Rivera Law Project, September 27, 2008, http://srlp.org/prisons-as-a-tool-for-reproductive-oppression-cross-movement-strategies-for-gender-justice/.

75. Elana Redfield, letter to Karen Pittleman, December 1, 2015, shared with authors.

76. Dorothy Roberts, "Prison, Foster Care, and the Systemic Punishment of Black Mothers," *UCLA Law Review* 59 (2012): 1476; Betsy Krebs and Paul Pitcoff, "Reversing the Failure of the Foster Care System," *Harvard Women's Law Journal* 27 (2004): 361; Beth E. Richie, "The Social Impact of Mass Incarceration on Women," in *Invisible Punishment: The Collateral Consequences of Mass Imprisonment*, ed. Marc Mauer and Meda Chesney-Lind (New York: New Press, 2002), 136.

77. Vivian Yee, "Suit Accuses New York City and State of Keeping Children in Foster Care Too Long," *New York Times,* July 7, 2015, http://www.nytimes.com/2015/07/08/nyregion/suit-accuses-new-york-city-and-state-of-keeping-children-in-foster-care-too-long/.

78. Dorothy Roberts, *Shattered Bonds: The Color of Child Welfare,* (New York: Basic Civitas Books, 2002), 103; Roberts, "Prison, Foster Care, and the Systemic Punishment of Black Mothers," 1477; Benjamin

Kerman, Madelyn Freundlich, and Anthony N. Maluccio, *Achieving Permanence for Older Children and Youth in Foster Care* (New York: Columbia University Press, 2009), 19.

79. Christina White, "Federally Mandated Destruction of the Black Family: The Adoption and Safe Families Act," *Northwestern Journal of Law and Social Policy* 1 (2006): 313; Natalie Pardo, "Losing Their Children: As State Cracks Down on Parents, Black Families Splinter," *Chicago Reporter,* April 6, 2011, http://chicagoreporter.com/losing-their-children-state-cracks-down-parents-black-families-splinter/.

80. Evan R. Meyers, Douglas C. McCrory, Alyssa A. Mills, Thomas M. Price, Geeta K. Swamy, Julierut Tantibhedhyangkul, Jennifer M. Wu, and David B. Matchar, *Effectiveness of Assisted Reproduction Technology,* Evidence Report/Technology Assessment no. 167, AHRQ publication no. 08-E012 (Rockville, MD: Agency for Healthcare Research and Quality, May 2008); "Assisted Reproductive Technology," *British Journal of Psychotherapy* 20, no. 4 (2004): 541; Carlos Simón, "Personalized Assisted Reproductive Technology," *Fertility and Sterility* 100, no. 4 (2013): 922.

81. Alexis Jetter, Annelise Orleck, and Diana Taylor, *The Politics of Motherhood: Activist Voices from Left to Right,* (Hanover, NH: University of New England Press, 1997), 286; "Genocide in the Caucasus: Sex-Selective Abortion," *Economist* 408 (2013): 54; Mara Hvistendahl, *Unnatural Selection: Choosing Boys Over Girls, and the Consequences of a World Full of Men* (Philadelphia: Public Affairs, 2011), 6; President's Council on Bioethics "Choosing Sex of Children," *Population and Development Review* 29, no. 4 (December 2003): 751.

82. Patricia Hill Collins, *Black Feminist Thought: Knowledge, Consciousness, and the Politics of Empowerment,* 2nd ed.(New York: Routledge, 2000), 178.

83. President's Council on Bioethics, "Choosing Sex of Children," 757–58; Kerry Lynn Macintosh, "Brave New Eugenics: Regulating Assisted Reproductive Technologies in the Name of Better Babies," *University of Illinois Journal of Law, Technology, and Policy* 2 (2010): 259; Naomi R. Cahn, "What Is Wrong with Technology?" in *Test Tube Families: Why the Fertility Market Needs Regulation* (New York: New York University Press, 2009), 165.

84. Richard Herrnstein and Charles Murray, *The Bell Curve: Intelligence and Class Structure in American Life,* (New York: Free Press, 1994).

85. Supreme Court of the United States, Transcript of Oral Arguments in *Fisher v. University of Texas at Austin,* December 9, 2015, http://www.supremecourt.gov/oral_arguments/argument_transcript .aspx.

86. Dean Hamer and Peter Copeland, *The Science of Desire: The Gay Gene and the Biology of Behavior* (New York: Simon & Schuster, 1994).

87. Lynn Weber, "A Social Framework for Understanding Race, Class, Gender, and Sexuality," *Psychology of Women Quarterly* 22 (1995): 18.

88. Oscar Lewis, "The Culture of Poverty," *Scientific American* (October 1966): 19–25; Office of Policy Planning and Research, U.S. Department of Labor, "The Tangle of Pathology," chapter 4, in *The Negro Family: The Case for National Action* (Washington, DC: DOL, March 1965).

89. Nick Loeb, "Sofía Vergara's Ex-Fiancé: Our Frozen Embryos Have a Right to Live," *New York Times,* April 29, 2015, http://www .nytimes.com/2015/04/30/opinion/sofiavergaras-ex-fiance-our-frozen-embryos-have-a-right-to-live.html.

90. Committee on Healthcare for Underserved Women, American Congress of Obstetricians and Gynecologists, "Reproductive and Sexual Coercion," Committee Opinion, no. 554, February 2013, http:// www.acog.org/Resources-And-Publications/Committee-Opinions /Committee-on-Health-Care-for-Underserved-Women/Reproductive-and-Sexual-Coercion.

91. Joanna L. Grossman, "Baby Mama: Appellate Court Declares Sherri Shepherd Is the Legal Mother of a Child Born via Her Surrogate," *Verdict: Legal Analysis and Commentary from Justia,* December 1, 2015,https://verdict.justia.com/2015/12/01/baby-mama-appellate-court-declares-sherri-shepherd-is-the-legal-mother-of-a-child-born-to-her-via-surrogate.

92. Amrita Pande, *Wombs in Labor: Transactional Commercial Surrogacy in India* (New York: Columbia University Press, 2014).

93. Mirah Riben, "American Surrogate Death: Not the First," *Huffington Post,* October 15, 2015, http://www.huffingtonpost.com/mirah-riben/american-surrogate-death-_b_8298930.html.

94. Brock A. Patton, "Globalization and the Lack of Federal Regulation of Commercial Surrogacy Contracts," *University of Missouri Kansas City Law Review* 79, no. 2 (2011): 514–19.

95. Ethics Committee of the American Society for Reproductive Medicine, "Consideration of the Gestational Carrier: A Committee Opinion," *Fertility and Sterility* 99, no. 7 (2013): 1839.

96. "Surrogate Mother Pay," *ConceiveAbilities,* n.d., accessed February 2, 2016 https://www.conceiveabilities.com/surrogates/surrogate-mother-pay; "Surrogate Mother Compensation," *Fertility SOURCE Companies,* n.d., accessed February 2, 2016 https://www.fertilitysource companies.com/surrogacy/surrogate-mother-compensation/; "How Much Do Surrogates Get Paid?" *Circle Surrogacy,* n.d., accessed February 2, 2016 http://www.circlesurrogacy.com/surrogates/how-much-do-surrogates-get-paid.

97. Andrea Dworkin, *Right-Wing Women* (New York: Perigee Books, 1983), 187.

98. Abby Brandel, "Legislating Surrogacy: A Partial Answer to Feminist Criticism," *Maryland Law Review* 54 (1995): 493–94; Martha Field, *Surrogate Motherhood* (Cambridge, MA: Harvard University Press, 1988), 78.

99. Sharyn Roach Anleu, "For Love but Not for Money?" *Gender and Society* 6, no. 1 (1992): 36.

100. Mark Tran, "Apple and Facebook Offer to Freeze Eggs for Female Employees," *Guardian,* October 15, 2014, http://www.theguardian.com/technology/2014/oct/15/apple-facebook-offer-freeze-eggs-female-employees.

101. Harriet Meyer, "Women are Being Given False Hope over Freezing Eggs," *Guardian,* October 24, 2015, http://www.theguardian.com/society/2015/oct/24/women-false-hope-freezing-eggs; P.-O. Karlström, T. Bergh, A.-S. Forsberg, U. Sandkvist, and M. Wikland, "Prognostic Factors for the Success Rate of Embryo Freezing," *Human Reproduction* 12, no. 6 (1997): 1263.

102. "Egg Donor Compensation," *Egg Donor America,* n.d., accessed February 2, 2016 https://www.eggdonoramerica.com/become-egg-donor/egg-donor-compensation; Bonnie Steinbock, "Payment for Egg Donation and Surrogacy," *Mount Sinai Journal of Medicine* 71, no. 4 (2004): 259.

103. Matthew Patrick, Allison L. Smith, William R. Meyer, and R.A. Bashford, "Anonymous Oocyte Donation: A Follow-up Questionnaire," *Fertility and Sterility* 75, no. 1 (2001): 135–36.

104. Jason Keehn, Eve Howell, Ruqayyah Abdul-Karim, Lisa Judy Chin, Cheng-Shiun Leu, Mark V. Sauer, and Robert Klitzman, "Recruiting Egg Donors Online: An Analysis of In Vitro Fertilization Clinic and Agency Websites' Adherence to American Society for Reproductive Medicine Guidelines," *Fertility and Sterility* 98, no. 4 (2012): 997; Jason Keehn, Eve Howell, Mark V. Sauer, and Robert Klitzman, "How Agencies Market Egg Donation on the Internet: A Qualitative Study," *Journal of Law, Medicine, and Ethics* 43, no. 3 (2015): 615. See also Shan Li, "Asian Women Command Premium Prices for Egg Donation in U.S.," *Los Angeles Times*, May 4, 2012; Heather Norris, "Wanted: Jewish Eggs," *Baltimore Jewish Times*, October 3, 2013; Cynthia Cohen, ed., *New Ways of Making Babies: The Case of Egg Donation*, National Advisory Board on Ethics in Reproduction (Bloomington: Indiana University Press, 1996).

105. Solana Larsen, "The Anti-Immigrant Movement: From Shovels to Suits," *NACLA Report on the Americas* 40, no. 3 (2007): 14.

106. Conor Dougherty, "Whites to Lose Majority Status in U.S. by 2042," *Wall Street Journal* August 14, 2008, http://www.wsj.com /articles/SB121867492705539109.

107. The U.S. government has a long-standing imperial policy of attacking or overthrowing democratically elected regimes in Central and South America that are not sufficiently subservient to U.S. economic interests, such as ones in Guatemala, Nicaragua, El Salvador, Chile, Brazil, and Venezuela. In addition, our "free trade" agreements such as NAFTA have helped deepen the poverty in Mexico, increasing drug violence and creating hundreds of thousands of unemployed people fleeing the violence and the poverty. See Ben Norton, "This Is Why They Hate Us: The Real American History Neither Ted Cruz nor the New York Times Will Tell You," *Salon,* November 18, 2015, http://www.salon.com/2015/11/18/this_is_why_they_hate_us_the_real_ american_history_neither_ted_cruz_nor_the_new_york_times_will_ tell_you/); Alexander Main, "The U.S. Re-militarization of Central America and Mexico," *NACLA Report on the Americas* 47, no. 2 (2014):

65–66; Gabriel Marcella, "The Transformation of Security in Latin America: A Cause for Common Action," *Journal of International Affairs* 66, no. 2 (2013): 67.

108. Erin Siegal McIntyre and Deborah Bonello, "Is Rape the Price to Pay for Migrant Women Chasing the American Dream?" *Fusion*, September 10, 2014, http://fusion.net/story/17321/is-rape-the-price-to-pay-for-migrant-women-chasing-the-american-dream/; Kathleen A. Staudt, Tony Payan, and Z. Anthony Kruszewski, *Human Rights Along the U.S.-Mexico Border: Gendered Violence and Insecurity* (Tucson: University of Arizona Press, 2009), 31.

109. Karina Braeck and Qingwen Xu, "The Impact of Detention and Deportation on Latino Immigrant Children and Families: A Quantitative Exploration," *Hispanic Journal of Behavioral Sciences* 32, no. 3 (2010): 351.

110. Maxine Baca Zinn and Bonnie Thornton Dill, *Women of Color in U.S. Society* (Philadelphia: Temple University Press, 1994), 68.

111. Jim Tankersley and Scott Clement, "It's Not Just Donald Trump: Half of Republicans Share His Views on Immigrants and Refugees," *Washington Post*, November 25, 2015, https://www.washingtonpost.com/news/wonk/wp/2015/11/24/its-not-just-donald-trump-half-of-republicans-shares-his-views-on-immigrants-and-refugees/.

112. Devin Burkhart and Leonard Zeskind, "The Tea Party Movement in 2015," Institute for Research and Education in Human Rights, 3, www.irehr.org/2015/09/15/the-tea-party-movement-in-2015/.

113. Kalina Brabeck and Qingwen Xu, "The Impact of Detention and Deportation on Latino Immigrant Children and Families: A Quantitative Exploration," *Hispanic Journal of Behavioral Science* 32, no. 3 (August 2010): 354.

114. Ayelet Shachar, *Birthright Citizenship: Citizenship and Global Inequality* (Cambridge, MA: Harvard University Press, 2009), 15.

115. Eric Benson, "The Border War on Birthright Citizenship," *Rolling Stone*, October 31, 2015, http://www.rollingstone.com/politics/news/the-border-war-on-birthright-citizenship-20151029. An estimated 295,000 children born in the United States in 2013 had at least one undocumented immigrant parent, a number that accounted for

8 percent of all domestic births in that year. Jeffrey S. Passel and D'Vera Cohn, "Number of Babies Born in U.S. to Immigrants Declines," Fact Tank: News in the Numbers, Pew Research Center, September 11, 2015, http://www.pewresearch.org/fact-tank/2015/09/11/number-of-babies-born-in-u-s-to-unauthorized-immigrants-declines/.

116. Jacqueline Bhaba, *Children without a State: A Global Human Rights Challenge* (Cambridge, MA: MIT Press, 2011), 43.

117. Manny Fernandez, "Hurdles as Immigrants Seek Texas Birth Certificates for Children," *International New York Times,* September 17, 2015, http://www.nytimes.com/2015/09/18/us/illegal-immigrant-birth-certificates.html; Pulma Rashe, "Statelessness: Living the South African Dream on Borrowed Time," UN High Commissioner for Refugees, October 10, 2011, http://www.unhcr.org/4e92e8bd9.html; Jessica P. George and Rosalind Elphick, *Promoting Citizenship and Preventing Statelessness in South Africa: A Practitioner's Guide* (Pretoria, SA: Pretoria University Press, 2014), 14.

118. Chris McGreal, "Anti-Obama 'Birther' Movement Gathers Steam," *Guardian,* July 28, 2009, http://www.theguardian.com/world /2009/jul/28/birther-movement-obama-citizenship.

119. Michelle Alexander, *The New Jim Crow: Mass Incarceration in the Age of Colorblindness* (New York: New Press, 2012), 59; Becky Pettit, *Invisible Men: Mass Incarceration and the Myth of Black Progress* (New York: Sage, 2012), 83; Andrea C. James, *Upper Bunkies Unite and Other Thoughts on the Politics of Mass Incarceration,* (Boston: Goode Press Books, 2013), 32.

120. James, *Upper Bunkies,* 40.

121. Ibid., 50–51. Some investigators believe that the need for foreign intelligence and support for the "War on Terror" means that money from the international drug and gun trade still funds covert operations for the United States. In the 1980s, the Reagan administration was accused of illegally providing guns to rebels trying to overthrow the legitimately elected government of Nicaragua in Central America. The administration finally acknowledged in 1986 that funds from cocaine smuggling aided the rebels they were supporting but denied that the drugs were shipped to the United States. A decade later in 1996, an investigative reporter, Gary Webb, discovered that the rebels' cocaine ended up in the

United States, which precipitated a foreign policy drug scandal for which no Reagan official was ever held accountable. One of the operators of the illegal scheme reported under oath that a plane running weapons out of New Orleans "was probably being used for drug runs into [the] U.S." on its return voyage. No proof has yet been found that confirms the current funneling of drugs into this country due to the War on Terror, although the burgeoning heroin epidemic suggests another reoccurring nexus between wars and drugs. For example, Afghanistan is the biggest supplier of opium in the world, a key ingredient in the rising heroin epidemic in the United States because heroin is processed from morphine, which is derived from the opium poppy. See National Security Archive, *The Contras, Cocaine, and Covert Operations*, National Security Archive Electronic Briefing Book no. 2, George Washington University, n.d., http://nsarchive.gwu.edu/NSAEBB/NSAEBB2/nsaebb2.htm. Also see Gary Webb, *Dark Alliance: The CIA, the Contras, and the Crack Cocaine Explosion* (New York: Seven Stories Press, 1998).

122. Michael Arria, "Nashville Prosecutors Have Made Sterilization of Women Part of Plea Deals," *AlterNet*, March 31, 2015, http://www.alternet.org/gender/nashville-prosecutors-have-made-sterilization-women-part-plea-deals-least-4-times-last-5.

123. "Virginia Revisits Its Barbarous Past by Coercing a Citizen to be Sterilized," *Washington Post*, July 4, 2014, https://www.washingtonpost.com/opinions/virginia-revisits-its-barbarous-past-by-coercing-a-citizen-to-be-sterilized/2014/07/04/6ee8021a-02d6–11e4-b8ff-89afd3fad6bd_story.html

124. "Bad Ideas Never Die, They Just Plea Bargain," *Bioethics News*, Bioethics Research Library at Georgetown University, April 18, 2015, https://bioethics.georgetown.edu/2015/04/bad-ideas-never-die-they-just-plea-bargain/.

125. Hannah Gold, "Instead of Protecting Women from Violence, We're Throwing Them in Jail," *Alternet*, May 6, 2015, http://www.alternet.org/gender/instead-protecting-women-violence-were-throwing-them-jail.

126. Daniel G. Saunders, "The Tendency to Arrest Victims of Domestic Violence," *Journal of Interpersonal Violence* 10, no. 2 (2014): 147;

see also Beth E. Ritchie, *Compelled to Crime: The Gender Entrapment of Battered Black Women* (New York: Routledge Press, 1996).

127. Rachel Gebreyes, "Marissa Alexander Looks Back on Her Time in Jail: 'I Was a Fish Out of Water'" *Huffington Post,* March 18, 2015, http://www.huffingtonpost.com/2015/03/18/marissa-alexander-jail_n_6895724.html.

128. Alyssa Figueroa, "Victims of Domestic Violence Getting Longer Prison Sentences Than Their Children's Abusers?" *Alternet,* October 26, 2014, http://www.truth-out.org/news/item/27057-victims-of-domestic-violence-getting-longer-prison-sentences-than-their-childs-abuser; Mark Hansen, "Liability for Spouse's Abuse: New theory Holds Mother Liable for Failing to Protect Children," *American Bar Association Journal* 79 (1993): 16; Sandra Kopels and Marcie Chestnut Sheridan, "Adding Insult to Injury: Battered Women, Their Children, and the Failure to Protect," *Affilia* 17, no. 1 (2002): 12.

129. Gold, "Instead of Protecting Women."

130. Barbara Gurr, *Reproductive Justice: The Politics of Health Care for Native American* Women (New Brunswick, NJ: Rutgers University Press, 2015), 107.

131. Protection of Unborn Children, U.S. Code 18 (2004), §§ 1841.

132. Jeanne Flavin, *Our Bodies, Our Crimes: The Policing of Women's Reproduction in* America (New York: New York University Press, 2008) 98–99; Tara Kole and Laura Kadetsky, "Unborn Victims of Violence Act: The Recent Developments," *Harvard Journal on Legislation* 39, no. 2 (2002) 215–16; U.S. Congress, House of Representatives, Subcommittee on the Constitution, Committee on the Judiciary, 107th Cong., 1st sess., "Unborn Victims of Violence Act 2001," 52.

133. Sheigla Murphy and Marsha Rosenbaum, *Pregnant Women and Drugs: Combating Stereotypes and Stigma* (New Brunswick, NJ: Rutgers University Press, 1999), 9; Katherine Beckett, "Fetal Rights and 'Crack Moms': Pregnant Women in the War on Drugs," *Contemporary Drug Problems* 22 (1995): 588; American Public Health Association, "Illicit Drug Use by Pregnant Women," Policy Statement No. 9020, *American Journal of Public Health* 8 (1990): 240, http://www.apha.org/policies-and-advocacy/public-health-policy-statements/policy-database/2014/07/03/10/56/illicit-drug-use-by-pregnant-women.

134. Lynn M. Paltrow and Jeanne Flavin, "Arrests of and Forced Interventions on Pregnant Women in the United States, 1973–2005: Implications for Women's Legal Status and Public Health," *Journal of Health Politics, Policy and Law* 38 (2013): 299–343.

135. Annaick Miller, "Using the 'War on Drugs' to Arrest Pregnant Women," Political Research Associates, September 17, 2015, http://www.politicalresearch.org/2015/09/17/using-the-war-on-drugs-to-arrest-pregnant-women/#shash.or3FxRyC.dpbs.

136. Jessica Mason Pieklo, "Murder Charge Dismissed in Mississippi Stillbirth Case," RH Reality Check, April 4, 2014, https://rewire.news/article/2014/04/04/murder-charges-dismissed-mississippi-stillbirth-case/; Katie McDonough, "Murder Charges Dismissed against Mississippi Women on Trial for Giving Birth to a Stillborn," *Salon,* April 3, 2014, http://www.salon.com/2014/04/03/murder_charges_dismissed_against_mississippi_woman_on_trial_for_giving_birth_to_a_stillborn/. In the 1980s, New York City funded twenty family rehabilitation programs to provide comprehensive services including drug treatment, case management, home visits by nurses, and early childhood intervention to drug-using (mostly crack cocaine) mothers. These programs were evaluated and found to be successful; see Stephen Magra, Alexandre Laudet, Sung-Yeon Kang, and Shirley A. Whitney, "Effectiveness of Comprehensive Services for Crack-Dependent Mothers with Newborns and Young Children," *Journal of Psychoactive Drugs* 31, no. 4 (1999): 321–338. http://www.tandfonline.com/doi/abs/10.1080/02791072.1999.10471763.

137. National Advocates for Pregnant Women, "NAPW Challenge to Wisconsin Law Will Go to Court," October 22, 2015, http://advocatesforpregnantwomen.org/blog/2015/10/victories_patel_update_tn_wrap.php.

138. Jessica Mason Pieklo, "Alabama, Jane Doe, and the Danger of Fetus-First Laws," *Rewire,* August 12, 2015, https://rewire.news/article/2015/08/12/alabama-jane-doe-dangers-fetus-first-laws/.

139. Flavin, *Our Bodies, Our Crimes,* 103–104.

140. Katha Pollitt, "Fetal Rights," in *Bad Mothers: The Politics of Blame in Twentieth-Century America*, ed. Molly Ladd-Taylor and Lauri Umansky (New York: New York University Press, 1998), 287.

141. Pollitt, "Fetal Rights."

142. Gold, "Instead of Protecting Women."

143. Eesha Pandit, "The Case of Purvi Patel: How Mike Pence Won His Crusade against Abortion in Indiana," *Salon,* August 4, 2016, http://www.salon.com/2016/08/04/the_case_of_purvi_patel_how_mike_pence_won_his_crusade_against_abortion_in_indiana/

144. Ed Pilkington, "Indiana Prosecuting Chinese Woman for Suicide Attempt That Killed Her Foetus," *Guardian,* May 30, 2012; Diana Penner, "Woman Freed after Plea Agreement in Baby's Death," *USA Today,* August 2, 2013.

145. Jessica Valenti, "The War on Drugs Has Reached into the Womb—and Threatens Abortion Rights," *Guardian,* June 30, 2015, https://www.theguardian.com/commentisfree/2015/jun/30/war-on-drugs-threatens-abortion-rights.

146. Dorothy Roberts, "Punishing Drug Addicts Who Have Babies: Women of Color, Equality, and the Right of Privacy," *Harvard Law Review* 104, no. 7 (1991): 1425; Jennifer Henricks, "What to Expect When You're Expecting: Fetal Protection Laws That Strip Away the Rights of Pregnant Women," *Boston College Journal of Law and Social Justice* 35, no. 1 (2015): 131.

147. National Women's Law Center, "Gender Injustice: System-Level Juvenile Justice Reforms for Girls," September 24, 2015, https://nwlc.org/resources/gender-injustice-system-level-juvenile-justice-reforms-girls/.

148. Flavin, *Our Bodies, Our Crimes,* 124–26.

149. American Medical Association House of Delegates, "Shackling of Pregnant Women in Labor," Resolution 203 (A-10), April 16, 2010, https://www.prisonlegalnews.org/media/publications/american_medical_association_house_of_delegates_resolution_203_(a-10)_shackling_of_pregnant_women_in_labor_2010.pdf.

150. Roxanne Nelson, "Laboring in Chains: Shackling Pregnant Inmates, Even during Childbirth, Still Happens," *American Journal of Nursing* 106, no. 10 (2006): 25.

151. Christopher W. Kuzawa and Elizabeth Sweet, "Epigenetics and the Embodiment of Race: Developmental Origins of U.S. Racial Disparities in Cardiovascular Health," *American Journal of Human Biology* 21 (2009): 2.

152. David Murphey and P. Mae Cooper, *Parents Behind Bars: What Happens to Their Children?* Child Trends, October 2015, http://www.childtrends.org/wp-content/uploads/2015/10/2015-42ParentsBehind-Bars.pdf.

153. Rickie Solinger, ed., *Interrupted Life: Experiences of Incarcerated Women in the United States* (Berkeley: University of California Press, 2010); Jodie Michelle Lawston and Ashley E. Lucas, eds., *Razor Wire Women: Prisoners, Activists, Scholars, and Artists* (Albany: State University of New York Press, 2011); Renny Golden, *War on the Family: Mothers in Prison and the Families They Leave Behind* (New York: Routledge, 2005).

154. James, *Upper Bunkies*, 75.

155. Flavin, *Our Bodies, Our Crimes*, 139. See also James, *Upper Bunkies*, 75.

156. Flavin, *Our Bodies, Our Crimes*, 152.

157. Christopher J. Mumola, "Incarcerated Parents and their Children," Bureau of Justice Statistics Special Report (Washington, DC: U.S. Department of Justice, 2000), 5; Flavin, *Our Bodies, Our Crimes*, 140; Barbara Bloom and David Steinhart, *Why Punish the Children?* (San Francisco: National Council on Crime and Delinquency, 1993), 26.

158. Barbara Bloom and Marilyn Brown, "Incarcerated Women: Motherhood on the Margins," in *Razor Wire Women*, ed. Lawston and Lucas, 55.

159. Ibid., 56; Flavin, *Our Bodies, Our Crimes*, 147.

160. James, *Upper Bunkies*, 81–82.

161. Flavin, *Our Bodies Our Crimes*, 151–53.

162. Ibid., 159.

163. Legal Action Center *After Prison: Roadblocks to Reentry: A Report on State Legal Barriers Facing People with Criminal Records* (New York: Legal Action Center, 2004) 12, lac.org/roadblocks-to-reentry/upload/lacreport/LAC_PrintReport.pdf.

164. Chanequa Walker-Barnes, "White Feminist Privilege and the War on Mother's Day" (blog), May 9, 2015, https://drchanequa.wordpress.com/2015/05/09/white-feminist-privilege-and-the-war-on-mothers-day/; Center for Restorative Justice Works, "Who We Are," Get on the Bus, accessed February 6, 2016, http://www.crjw.us/who-we-are/.

165. "Race, Class, and the Atlanta Housing Market," in Larry Keating, *Atlanta Race, Class, and Urban Expansion* (Philadelphia: Temple University Press, 2001), 42; Timothy J. Lombardo, "The Battle of Whitman Park: Race, Class, and Public Housing in Philadelphia, 1956–1982," *Journal of Social History* 47, no. 2 (2013): 404.

166. Naikang Tsao, "Ameliorating Environmental Racism: A Citizen's Guide to Discriminatory Siting of Toxic Waste Dumps," *New York University Law Review* 67, no. 2 (1992): 366; Dorceta E. Taylor, *Toxic Communities: Environmental Racism, Industrial Pollution, and Residential Mobility* (New York: New York University Press, 2014), 6.

167. Jeremy C. F. Lin, Jean Rutter, and Haeyoun Park, "Events That Led to Flint's Water Crisis," *New York Times,* January 21, 2016.

168. Alison Hope Alkon and Julian Agyeman, *Cultivating Food Justice: Race, Class, and Sustainability* (Cambridge, MA: MIT Press, 2011), 8; Rachel Slocum and Arun Saldanha, eds., *Geographies of Race and Food* (Surrey, UK, and Burlington, VT: Ashgate, 2013), 248.

169. Lance Freeman, *There Goes the 'Hood: Views of Gentrification from the Ground Up* (Philadelphia: Temple University Press, 2006), 1; Sabiyha Prince, *African Americans and Gentrification in Washington, D.C.* (Surrey, UK, and Burlington, VT: Ashgate, 2014) 100.

170. Alkon and Agyeman, *Cultivating Food Justice,* 27; Prince, *African Americans and Gentrification,* 104.

171. See Ta-Nehisi Coates, "The Case for Reparations," *Atlantic,* June 2014; Beryl Satter, *Family Properties: How the Struggle Over Race and Real Estate Transformed Chicago and Urban America* (New York: Picador, 2010); Jonathan Glick, "Gentrification and the Racialized Geography of Home Equity," *Urban Affairs Review* 44, no. 2 (2008): 280.

172. Richard Fausset, "Clayton County Loses Vital Bus Service, Link to Atlanta," *Los Angeles Times,* April 1, 2010 http://articles.latimes.com/2010/apr/01/nation/la-na-georgia-bus1–2010apr01.

173. T. Rees Shapiro, "Arlington School Officials Stick to Tighter Bus Plan despite Parents' Complaints," *Washington Post,* August 31, 2012, https://www.washingtonpost.com/local/education/arlington-school-officials-stick-to-tighter-bus-plan-despite-parents-complaints/2012/08/29/a45a83bc-f204–11e1-a612–3cfc842a6d89_story.html.

174. Andrea Simmons, "GA: Legislators Pondering a MARTA Expansion Referendum," *Mass Transit Magazine,* November 11, 2015, http://www.masstransitmag.com/news/12137152/legislators-pondering-a-marta-expansion-referendum.

175. "From the Archives: Metro Fleshes Out Expansion Proposal; Georgetown Stop Would Be Included on New Blue Line," *Washington Post,* October 19, 2001, https://www.washingtonpost.com/local/metro-fleshes-out-expansion-proposal-georgetownstop-would-be-included-on-new-blue-line/2014/07/28/63af6d34–1681–11e4–9e3b-7f2f110c6265_story.html.

176. Center for Neighborhood Technology, "Transit Deserts in Cook County," Transit Future Campaign, July 10, 2014, http://www.cnt.org/sites/default/files/publications/CNT_TransitDesertsCookCounty_0.pdf.

177. Monica Simpson, "Considering Motherhood and Murdered Black Children: Thinking of Becoming a Mom in the Era of Tamir Rice and Rekia Boyd," *Ebony,* August 18, 2015, http://www.ebony.com/life/considering-motherhood-and-murdered-black-children-503#axzz3s4H6QDDh; Phillip Jackson, "Tears of Black Mothers," *New Pittsburgh Courier,* April 28, 2004; Aisha Sultan, "Black Moms Tell Audience How They Fear for Their Sons," *St. Louis Post-Dispatch,* September 28, 2014, http://www.stltoday.com/lifestyles/relationships-and-special-occasions/parenting/aisha-sultan/black-moms-tell-audience-how-they-fear-for-their-sons/article_050d4db8–8155–568a-93d3–20ec1d10f7a4.html.

178. "Tanya McDowell, Homeless Woman, Arrested for Sending Son to School Using Babysitter's Address," *Huffington Post,* April 18, 2011, http://www.huffingtonpost.com/2011/04/18/tanya-mcdowell-homeless-w_n_850571.html; Andrea Canning, "Ohio Mom Kelley Williams-Bolar Jailed for Sending Kids to Better School District," *ABC News,* January 26, 2011, http://abcnews.go.com/US/ohio-mom-jailed-sending-kids-school-district/story?id = 12763654. In Georgia, enrolling a child in a school district where the child doesn't have residence can subject the adult to up to five years' imprisonment. John D. Barge, Georgia State School Superintendent, "Guidance for the

Student Enrollment and Withdrawal Rule," September 13, 2012, 27, https://www.gadoe.org/External-Affairs-and-Policy/Policy/Documents/Guidance%20for%20Student%20Enrollment%20and%20Withdrawal%20Rule.pdf.

179. Associated Press in Albuquerque, New Mexico, "Albuquerque Boy Arrested for Burping Must Digest Suspension, Court Rules," *Guardian,* July 30, 2016, https://www.theguardian.com/us-news/2016/jul/30/albuquerque-boy-arrested-burping; National Council of La Raza, "School-to-Prison Pipeline: Zero Tolerance for Latino Youth," fact sheet prepared for Models for Change: Systems Reform in Juvenile Justice, 2011, https://www.sccgov.org/sites/pdo/ppw/pubs/documents/zerotolerance_factsheet22011.pdf.

180. Tierney Sneed, "Study: Black Students –Not Crime—Determine If Schools Get Security," *TPM News,* November 4, 2015, http://talkingpointsmemo.com/news/study-race-school-security.

181. Aaron Kupchik, "The School to Prison Pipeline: Rhetoric and Reality," in *Choosing the Future for American Juvenile Justice,* ed. Franklin E. Zimring and David S. Tanenhaus (New York: New York University Press, 2014), 96–97. Chris Zubak-Skees and Ben Wieder, "A State-by-State Look at Students Referred to Law Enforcement," Center for Public Integrity, April 10, 2015, http://www.publicintegrity.org/2015/04/10/17074/state-state-look-students-referred-law-enforcement. Even the basic human right to an education is challenged at the state level. In 2014, the Michigan Court of Appeals ruled that the state of Michigan has no legal obligation to provide a quality public education to its students, denying that there is a compelling state interest in the provision of education to all children. Because the case was brought on behalf of African American students in Detroit, dog whistle politics again undermined the human rights of all children as the court chose to sacrifice public education on the altar of a minimalist government role in society, a goal of the right wing.

182. Sue Bradford Edwards and Duchess Harris, *Black Lives Matter* (Minneapolis: Abdo, 2016), 55. See also Michelle Alexander, *The New Jim Crow.* Also see, Children's Defense Fund, "The Cradle-to-Prison Pipeline Campaign," http://www.childrensdefense.org/campaigns/cradle-to-prison-pipeline/.

183. Julie Cwikla, "The Trials of a Poor Middle School Trying to Catch Up in Mathematics—Teachers' Multiple Communities of Practice and the Boundary Encounters," *Education and Urban Society* 39, no. 4 (2007), 561; Editorial Projects in Education Research Center, "Issues A-Z: Achievement Gap," *Education Week,* July 7, 2011, http://www.edweek.org/ew/issues/achievement-gap/.

184. Kristin Rawls, "The Ugly Truth about 'School-Choice," *Salon,* January 24, 2012, http://www.salon.com/2012/01/24/the_ugly_truth_about_school_choice/.

185. Massachusetts Teachers Association, "Reasons to Oppose Lifting the Cap on Charter Schools," n.d., accessed February 7, 2016 http://www.massteacher.org/issues_and_action/charter_schools/charter_school_messages.aspx.; Tim Walker, "Don't Know Much About History: Controversial Changes May Be in Store for Your Textbooks, Courtesy of the Texas State School Board," *National Education Association,* n.d., accessed February 7, 2016, http://www.nea.org/home/39060.htm; Yanan Wang, "Workers or Slaves? Textbook Maker Backtracks after Mother's Online Complaint," *Washington Post,* October 5, 2015, https://www.washingtonpost.com/news/morning-mix/wp/2015/10/05/immigrant-workers-or-slaves-textbook-maker-backtracks-after-mothers-online-complaint/.

186. Dale Russakoff, *The Prize: Who's in Charge of America's Schools?* (Boston: Houghton Mifflin Harcourt, 2015); John Kuhn, *Fear and Learning in America: Bad Data, Good Teachers, and the Attack on Public Education* (New York: Teachers College Press, 2014); Dale Russakoff, "Schooled: Cory Booker, Chris Christie, and Mark Zuckerberg Had a Plan to Reform Newark's Schools. They Got an Education," *New Yorker,* May 9, 2014, http://www.newyorker.com/magazine/2014/05/19/schooled.

187. Katsi Cook, "Our Bodies, Our Stories," Our Bodies, Ourselves, http://www.ourbodiesourselves.org/about/contributors/katsi-cook/.

188. Robert D. Bullard, *Dumping in Dixie: Race, Class, and Environmental Equality* (Boulder, CO: Westview, 2000); Gordon Walker, "Globalizing Environmental Justice," *Global Social Policy* 9, no. 3 (2009), 357; David N. Pellow, *Garbage Wars: The Struggle for Environmental Justice in Chicago* (Cambridge, MA: MIT Press, 2002); Rachel Stein, *New Perspectives on Environmental Justice* (New Brunswick, NJ: Rutgers University Press, 2004); Carolyn Finney, *Black Faces, White Spaces: Reimagining the*

Relationship of African Americans to the Great Outdoors (Chapel Hill: University of North Carolina Press, 2014).

189. Victor Luckerson, "More Women Aren't Having Children, Survey Finds," *Time,* April 7, 2015, http://time.com/3774620/more-women-not-having-kids/; U.S. Census Bureau, "Historical Table 1: Percent Childless and Births per 1,000 Women in the Last 12 Months: CPS, Selected Years, 1976–2014," accessed February 7, 2016 http://www.census.gov/hhes/fertility/data/cps/historical.html.

190. "Use It and Lose It: The Outsize Effect of U.S. Consumption on the Environment," *Scientific American,* September 14, 2012, http://www.scientificamerican.com/article/american-consumption-habits/; see also Peter Dauvergne, *The Shadows of Consumption: Consequences for the Global Environment* (Cambridge, MA: MIT Press, 2008).

191. Betsy Hartmann, *Reproductive Rights and Wrongs: The Global Politics of Population Control* (Boston: South End Press, 1995).

192. Jade Sasser, "From Darkness into Light: Race, Population, and Environmental Advocacy," *Antipode* 46, no. 5 (2014): 1243.

193. "Girl Disrupted: Hormone Disruptors and Women's Reproductive Health, A Report on Women's Reproductive Health and the Environment Workshop" (Bolinas, CA: Collaborative on Health and the Environment/Commonweal, January 2009); Kristen Iversen, *Full Body Burden: Growing Up in the Shadow of Rocky Flats* (New York: Crown, 2012); T.J. Woodruff, A.R. Zola, and J.M. Schwartz, "Environmental Chemicals in Pregnant Women in the U.S.: NHANES 2003–2004," *Environmental Health Perspectives* 119 (June 2011): 878–85; Robert Bullard, ed., *The Quest for Environmental Justice: Human Rights and the Politics of Pollution* (San Francisco: Sierra Club Books, 2005).

EPILOGUE

1. US Women and PrEP Working Group, "Position Statement Update," December 2015, 3, http://www.sisterlove.org/wp-content/uploads/2015/11/US-Women-and-PrEP-Updated-Statement-_Final2-1.pdf.

2. SisterLove, Inc., Positive Women's Network–USA, and National Women's Health Network, *Ryan White and the Affordable Care Act: Advocat-*

ing for Public Healthcare for Women Living with HIV, March 2015, https://pwnusa.files.wordpress.com/2015/03/nwhn_pwn_sl_rw_brief_final.pdf.

3. Ibid.

4. White House Office of National AIDS Policy, *National HIV/AIDS Strategy for the United States: Updated to 2020,* July 2015, https://www.aids.gov/federal-resources/national-hiv-aids-strategy/nhas-update.pdf; US Women and PrEP Working Group, "Position Statement Update," 3.

5. US Women and PrEP Working Group, "Position Statement Update," 3; see also 30 for 30 Campaign, "Integrating HIV and Sexual and Reproductive Health Service Provision: A Proven Strategy for Providing More and Better Health Care to Women Living With and at Risk of HIV/AIDS," briefing paper, January 2016, http://30for30campaign.org/wp-content/uploads/2016/01/30-for-30-report_Integraton_HIVrepro_FINAL_Jan21_2016.pdf.

6. LGBTTQQIA stands for Lesbian, Gay, Bisexual, Transgender, Transsexual, Queer, Questioning, Intersex, Asexual.

7. This dynamic can be compared to the way that the experiences of the Freedom Riders in 1961 were co-opted to promote the antiabortionists' Black genocide campaigns.

8. Keisha La'Nesha Goode, "Birthing, Blackness, and the Body: Black Midwives and Experiential Continuities of Institutional Racism" (PhD diss., Graduate Center, CUNY, 2014), http://academicworks.cuny.edu/gc_etds/423.

INDEX

Abbott, Grace and Edith, 26
Abortion: access to, 34, 132; and
  Asian Americans, 134; and "back
  alley butchers," 45; and Black
  Lives Matter, 259; as class
  privilege, 131; and coercion, 91,
  135; and communities of color,
  134; constraints on, 62; criminal,
  44, 45, 245; death rate, 45;
  debates, 62, 64; decision, 62, 186;
  delayed, 135; as economic
  decision, 135; and economic
  inequality, 134, 186; of female
  fetuses, 134, 205; funding
  restrictions on, 80, 128, 137, 141;
  and Great Depression, 34; and
  Hyde Amendment, 128–39; and
  infanticide, 205; and insurance
  coverage, 138; and intimate
  partner violence, 153; and law
  enforcement, 44; legal status of
  in nineteenth century, 23; and
  medical necessity, 138–39; and
  misoprostol, 223; and personal

goals, 154–55; and poverty, 135–36,
  138, 140, 153, 186; practitioners, 45;
  primacy of, 64; and racism,
  134–35; rates of, 44; self-induced,
  34, 222–23; and sensationalism,
  44; severed from health services,
  132; and sex selection, 134, 205;
  under slavery, 20; trials, 144; and
  unintended pregnancy, 153–54;
  and white supremacy, 134; and
  women of color, 45
Adams, Charles Francis, Jr., 22
Adams, Jill, 139–40
Addams, Jane, 26
Adoption, 201–5; and coercion, 202;
  decline of, 48; practice of
  (1951–1975), 92; and racialized
  policies, 43–44; and reproductive justice, 201–5; resistance to,
  48; rise of international
  strategies for, 48; and rise of
  white single motherhood, 48
Adoption and Safe Families Act
  (1997), 227

325